51563

At thirty-nine, Helen Hayes has been on the stage thirty-four years. In a series of charming and heart-warming letters addressed to Miss Hayes' nine-year-old daughter, Mary, Mrs. Brown retraces the path that Helen Hayes followed from a Washington side street to become one of the First Ladies of the American Theatre.

For anybody who has the slightest interest in the theatre, this book is required reading. Every page is full of the glamour of backstage life. The accounts of Miss Hayes' childhood experiences with Lew Fields and Vernon Castle, her appearances with John Drew and William Gillette, her debutante days, and her stardom in such triumphs as *Coquette, Mary of Scotland* and *Victoria Regina* are told with humor and intimate details that will delight Miss Hayes' country-wide public. And the stories of her romance with Charles Mac Arthur and her adventures in Hollywood are in the nature of new revelations of her personality and activities.

There is a disarming introduction by Charles Mac Arthur, and the book is profusely illustrated.

Letters to Mary

Helen Hayes, Mary Mac Arthur and Catherine Hayes Brown

[VANDA

Letters

to

Mary

BY CATHERINE (HAYES) BROWN

with a *Foreword* by *Charles Mac Arthur*

RANDOM HOUSE · NEW YORK

FIRST EDITION

FOR

RUTH GORDON

with my love and gratitude.

List of Illustrations

Foreword

I CANNOT call her my mother-in-law. That double-hyphen-ated epithet doesn't fit her in the least.

Not once in the eleven happy years since I robbed the roost has she admonished, heckled or even advised me in the conduct of my affairs with her only begotten child. It follows that I am very fond of Catherine Estelle Brown, though her full name startles mine eyes as I type it down. "Brownie" it is, was, and ever shall be, to me and her other friends named Legion.

So many interests have lately taken the place of her real life work—that of hoeing and watering Helen Hayes until she came to flower—that getting her out to see us nowadays almost requires a subpoena, unless it be Christmas or a birth-day. But I've noticed one exception to this rule: any hint of our daughter Mary's debut in any one of the lively arts. That brings Brownie on a fire engine, whether the event takes place in New York or California.

So far Mary's public appearances have ranged from a piano recital, in which she performed with a blacksmith's energy and a little girl's charm, to a stage appearance with her mother in *Victoria Regina*. Mary enacted the role of the seven-year-old Princess Ena. She had no lines, but we robbed another actress of two, in the hope that our child might wring the heart of Seattle. The lines were: "You were wonderful, Grandmama" and "Yes, Grandmama."

Her having lines to say was Brownie's suggestion. Helen was seven when she first appeared on the stage and Mary was now seven. Brownie had recently seen some child actresses and wanted to be reassured. *Ergo*, like a retiring Field Marshal, she waved her baton and summoned up the Class of 1940.

Our daughter went on for one night and was yanked, as the saying goes in our profession. Brownie cannot stand an amateur, and Mary, at seven, showed all of the signs. Mary may not know it, but it was her last chance to be Ellen Terry. Or her Mother.

I think that this hatred of amateurishness, or what we call Ham around the house, is my greatest tie to Helen's mother, next to Helen, herself. Neither one of us wants Mary to become an actress, but if she ever makes that important step in Brownie's lifetime (and long may it wave!) she will never be a ham—and live.

Brownie's recognition of ham, always unspoken, but always implicit in a look, has sometimes changed my views about life. Once or twice it has even changed my views about myself.

Take it away, Brownie!

CHARLES MAC ARTHUR

Chronological List of Helen Hayes' New York Appearances

Old Dutch	⎫	1908 and 1909
The Summer Widowers	⎬ Lew Fields	1909 and 1910
The Never Homes	⎬ Musical Comedies	1910 and 1911
The June Bride	⎭	1912
The Prodigal Husband (Star: John Drew)		1914 and 1915
Pollyanna (On tour only)		1916 and 1917
Penrod		1917 and 1918
Dear Brutus (Star: William Gillette)		1918 and 1919
Clarence (with Alfred Lunt and Glenn Hunter)		1919 and 1920
Bab		1920 and 1921
The Wren		1921
Golden Days		1921
To the Ladies		1922 and 1923
We Moderns		1924
Dancing Mothers		1924 and 1925
Quarantine		1925
Caesar and Cleopatra		1925
Young Blood		1925
What Every Woman Knows		1926 and 1927
Coquette		1928 and 1929
Mr. Gilhooly		1930
Petticoat Influence		1930 and 1931
The Good Fairy		1931 and 1932
Mary of Scotland		1933 and 1934
Victoria Regina		1935 to 1939
Ladies and Gentlemen		1939

This list does not include summer-stock engagements or motion-picture commitments.

Letters to Mary

Mary darling, I am going to write you a lot of letters about your mommy, who was my Helen Hayes.

I shall start from the day of her birth, maybe even before that, but I want to tell you every little thing I can recall, about things only I know.

I hope you will like them.

With all my love to you,

Grandma

Mary darling, In the year 1900 on October 10th, in Washington, D. C., there was born to Francis Van Arnum Brown and Catherine Estelle Hayes Brown, a daughter who a month later was christened Helen Hayes Brown. That was your mother. She wasn't pretty as most babies are, because she had a dreadful shock of straight black hair and heavy eyebrows that grew so close over her nose that it gave her an owl-like expression. Those brows, however, overhung the most beautiful deep blue eyes, for which I have always been so grateful. You know, the poet says, "the eyes are the windows of the soul," and your mother's soul came through those windows and made her truly beautiful.

The hair and eyebrows worried me more than anything, but Graddy Hayes, my mother, told me they would both wear off, and much to my amazement they were practically gone by the time she was two years old. She was so tiny that she was always being credited with being smarter than she really was for her age. I think almost from the day she was born she started to act. When she was about two years old I discovered her, with a ribbon which had come untied from the top of her head, tossing it back and forth over her shoulders as if it was a braid. Strangely enough, in all her early years at make-believe, I never saw her watch herself in a mirror. She was almost twelve years old before she played with other children. When I would suggest going out into the yard with the girls and boys in the neighborhood, she would always say they were "noisy." Now that she is thirty-nine, I know this has been a phobia; she still can't bear crowds or noise.

Your mother came of very middle-class people, but on both sides there was a certain amount of good background. My mother had great artistic ambitions for me, took me to see all the best in plays and actors, had me taught piano, then banjo, and finally painting. None of these seemed to be my forte. My one desire was to go to as many plays as she could take me. This was no real hardship for her, for she loved the theatre and I was the only one of her children who enjoyed it as much as she did. The only ones who

4

suffered from this extravagance were the family, for mother would market for cheap cuts and not-so-fresh vegetables, then having done this bit of cheating we would go off happily to a matinee. I had a great sense of mimicry and amused my brothers and sisters with a perfect imitation of the star in the afternoon's play. Because of this my mother thought I would be an actress some day and I, flattered by this thought, made up my mind I would be. Years later, I was to find out the difference between an imitation and a God-given gift.

All my love, dear,

Grandma

MARY DARLING, I just want to tell you this one little story to illustrate how four generations were made so much happier through Mommy's great career. Graddy Hayes, your great-grandmother, had wonderful dreams for me and although I disappointed her they came true through Mommy. She was almost deaf but she managed to overhear the greatest amount of comments and glowing things about Mommy while she would be seated in the second row at every matinee in which Mommy appeared. From the moment Mommy made her appearance Graddy Hayes would begin to cry and what with taking off her glasses to wipe them, blowing and wiping her nose, turning right and left and completely around to tell everyone in her vicinity "that's my grand-daughter" in a whisper so loud that it was distinctly heard on the stage—what with all these goings on, the family never knew how she could hear the play. I knew the secret. All plays done in stock were those that had been done the seasons before and as Graddy Hayes attended the theatre regularly, seeing all the best up to a few weeks before her death at seventy-eight, she was already familiar with the story. My friends used to say that her pride in Mommy on the stage was ten times more satisfying than the plays. Mommy once asked me to tell Graddy not to whisper so loud, but I just couldn't stop her because she did it on purpose; she *wanted* to be heard all over the theatre!

I must describe her as she looked and dressed then. She was very tall and very erect and never walked, always strolled. I often tried to imitate this stroll but it was impossible, for it was as if she was going to make an obeisance to a royal person at the end and so must not hurry. To the theatre she always wore her heavy black silk dress that touched the ground and was never held up, no matter what the weather. It had a little white ruche at the neck, held by an old-fashioned coral pin. She would tell each of her children how she received this pin, each story different, but all most fantastic. We never compared these stories until after she had gone, so we never knew the true one. She wore a tiny black bonnet, far back from her high brow, with a white or black egret and with black ribbons tied under her chin just like the bonnet Mommy wore in the last scene of *Victoria Regina*. Her face was like old parchment, but she had strangely young and enthusiastic gray eyes. I once asked her if worry had given her all those wrinkles, but she said, "Indeed, no, they came from laughing." She was a magnificent liar.

To go back to her "performances" at the matinees, they never varied. After the play she would put on her bonnet very leisurely, tie the ribbons in a bow under her left ear, so the coral pin would show, gather up a soppy handkerchief, see that her chatelaine pocket-book was securely fastened to her skirt, put on one right-hand glove and carry one right-hand glove. She never wore but one glove, for she was always losing one and so had the greatest collection of right-hand gloves ever known. Then would begin her majestic stroll up the aisle. She would regale us throughout supper with the things various ladies had said about Helen, *ad infinitum*, and always so fulsome that I'd have to spend the rest of the evening explaining to Mommy that Graddy Hayes couldn't possibly have heard these things because she was too deaf. It was amazing the area she covered in her imagination, in that slow stroll up one aisle.

When Graddy Hayes was about sixty-nine, Bernhardt was making a tour of the United States in a series of scenes from some of her most famous plays. The tickets were frightfully expensive, but I bought two in the gallery for Mommy and me. Graddy Hayes kept talking of the time she took me to see Bernhardt when I wasn't any older than

Mommy and with such longing in her voice and eyes that I asked if she would like to go. I pointed out that it was way up in the gallery and not only would she not hear Bernhardt, but wouldn't understand her, since it was in French. She answered, "Bernhardt is so great that all one has to do is listen to that glorious voice and watch those expressive arms and you know everything she is saying."

It was impossible to get another seat, so Mommy had to be satisfied with my imitations of the famous face and arms. Every once in a while Graddy Hayes would correct me to say, "This is what Bernhardt meant." I'm confident Mommy preferred Graddy's interpretation to mine, for with the vivid imagination that the Hayeses seemed to be born with, she added her own touches to the scene. She might have been a great actress if she hadn't had such a large family, and it took all her time to do the best she could for us. You know, it's said that heredity skips a generation, but though my father insisted that I be named for his cousin, the great Irish soprano, Catherine Hayes, nothing came of that adage as far as I was concerned. My father was a great Shakespearian student, and if he had a nip or two he would recite and act all the great scenes from most of Shakespeare's plays. I was always his sole enraptured audience.

All my love,

Grandma

MARY DARLING, One day when Mommy was about four or four and a half years old, I fixed her tub, put her in it and left her to play while I finished my bedroom work. In those days our bathtubs were not built-in ones but stood on legs and had a space between them and the wall. By and by when I returned to the bathroom to lift her out, for she was too tiny to get out herself, I found her with a hand towel draped about her head, à la Egyptian, and a large towel across the tub and in her hand a palm-leaf fan which she was waving slowly as she lay back in the tub. She wasn't at all self-conscious at being caught and when I asked her what or who she was, she said without any hesitancy, "I'm Cleopatra in her bath." This answer rather puzzled me, for I couldn't understand where she had ever heard of Cleopatra, until I recalled taking her to an art gallery, where there was a painting of "Cleopatra in Her Barge." She evidently thought I had mispronounced "bath." She was constantly being someone and, rather prophetically, it was always a royal character. I say prophetically because in after years her greatest characterizations were queens.

When she was around five years of age, I entered her in the Misses Hawke's dancing class, not to be a dancer, but to correct a turned-in toe and to give her poise. Her first public appearance was in a little dance that had no name except pas seul. For this occasion, Aunt Mamie, my sister, made her one of the most exquisite little frocks I have ever seen. Well, when Mommy's music cue came she went on

9

gaily enough, but after a few steps around she tapped her forehead, as was her habit when she couldn't remember, then she walked off the stage to the tragic disappointment of Aunt Mamie, who felt all of her work on the dress had gone for naught.

The next child went on to do her little number, and when she was half way through it Mommy said to me, "Now I remember all the steps, so I will go on again." Sadly I told her it was too late. She was terribly distressed about disappointing Miss Hawke and me, but not at all ashamed or self-conscious.

The next year Miss Hawke gave her a Dutch song and dance to do in her annual exhibition. She wore a little Dutch peasant dress and wooden shoes. The song was about a little girl left by the Zuyder Zee when her sweetheart went to America. When I was teaching her the words of the song I suggested she let tears be in her voice and at rehearsals she would turn on a little sob at just the right place. The day of the public performance I said to her just as she was about to go on, "You know, dear, when you cry your nose invariably runs a bit, so if I were you at the end of the last chorus, I'd pick up my little apron and wipe my nose on it. It will be a perfectly natural touch." She did it just as I suggested and the entire theatre applauded more than for any other number and Miss Hawke nearly fell into the pit with delight. From that time on Miss Hawke only thought of her as the actress of her class and not as a dancing pupil. A year later she gave an impersonation of the

Gibson Bathing Girl which I had seen Annabelle Whitford do in the Ziegfeld Follies. It was in this impersonation that Lew Fields saw her and wrote the manager of the theatre that if ever the parents of this child should consider allowing her to go on the stage, he wanted to be the first to see her.

Good night, dear,

Grandma

Mary darling, I want to tell you of a funny incident in Mommy's "private" life before she went on the stage. I had punished her for something. I'm sure it was a trivial thing, for she never did a really bad thing in her life. I think I was just irritable, because I had to do my own work and I was a bad housekeeper. After about a half hour I went into her room with the full intention of ignoring our recent disagreement. She ran behind a standing radiator and with real hatred in her eyes she said, "Don't come near me. You are not my mother. A real mother couldn't be so cruel." I don't think I've told you that Mommy never talked baby talk. Well, I just left her and went on with my work. In a short time she came to me to say she was going away forever. She was so tiny she couldn't open the door, so I opened it and said I hoped she would find her real mother and bade her good-bye. I knew she wouldn't go far and that she was perfectly safe, for she had never crossed the street alone. A short time later there was a knock at the door and there she stood, not a tear in her eye and said, "I will have to have five cents for carfare because my mother lives a long way from here." I gave her the five cents, much to her surprise and consternation, for I'm sure she thought I would coax her to remain, but I didn't. I gave her the nickel. Away she went and after about a half hour I got worried and went to look for her. We lived at that time in one of a row of apartment houses that had lawns with benches between each one and I expected to find her in the one next to ours. I looked in the first lawn, the second, and the third and she wasn't in any of them. I began to be terrified. I hurried to the fourth lawn, and there sat Mommy with only her big bow visible over the bench. I slowed down to imitate Graddy Hayes' stroll and said quite casually, "Oh, there you are. I'm going to the grocer's. Would you like to come along?" The play was over. She was Helen Hayes Brown again. She never mentioned the nickel I gave her and I was a bit mystified as to its disposition. I couldn't ask her about it for fear of reminding her of her scene; so when we reached the grocer's I said, "I don't believe I have enough money." Her face glowed as she handed me the nickel, saying, "Buy whatever you want with my five cents."

All my love, dear,

Grandma

P.S.—I must tell you a funny story about Mommy when I

entered her in the Holy Cross Academy at the age of five. The Mother Superior said, "Why, she's only a baby but we'll take her." I asked Mommy, after she had been there about a week, what musical instrument she would like to learn and she promptly said "the hark." Bear in mind, at this time she had not been on the stage, only her dancing school entertainments, but she immediately visualized herself as an angel seated at a beautiful gold harp, playing heavenly music. I got rid of that "dream" by telling her it would be impossible to carry a harp around until she was much larger.

Grandma

MARY DARLING, In reading over my letters to you I feel that I ought to tell you exactly how it came about that Lew Fields saw Mommy, because this was the first step in the destiny that was to be hers. The Misses Hawke gave a "May Ball" each year at the Belasco Theatre in Washington and it was always sold to some pet society charity. Lew Fields was playing that week in a musical called *It Happened in Nordland*, and he very generously loaned Miss Hawke a beautiful arbor covered with flowering vines to be used in one of her numbers. Not to be outdone in generosity Miss Hawke invited him to the matinee. Much to everybody's amazement, he came.

I had seen many of these affairs and noticed that invariably when a child finished a number he or she would drop out of character and either run off in tears or be frightened by the applause. I told Mommy to be sure to stroll off with the same blasé manner she had held throughout the song. In a way this was bad advice, for the applause was tremendous, and since no child had ever been known to take an encore or a bow in those entertainments, it ruined the next child's number. The audience refused to let Mommy leave the stage, and after about seven or eight bows someone standing in the wings said to me, "She had better drop out of character or the audience will keep this up all afternoon." People told me that Mr. Fields laughed at Mommy until the tears rolled down his cheeks. He told me afterward that he had never seen anything so funny as that baby's poise. I wish you could have seen her. She looked like a little black beauty spot that the ladies wore in those days. Her bathing suit was black taffeta cut very low and sleeveless. Her head was piled high with puffs which I had bought at the five-and-ten-cent store. Mr. Fields told me he rushed home and wrote the "famous" note to the manager, which led to four of her happiest seasons in the theatre.

My love,

Grandma

P.S.—This is the funny song Mommy sang:

Why do they call me the Gibson Girl,
the Gibson Girl, the Gibson Girl?

What is the matter with Mr. Ibsen,
  why Dana Gibson?
Just wear a blank expression
And a monumental curl
Walk with a bend in your back and
They'll call you a Gibson Girl.

Grandma

M ARY, MY SWEET, I am going to tell you about Mommy's
first professional appearance. Mr. Fred Berger had a company in Washington known as the Columbia Players.
They needed a small child for the part of Prince Charles
in The Royal Family, and in Mommy's presence they
asked me if I would let her try it. She begged me to,
and with many misgivings I promised to teach her the part,
for she, of course, couldn't read at that age—five years. I
kept forgetting it was the part of a boy she was to play, but
she would interrupt some direction I would give to say, "A
boy wouldn't do it that way, Mother," and instinctively
she was right. She only rehearsed a week, but by the opening night she was playing the part in her own way and there
was nothing of my direction left. This led to Mr. Berger's
finding other plays in which Mommy would have larger
parts.

When she was in her seventh year Mr. Berger decided to put on *Little Lord Fauntleroy*. It is a tremendously long part and though she had only a week in which to study and rehearse it, she was letter perfect. They had a dress rehearsal on Sunday and to the horror of the director and the entire cast Mommy would hesitate before many of her speeches and then tap her forehead in that funny little way. I knew Mommy knew her part, but nothing I could say to the director would reassure him and unbeknown to Mommy they wired New York for a young girl who had played it years before. I took Mommy up to her dressing room, and we went over the scenes that she had stumbled over at the rehearsal and there wasn't a moment's hesitancy in answering her cues. The character man, who was to play the old Earl, Fauntleroy's grandfather, came to his dressing room and, thinking we had gone home, called to another member of the cast, "Well, we will have a week's vacation. That child will never know a line tomorrow night and there will be no show." Mommy looked at me and if there had been tears in her eyes I think I'd have gone in and killed that man, but all the fighting Irish was shining out of them and she whispered to me, "You know I know it." Well, that week proved that Mommy was a genius, for she not only was letter perfect, but she had to prompt the entire cast throughout the week. Props were forgotten, but it never fazed her. She would make up lines to cover up the oversight.

Now, Mommy showed such a sense of improvising that

from then on I knew she could extricate herself and the company from any ticklish situation. There was a scene in which she showed the old Earl the gifts her poor New York friends gave her when she was leaving them to live with him. One gift was a large red bandana handkerchief. She searched in all her pockets, but no hanky. I was standing in the wings and couldn't believe my eyes, for I remembered putting it in her pocket the last thing before she went on the stage. Mommy said finally, "I guess I left it in my room. I will show it to you after a while," and then proceeded to put in such a scene describing the hanky mentioned that the Earl thought she would never finish and, in truth, she was so frightened, she did not know how to end it!

She had a long scene with the Earl after that in which she had to leave the stage to get a pair of crutches intended for the Earl, but which the property man neglected to have behind the window curtains for that scene. Her line was, "I've got a present for you, Grandpa." When she couldn't find them she began looking around. She saw the property man waving them in the wings so she walked down to the Earl and said as she ran to get them, "Oh, I know what, I left them in the hall." By this time the Earl was in a state of terror. He didn't know what would happen next or just what Mommy would do when it did happen. He made no attempt to help her out, just stood there waiting. As the scene drew to a close, the old Earl said he would go to bed. Fauntleroy said, "Lean on me, Grandfather," and they

17

started across the stage that way. Just as they got in the middle of the stage Mommy suddenly saw the bandana coming out of the leg of her trousers. I had put it, not in her pocket, but between the trousers and her stomach. She pulled it out and said, "Why, here's my bandana. Isn't it beautiful, Grandfather?" By that time they had reached the wings and the curtain fell. We were all wrecks, but Mommy was only cross with me, for making such a mistake.

In the rest of the play the Earl himself saw to it that all the properties were in their places. After that, in spite of her extreme youth, they treated Mommy with the greatest respect and admiration! I would have the members of the company to dinner frequently and Mommy would sit absorbed and fascinated by their experiences in the theatre. When she and I were alone she could talk of nothing else, but strangely enough, the children of the neighborhood couldn't get a word out of her about her work. Today she would rather not talk of the theatre to one who is not of it.

All my love, dear,

Grandma

MARY DARLING, I have just remembered something that happened in the Columbia Stock Company when Mommy was in her sixth year which helped to confirm everybody's previously formed opinion that the theatre was truly to be her life. She was to play four-year-old Claudia in the first act of *The Prince Chap*. There was no woman in the regular stock company to play the mother, who was supposed to be dying of tuberculosis and finally, in a moment of sheer weakness, I was persuaded to go on in the part. For, as the manager said, as the final straw to break down my objections, "Only a mother could feel this part truly." This play proved to me beyond a shadow of a doubt that any talent Mommy had for acting was God-given, for certainly after eight performances I was just as bad and self-conscious as I had been at the first rehearsal and never at any moment did I forget that I was Mrs. Catherine Hayes Brown making a fool of herself and suffering accordingly. As Mommy had always insisted that I stand in the wings so she could see me during her performances I asked her if she could be in the wings while I was on the stage so she could tell me if I was all right. I made my entrance before Mommy, for I was supposed to ask the Prince Chap, who had been a friend of my dead husband, to take my child and raise her as his own; that we were so poor we were practically starving. I died in that scene and the Prince Chap carried me to the couch, legs exposed, as the curtain fell. Mommy made her entrance in the next scene, but as I came off she said, "You cried beautifully, Mother, but you shouldn't wear silk stockings if you are poor." No one else had noticed this discrepancy. Wasn't that wonderful?

All my love, dear,

Grandma

P.S.—I think this would be a good time for me to try to remember the plays Mommy appeared in during her six years with the Columbia Players, also the members of the company. Her very first part, as I think I wrote you before, was Prince Charles in *The Royal Family*; then the principal child in *A Poor Relation*; Claudia in *The Prince Chap*; a boy in *The Servant in the House*; Little Lord Fauntleroy in the play of that name, and the dual role in *The Prince and the Pauper*. I think these were all the child parts she played in stock.

Now these were the actors Mommy appeared with during this time; some were famous and some have become famous since then: Miss Julia Dean, Miss Ruth Chatterton, Miss Ollie Cooper, Miss Dorothy Bernard, Miss Clara Blandish, George Barbier, William Carlton, Willard Robinson, Reginald Sheffield, Orme Caldara, A. H. Van Buren and John Kline. Also in the Columbia Stock Company from time to time, though Mommy didn't appear with them, were Miss Jane Cowl, Frank Craven and Miss Marie Nordstrom.

Grandma

MARY DARLING, This is one of many letters I'll have to write you willy-nilly. By that I mean no connection of thought. It has been said of me that in talking I've never

Helen Hayes at the time of her debut, at the age of 3

stuck to one subject until I finished it. In other words, I'm like a mountain goat jumping from crag to crag. Bear with me and I'm quite sure eventually, if you have anything of your mother's imagination (and I think you have), you will get a clear vision of Mommy growing up and into this grand and glorious position that is hers.

Grandpa Brown belonged to the Elks, a fine organization doing a great deal of charity work. In order to keep their treasury filled with money to carry on these many charities, they gave frequent entertainments. Now this was the day when vaudeville flourished. Children were taken to vaudeville because it was clean good fun. As nearly every member of the Elks had a potential actress in the family, the Elks Benefit was a grand way to show them off. I wonder what has become of all the toe dancers, tap dancers and coon shouters I saw and heard at those affairs. Another thing I wonder about is what happened to the throats of these same coon shouters, some not more than eight years old, who because they thought or had been told they must be heard to the farthest ends of the earth, sang these songs so raucously that not only were their throats in danger of being ruined for life but their listeners were threatened with deafness as well. Grandpa, because Mommy had done many songs in Miss Hawke's affairs, thought I should let her do something for the Elks. Now though Mommy sang in her impersonations no one ever heard one word; it wasn't necessary, for her pantomiming was so eloquent. Grandpa thought me snobbish because I wouldn't let

Mommy appear in these entertainments, but I knew the majority of people who were *compelled* to buy these tickets would not understand the beauty and simplicity of her burlesquing.

I know it was Grandpa's great pride in Mommy that made him want her to appear for his Brother Elks. He was sure she'd outshine every other child. I dreaded the mention of an entertainment in the offing. The arguments would start all over again, frequently before Mommy, who was all for appearing because it was to be before an audience. I don't want to seem to be taking credit for anything that Mommy is today, but you see I had been taken by my mother to see only the best in acting and if Mommy was going to act she, too, must see the best and appear only with the best. I'm afraid all this was done for my own aggrandizement. I'm positive Mommy would have followed her destiny no matter what she did, or what she appeared in. There are many more interesting things about Mommy at this time but I can't recall them for this letter. As I think of them, I'll write you.

All my love,

Grandma

P.S.—About this time Mischa Elman gave a violin concert in Washington and Mommy and I went and sat almost on the roof of the theatre to hear him. At this time Mommy hadn't taken up the study of the violin but she and I were considering it, when we could bring Grandpa

Brown around to our way of thinking. All through the concert Mommy was so restless, and between numbers I noticed her eyes were very bright and she had a very high color in her cheeks. I thought it was the "artist" in her that was coming out. After the concert when we were on the street car Mommy kept up a running fire of babble and kept getting redder and redder. When we walked into the house I pointed to Mommy and said to Grandpa Brown, "Look what one violin concert has done to her. You can't deny her a violin any longer." He said, "This is another one of your crazy ideas. She is no more interested than I am. She's got the measles." And she had!

Grandma

MARY DARLING, Mr. Fred Thompson, the stock director, persuaded me to bring Mommy to New York to see the big producers, which I did in the fall just before her ninth birthday. The very first time Mommy and I came to New York to look for an engagement the Thompsons advised us to go to Mrs. Martin's theatrical boarding house. We arrived at the old Pennsylvania Station, Sunday noon, having ridden in the day coach from Washington. Mr. Thompson had given me the address of Mrs. Martin on West Forty-fifth Street and I had it on a card which I held in my hand so it would be convenient to refer to for the street numbers. I also carried a large and heavy straw suitcase.

We walked along Thirty-fourth Street to Broadway, and that, by the way, was the only sign we found in our long trip to Forty-fifth Street. In those days the street signs were on the sides of buildings. Half the time I couldn't make them out. There were so many street cars there that I was afraid to get on one for fear of going in the wrong direction. Having heard of the "wickedness" of New York I told Mommy we wouldn't ask anyone to direct us except a policeman, but, like the street signs, I couldn't find one. I'd transfer the bag from one hand to the other and Mommy would skip around and take my free hand. From time to time I would stop to look in a store window, not with any interest in anything it contained, but to rest my arm from the strain of the suitcase. Mommy didn't want to stop for anything, and when I explained I must rest once in a while, she said, "Couldn't we get on a street car that is going in the same direction we are?" I said, "I don't dare, for you know how street cars in Washington don't always go straight ahead on one street, but frequently turn corners. We'd surely get lost then." Mommy said, with great forbearance, "Well, rest when you like. I'll wait for you."

From the time we got off the train Mommy walked in the clouds, for to her we were in the city whose only business was the theatre. Finally, after walking miles, it seemed to me, I saw a policeman and asked him to direct us to Two Hundred and Thirty-nine West Forty-fifth Street (where the Music Box Theatre stands today). He explained that

24

we were at Forty-second Street now and had only three blocks more to go, then turn left. Mommy said, "We just got in from Washington, D. C." He said, "Now if you had gotten in a cab at the station, given the address to the driver, you'd have had no trouble at all." He didn't know I had only fifty dollars which Grandpa had given us under protest, for he thought this idea of the theatre was the maddest he ever heard. This fifty dollars was to last us until we returned to Washington. He had bought us round trips. Mommy rode half fare.

Good night, dear,

Grandma

MARY DARLING, Since the fifty dollars had to last us for our stay in New York, we took one of Mrs. Martin's cheapest rooms, but nothing could dull Mommy's enthusiasm. After a sleepless night she wanted me to start the rounds of managers practically at the crack of dawn. We were told by Mrs. Martin that we wouldn't find anyone in theatrical offices until after ten o'clock. She suggested that we go to some agencies. In those days it was almost impossible to get engagements unless you were registered with an agent who took ten percent of your first five weeks' salary. There was a woman, a Mrs. Kelly, who had the best child agency of that day, so I took Mommy there and was horrified to see the waiting room filled with girls and boys ranging from the age of five to fifteen and in most instances unaccompanied by an older person.

They resented us immediately, for to them we were aliens; they had never heard of Helen Hayes Brown and even Mrs. Kelly let me know that she would give the preference to one of her older clients. She told me I could take a seat and if anything came in she would let me know. I'm afraid I was a bit snobbish and said I didn't know it was an employment agency and flounced out with Mommy.

We never went back there. Someone told me I ought to go to see the casting man at the Charles Frohman office as he was casting the Maude Adams *Peter Pan* play. Well, after braving a horrid little snip of an office boy who wanted to know if we had an appointment—and I lied and said "yes"—we were taken to a man who was seated at a desk and did not even look up as he said, "I have nothing for her in any play." Years later he was Mommy's stage manager when she was a star.

I had gone to other dramatic producers with Mommy, but few were even interested enough to ask what she had done. In those days child actresses were becurled, frequently bleached and always wore dresses that just barely covered their bottoms, so a child who had straight ash-blonde hair and a face whose beauty came from within as Mommy's did and who was dressed as a little girl and not as a French doll made no impression on these "astute" men. We had been going the rounds of managers from

26

early morning, that is, from ten o'clock until five, for almost a week. Our money was getting low and my morale even lower, for I was frightened at what it might do to Mommy, so I told her we would go home Saturday. She was heartsick, for even then she knew she would land if she persisted.

We had dinner on Thursday night with Mr. and Mrs. Thompson, who had persuaded me to bring her to New York. During dinner Mr. Thompson berated me for not making a better selling talk about Mommy. He said I didn't know how good she was, and therefore couldn't convince the managers. I said, "Oh, I know she is good and Lew Fields wrote if ever her parents considered putting her on the stage to bring her to him." Mr. Thompson threw up his hands and asked me why I hadn't gone to him. I was thunderstruck that he should suggest a musical comedy producer. He said, "The part wouldn't necessarily be with him; the Shuberts are the biggest producers in the theatre today, and Fields can make them jump through a hoop for him." Well, Mommy couldn't sleep that night with excitement. I couldn't either but for a different reason. I was very skeptical that it would lead to anything, for it was more than a year since Fields had written that letter and I was afraid another disappointment would crush Mommy. Here I must tell you a noticeable thing in Mommy's character during this time.

I was afraid all these rebuffs might do something terrible to her sensitive nature, but she kept explaining to me it wasn't their fault. They didn't know anything about her. Bear in mind this wasn't conceit but a great honesty in what she had to give. I was so disheartened when I was getting her ready to go to see Mr. Fields that I took no pains at all with our appearances. Mommy, on the contrary, needed no adornment. Her face was aglow. Instinctively, she knew Mr. Fields would remember her. We got to his office to be greeted by another office-boy barrier, who said Mr. Fields was in his office talking to Miss Lotta Faust and that he didn't know how long they would be. We could sit on the bench and wait if we liked. I was all for going, but not Mommy. So we waited. We could hear Mr. Fields and Miss Faust laughing in his office and my spirits kept getting lower because I hadn't primped a bit. You see, I remembered Miss Faust was a famous beauty of the Spanish type, and I felt it would be an awful let-down for Mr. Fields to be faced by such a frump as I looked.

Well, in about half an hour they came out of his office and they passed us without a glance. He took her to the elevator and returned to the room. I jumped up and without waiting for him to look at me I thrust a photo of Mommy taken as the Gibson Bathing Girl under his nose and said, "Do you remember this child?" He looked at it and said, "My, my! I'm glad you brought her to me. Come right into my office." I don't think my mind registered one thing of that interview until we found ourselves going down in the elevator, to which he escorted us as graciously as he had Miss Faust, with a contract in my hand for

28

Mommy to play Little Mimi in his Fall production of *Old Dutch* at fifty dollars a week. Mommy's only comment was, "My, that's a lot of money," and I answered, "Yes, dear. It is."

We returned to Washington the next day, practically broke, but wildly excited. We wondered how we could wait until September, when Mr. Fields said he would send for us.

All my love,

Grandma

MARY DARLING, I guess that month and a half was the longest in any calendar to Mommy, me and even Grandpa Brown. His suspense was from another cause. We were useless to him as companions, for we talked of nothing but New York and Mommy's engagement. We wondered how long the part would be and Mommy was quite sure it would be equal to the prima donna's for that amount of salary. When the wire came telling Mommy to report for rehearsals, a few days later, I could see the relief in Grandpa Brown's eyes as he put us on the train. He even staked us generously until Mommy should begin receiving her salary. This time we did not go to Mrs. Martin's but to an inexpensive hotel that had been recommended to us. Mommy wanted to go back there, where she could boast of her engagement to people who had known her only when we were going from office to office, but I was adamant.

The day of the first rehearsal, Mr. Fields took Mommy's hand and introduced us to everyone. I was puzzled by the expression on most of their faces, but I learned later Mr. Fields had told them she was the greatest child comedienne he had ever seen. There was reason for their doubtful looks when they saw this obviously shy and serious child. That day she met Victor Herbert, who had composed the score for *Old Dutch*; Ada Lewis, a great comedienne; John Bunny, Fritz Williams, Vernon Castle, Charles Judels, and Alice Dovey, an exquisite prima donna.

The moment the director handed the part of Mimi to her, she went off to study it in the wings. The first day the part was very tiny but it kept getting longer and longer as the days went by. Mr. Fields was constantly having more written in for her.

In a short time all of the company were discussing Mommy's work with her as if to a grown-up and not as though they were talking to a child. Her comedy scenes and burlesques were played with such seriousness that they were twice as funny as the author had expected them to be. She loved every minute of those days of rehearsals, and when we returned to our room at night, she would go over her lines again and again, each time reading them with a different inflection. Veteran comedians have said to me, "I wish I had half Helen's sense of comedy. She never overplays and never strikes a false note." Even at that stage in her career she gave the audience credit for having a sense of humor and did not lay it on thickly nor did she ever anticipate a point for her audience.

Much love, darling,

Grandma

MARY SWEET, I had great difficulty in getting Mommy into a convent when she went first to play in New York. I preferred convents to private schools for her, since she was definitely going to have a career in the theatre and accomplishments were more important than arithmetic in that sphere.

Because she would have to make up her rest in the mornings and because of a mid-week matinee, I felt some arrangement would have to be made for her lessons in the school outside of classes. Well, I went from convent to convent and the moment I would explain my reason for Mommy to have special lessons, there would be a noticeable shudder; the "stage child" could certainly not be educated in their school! It's true, I applied only to the schools where the scholars were of the best families. I persisted in trying all convents first, because a great spiritual foundation was one of Mommy's biggest assets and, though they got a great deal more catechism than was necessary for one's battle with life, I knew I could or she would temper it to her own

31

purposes. I finally entered her in the Dominican Convent on East 68th Street, where she had the undivided attention of four teachers, nuns. They adored her and were constantly planning entertainments in which she must recite long poems and which always made her most self-conscious.

I don't think I ever told you, but Mommy was never taught nursery rhymes as a child because I had been made to suffer too much by my friends who, the moment I'd call, would literally drag their frequently protesting offspring in to recite "Hickery Dickery Dock" or some other equally silly doggerel. I would take a solemn oath to myself that if I ever had a child it would never do a parlor stunt.

Mommy has never lost contact with the nuns of that first convent in New York, or those of the convents she attended in Washington. Though the nuns have been sent to other convents throughout the country, she always visits them when she is in or near their school.

She decided she would study the violin and would have been a really good player if her trouping days hadn't interfered with her practicing or rather the occupants of adjoining rooms in hotels hadn't objected to the hideous noises that only a beginner on the violin can make. I afterward had her taught piano but she made no particular advancement beyond "The Scarf Dance."

I forgot to tell you, when Mommy was about eight and in her third year in the convent, I engaged a French visiting governess for her. While the nuns taught her French, it was in a class, and when she left school that was the end of the French, for I had no knowledge of that language. Mlle. Pelletier would take her on long walks in which only French was spoken, consequently Mommy's accent was the purest. When I first suggested this she begged me not to make her speak French to anyone, and this was the only thing she was self-conscious about at this age. I said, "Suppose you are cast in a play in which you have to speak French, you'll have to study it then and it will be harder to learn." That was enough reason for her. When she was in *Old Dutch*, Vernon Castle said something to her in French and to his amazement she answered him perfectly in the same language. He told this to Mr. Fields—they were always telling each other something she had done—and so when *The Summer Widowers* was being written, Mommy was given a line to say to a maid in French. This line wasn't much, but the incongruity of this tiny child speaking pure French in a musical play that was almost pure New Yorkese throughout invariably got a tremendous round of applause as she made her exit.

All my love, dear,

Grandma

MARY DARLING, After *Old Dutch* opened all the cast played games with Mommy and they were acted as seriously as if it were a play they were in. For instance, Vernon

33

Castle carried on a surreptitious correspondence with her, first as an ardent husband who was appearing in the same play with her, then as a jealous one. Sometimes she would find these notes stuck in the mirror; sometimes Vernon's dresser would give her one very formally as she was coming off her scene. She would rush to her dressing room and answer it in the same spirit, but using an imagination that all of us marveled at. It reached the point where they didn't speak at all, but the notes would fly furiously. You see, dear, even in her "game" plays Mommy treated and acted them as real performances and, with the co-operation of her fellow actors, was learning all sorts of emotions.

All my love, dear,

Grandma

P.S.—I really think that Vernon Castle was Mommy's real "first love," for the day he introduced Irene Foote as his fiancée Mommy's jealousy was "painfully" evident to all of us. Time heals all wounds, for now Irene Castle McLaughlin is one of Mommy's dearest friends.

Grandma

MARY DARLING, I thought you would like to know how Mommy occupied her time between scenes when she first went with Mr. Fields. There were about ten children in

34

Old Dutch but they were only atmosphere. They were all very sweet children but, being perfectly normal and natural ones, they could hardly wait to get off the stage, rush downstairs to the basement of the theatre and romp and play together. Mommy, having the responsibility of a real part, never joined them in their games, but would visit with the other principals, watching them make up or discussing with them what they did on the stage when they were little like her. She was always regretting that she hadn't been born fifty years before so she, too, could have had some of these experiences to talk about. This was a secret joke among the ladies of the cast for there wasn't one of them fifty years old. They invariably prefaced their stories with, "Now this was about fifty years ago." If they didn't want to be bothered with her, she found compensation by standing in the wings, watching her fellow actors work. Mommy was so observing that she could tell immediately when they would change a bit of "business" and would always ask them why they had. Sometimes they were unconscious of having played the scene differently but always asked her which she liked best. At first, when I found this out, I was afraid she might get an exaggerated idea of the value of her opinions, but she never once boasted that they had followed her suggestion. To her it was everyone standing together for the good of the play, and to this day Mommy will treat with the most sincere consideration any suggestion or advice, no matter what the source.

If I couldn't find her in a dressing room or in the wings

there was one other place she loved above all, the wardrobe room. The wardrobe mistress was a queen who ruled over this fairy kingdom. Miss Ada Barclay was the queen and held Mommy spellbound by her descriptions of other gorgeous costumes which she had had charge of throughout her many years with musical comedies. As Miss Ada would be mending a costume, a sequin or two would drop off and Mommy would gather them all up and hoard them as if they were jewels. Ada Lewis had a comedy scene in *Old Dutch* in which the comedian tore a large bow of red tulle off her neck. It was necessary for a fresh bow to be made every night, so Miss Ada, who adored Mommy, permitted her to make the bow. Sometimes the bow wouldn't be torn very much and Mommy would suggest to Miss Ada that she could retie it so the tear wouldn't show. Miss Ada would say, "Well, that's fine," and Mommy would come up to me and say, "I saved a bow for Miss Ada tonight." She would watch this scene, confident the bow was the one she had restored, and rush down to Miss Ada to say, "You couldn't notice the tear at all." By the end of the season I am sure Mommy thought she had saved Miss Ada yards of tulle.

All my love,

Grandma

P.S.—Another job, self-appointed, was to see that John Bunny, who was a great gourmand, and would take sound

Helen Hayes in *The Prodigal Husband*, with John Drew

naps between scenes, was awakened in time for his cue. A stagehand was appointed to waken him on time, but Mommy watched the stagehand for fear he would forget and, "Then," she said, "Mr. Bunny would be embarrassed to find that he had slept through the scene!" Once, the stagehand disappeared purposely just before Mr. Bunny's cue and Mommy shook him, saying, "It's almost time, Mr. Bunny." She was trembling with joy. *She* had "saved" the show.

Grandma

M<small>ARY</small> <small>DARLING,</small> When Mommy opened in *Old Dutch* she was too small to see in the mirror to put her make-up on, and of course she insisted she had to put it on herself. There was nothing to do but lift her up on the shelf and there she sat before the mirror and with a make-up box holding every known color of grease paint, eye shadow and rouge, which Vernon Castle had given her, she prepared herself for the performance. Though she put on the most simple make-up it was a long and serious business and we were always at the theatre before anyone else. The older members of the cast would use all sorts of excuses to watch this process.

The night you went on as Princess Ena in Mommy's

play, *Victoria Regina*, you, too, insisted upon putting your own make-up on and it was a beautiful job.

Love,

Grandma

P.S.—If an actor visited the lady in her dressing room in those days he would knock and say, "Are you decent?" This meant "Have you a dressing-gown on?" Vernon Castle would bring a new supply of grease paint and say to Mommy, "Darling, are you visible?" Mommy's answer to this would always be, "Quite."

Grandma

MARY DARLING, This letter is to tell you about Mommy's play-time, midnight on Broadway. After the play was over she would rush to get her make-up off.

Old Dutch was playing at the Herald Square Theatre at Broadway and Thirty-fifth Street. Mr. Fields' brother Charlie, a big overgrown "boy" of about forty years of age, would be waiting for us inside the stage door and we three would start up Broadway for the Forty-second Street cross-town car (we lived on Lexington Avenue then) and suddenly Charlie would push Mommy's hat down over her eyes and run as fast as his fat legs would carry him to hide in a door way. This ludicrous performance between this very big man and Mommy no bigger than a peanut would continue all the way up to Forty-second Street. I was frequently left blocks behind, and if it was a snowy night, while waiting for me to catch up, a snowball fight would ensue in which the crossing policeman always joined. Charlie would put us on the car, with the assistance of the policeman, with yells and shouts of who was the winner in the battle. You would never recognize this joyous little girl as the same serious child of the theatre. I always felt Mr. Fields had given Charlie his order to see us safely on the street car, but certainly the games were Charlie's way of getting payment for his chore.

Mommy didn't stay at fifty dollars a week very long. Dear Mr. Fields was always raising her salary five dollars a week, and after that first contract we never had another one with him. His word was sufficient. I never discussed salary with any manager up to the time Mommy arranged her own contracts, except once with the Theatre Guild. I'll tell you about that when I reach that period in her career. The managers paid her what they thought the part was worth, but invariably after the play opened the critics would give her special notices, and I would find an increase in her salary envelope at the end of the week. For instance, the following criticism is quoted from Charles Darnton in the *Evening World:*

. . . Mr. Fields' best moment comes at the end of the first act, when in the hope of being able to pay for a telegram, he asks the little girl to whom he has given his last franc what she has done with the money. She looks up from his lap to tell him she has spent it for flowers to crown the impostor who has taken his name along with his pocketbook, whereupon he straightens out his legs and lets her slide to the ground without a word.

In this clever tot Mr. Fields has the greatest leading woman of her size. With a youngster only a head taller than herself she tumbles the house into laughter as she goes through the soulful pantomime of a sentimental song which two lovers are voicing on the other side of the stage. The longing in her dreamy eyes and the yearning in her outstretched arms make her seem more than seven. This kiddie knows a thing or two! She does a capital bit of burlesque.

I can't ever be grateful enough to Mr. Fields for his love and encouragement of Mommy. Her four seasons with him, because of his care, made her think and believe that the theatre was the most beautiful life to live, and today she still thinks the stage the most glorious place in the world. When in later engagements she was confronted with the petty jealousies and unpleasantnesses that are bound to come in any profession, she just didn't recognize them and soon they would disappear. I don't mean to imply that she was stupid or namby-pamby, but she had never envied anyone anything and so didn't suspect it in anyone else.

Good night, dear,

Grandma

M ARY DEAR, This is about Mommy's first moving picture. The same Fred Thompson who had persuaded me to bring Mommy to New York became a director for the Vitagraph Company with a studio somewhere in Brooklyn. Mommy was in *Old Dutch* when Mr. Thompson called me up and asked me to let her appear in a picture; they were silent, of course, in those days. I was horrified, but at the same time felt so grateful for all his interest in Mommy that I didn't know how to refuse. You see, in those days movies were considered a step down for an actor! No good actor would appear in them, only an actor who couldn't get work in his profession would stoop to such a thing! Now, I know, that at the bottom of this contempt was a fear of what inroads pictures would make in the business of acting, for you could see a picture for twenty-five cents and even as low as five cents in some houses.

Well, I took Mommy over to the studio and, to my horror, whom did I see there but John Bunny? (He afterwards became one of the funniest men in pictures.) I, at first, thought he was there as a visitor and begged him not to tell anyone he had seen Mommy there. He said to Mommy, "I will make a bargain with you. If you don't tell on me, I won't tell on you."

Mommy's first picture was in support of a famous collie dog, Jean. I think she was even smarter than Rin Tin Tin but she was always so busy becoming a mother that R.T.T. got the inside track. Some weeks after Mommy had finished the picture, during our matinee, one of the company said, "Why don't you take Helen across the street to see a picture that's showing there? She will enjoy it, I'm sure." I should have suspected something, for actors thought it beneath them to recommend a picture then. Sure enough, when we saw the name of the picture as we went to buy our admission, it was *Jean and the Calico Doll*, Mommy's picture. We crept in, watched it to the bitter end and crept out. We were ashamed to go to the theatre that night, but everyone was sweet to Mommy about it. Vernon Castle said he thought she was a better actress than Jean. All of them blamed me though and predicted it would spoil her work, but you know it didn't.

All my love,

Grandma

Mary darling, I want to tell you of the fun we used to have when we went on tour with Mr. Fields. In the company were two young girl dancers known as the Hess Sisters. They were such sweet girls and very sensible about their work. They didn't want to spend their whole life dancing, so they made hay while the sun shone by economizing in every way and sending as much of their salary home as they possibly could. They suggested that we double up in hotel rooms whenever we could. This was in the day

42

of two *double* beds in a room. Well, although Mommy was getting one hundred dollars a week then, our expenses on tour were double what they were in New York, so I was glad of this arrangement.

In order to keep limbered up they would get up very early and practice all the Russian dance exercises. This meant holding onto the foot of the brass bed—they were always brass beds then—squatting as low as possible, extending first the right leg off at the side, then the left one. When Mommy would hear them she would jump up and grab the top rail of our bed, and because she was so tiny and since she had to cling to the rail, she could only squat half way down. It was such a funny sight, the girls with cold cream still on their faces and hair in curlers, that I never failed to waken thoroughly. There was one position in which Mommy could squat low enough, because one extended one's arms from the sides and shot one's right leg from the knee directly in front, then the left one; but because she had nothing to hold onto she spent most of this exercise after the squat on her back. She kept at it though that entire season and it was about the only accomplishment that got the best of her.

The girls nearly always had breakfast in the room—raw fruit, milk and cold cereal which they brought in the night before. Mommy and I would go to the coffee room in the hotel or some restaurant in the neighborhood. I had to have coffee and Mommy had to have stewed fruit and a hot cereal. Then, unless Mr. Fields would invite us for an auto

43

ride into the country, we four would go for a long walk or go through the big shops. The girls had exquisite taste and dressed beautifully. It was because of the latter that makes what I'm going to tell you the more incongruous.

After our walk Rea, who was older than Hannah, would leave us to do the marketing for dinner. She would return to our joint room loaded down with brown paper bags bulging with Uneeda Biscuits, salami with garlic, canned beans, cold roast beef, canned tomatoes, which the sisters ate raw, and a quart bottle of milk. Mommy would set the table with our five-and-ten-cent-store cutlery and a lunch cloth which I carried along. One week we were playing a city in which a big convention was being held, and all the reasonable hotels that were convenient to the theatre were packed. We had to go to the big one at which Mr. Fields was stopping. We arrived there Monday afternoon, so had no time to go for a walk, but Rea, in honor of the grand hotel, dressed herself more beautifully than ever and sallied forth to market. When she returned, it seemed to me she had never bought so much before or that a quart of milk could be so large, for instead of having her purchases in two bags they were in an enormous brown bag, unmistakably delicatessen. Besides the milk bottle which was inches above the opening, there was a long loaf of French bread sticking out. I said, "Oh, Rea, how could you come through the lobby of this swank hotel with that load?" She said, "I didn't buy the lobby!" Those girls taught Mommy a lot in honesty and simplicity. This friendship lasted long after

Mommy had left Mr. Fields and until the girls married and had other responsibilities.

All my love, dear,

Grandma

Mary sweet, What I am going to tell you now is only one of the instances of Mr. Fields' love and great admiration of Mommy's ability. In most of the cities in which *Old Dutch* played the laws weren't so strict about children under sixteen appearing on the stage, but as we neared Chicago, where we hoped to have a long run, our advance man wired Mr. Fields that Mommy positively could not appear. Mr. Fields sent to New York for a midget to join us and rehearse the scenes which Mommy had with him, before we reached Chicago. After three or four rehearsals with the midget Mr. Fields said, "I just can't play those scenes without Helen." He said he had a friend in Chicago who was high up in the city's politics and he would get in touch with him and see if there wasn't something to be done about Mommy playing the entire engagement.

Well, whatever wires were pulled, Mommy did appear straight through the Chicago engagement. As the season drew nearer to a close, Mommy began to worry about leaving Mr. Fields, for at this time we had heard about a new musical called *The Summer Widowers* which he was pre-

45

paring to open in the spring for a summer run. One night he said to Mommy, "I hope you aren't too tired as you won't have much of a rest after you close in this, for you begin rehearsals in my summer show immediately." Mommy said with eyes shining, "Am I going to be with you again?" He said, "You are going to be with me as long as I can find a play to put you in." It was in this play that the "real affair" started with Vernon Castle.

Good night, dear,

Grandma

M ARY DARLING, Mr. Fields had a way of transferring the cast of one play into his next whenever possible, so, in addition to Vernon Castle and his wife, Irene, Alice Dovey, still our prima donna, Charles Judels and Mommy (Mr. Fields of course was the star), there were again Irene Franklin, Angie Norton, Paul Nicholson, Flavia Acaro, Will Archie, Joseph Santley and his wife, Ivy Sawyer, and a famous blackface comedian, Willis Sweatnam.

Each season with Mr. Fields Mommy would arrive at the theatre for rehearsal and three days after receiving her new part she would be letter perfect. From then on she would allow herself to day dream, and frequently when her cue would come, she would begin tapping her forehead for her lines. This was all right and understood while Mr.

Fields kept the same director, but during rehearsals of *The Summer Widowers* Mr. Fields had a disagreement with his old director and brought in a new one. Mommy and Will Archie had one of the funniest scenes in the whole play. Mommy walked on, gave her opening line, then dried up and began tapping her head. Will Archie would prompt her and go on with his next line. After the third head tapping the director yelled, "Send out and get another child. That kid will never get through with this." You have never seen anything so horrified as the faces of the cast. Mommy only looked amazed. Fortunately, Mr. Fields and I were sitting in the back of the theatre and Mr. Fields rushed down and shouted as he ran, "Let the baby alone. She knows the play backward. I'm responsible for her." He told the director that he was sure Mommy had some Scotch or Jewish blood in her as she had to see two dollars in every seat before she could act.

Good night, sweet,

Grandma

Mary darling, I don't think I ever told you about a piece of business Mommy substituted for a direction she had gotten in her "tart scene" as it was known in *The Summer Widowers*. Will Archie, who played opposite Mommy (he was twenty-three and Mommy was ten but

47

he was only about a head taller than she was), made his entrance from one side of the stage dressed as a little boy. Mommy made her entrance from the other side of the stage looking like a little French doll. They met in the center of the stage and their dialogue follows:

Billy: Look what I got for going on an errand. A raspberry tart.
Psyche Finnegan (Mommy): Are you sure it's raspberry?
Billy: Here, take a bite and see.
Psyche (taking a bite): I think it's blackberry. (Then taking a bite and another, guessing a different flavor after each bite until the last of the tart is consumed) Yes. You were right. It was raspberry.

She was told to dust her hands together to get rid of any remaining crumbs and stroll off. Once at a rehearsal she asked Billy if he minded if she wiped her hands on his sleeve instead of dusting them together. Now Will Archie was an old-timer and he told me afterwards that that bit of business was nothing short of inspired. He told Mommy to be sure to do it at the next rehearsal without telling it to a soul. This was before the new director came in, and as Mr. Fields and Mr. Wayburn left Mommy pretty much to herself, she had no fear of changing a piece of business without consulting either of them. I have never seen anyone laugh so loud or applaud so much as those two men, and, of course, they told Mommy to put that crowning "bit of insult" in for keeps.

Will Archie had to wait seconds for the audience's applause to die down in order to make his exit with the line: "You can't trust no woman."

I mention this to illustrate how Mommy was always thinking of different ways to make her part more convincing. She was sure that that was what that "brat Psyche" would do. How wise Mr. Fields was about Mommy! He never gave her a direction until he asked her what she would do under those circumstances. If what she did wasn't as funny as he thought it could be he would say, "Suppose you try it this way."

Mommy wasn't so smart in everything, for she could be as dumb as the next one at times, but she had a natural instinct for comedy.

All my love, darling,

Grandma

MARY DARLING, The year we reached Chicago for a run with *The Summer Widowers* Mr. Fields' "influence" was out of office, so a midget was engaged to take Mommy's place. All the song numbers that Mommy pantomimed had to be cut out, but because the "tart scene" was so funny that was kept in. Mommy and I left the company just before the opening in Chicago and went to Saranac Lake to visit the Fred Bergers. It was while we were there that Mommy received this "cruel letter" from Vernon:

My dear Miss Hayes:
I'm very sorry, but it had to come sooner or later. *I want a divorce.* To begin with, you had no right to leave me as you did, and, another thing, I am in love with the little woman who plays your part. She sings "Those Were the Happy Days" much better than you do and she is younger. My best love to your mother and please return my twelve dollars. Tag!
                                                    Vernon Castle

We rejoined the company after it closed in Chicago and Mommy had a long happy tour until the spring.

Mommy was engaged for Mr. Fields' next fall production *The Never Homes*, but while she had a happy time and made more stanch friends, it wasn't the same to her without Mr. Fields. After *The Never Homes* she was engaged for *The June Bride*, which had a very short life. It was in this play that Mr. Fields gave Mommy her first real solo. You couldn't hear what she sang beyond the first two rows, but her pantomiming brought her three and four encores.

From the time Mommy was eight years old she was a real trouper; and how she loved that part of it! 1908, 1909, 1910, 1911 and 1912 were interspersed with road tours, but as Mr. Fields had big musical comedies he, of course, only played large cities, and so traveling and hotel accommodations were of the best. Between 1912 and 1914 Mommy went back to Washington and to the Dominican Nuns at the Sacred Heart School. She was held in great awe by the pupils and oddly enough the nuns never tired of hearing her experiences in the "gay" theatrical world. This was something Mommy could never understand, for it never occurred to her that she was of another world than theirs. It rather spoiled her fun, for they seemed to think she would be bored by their games and she was seldom included.

My love,

Grandma

MARY DARLING, One night in 1914, I was entertaining some friends at bridge and had planned a buffet supper afterward. A telegram was handed to me during a rubber. It read, "Bring Helen Hayes Brown to Charles Frohman's office in the Empire Theatre Building for an important part in a play with John Drew. Report at eleven o'clock tomorrow morning." If I live to be a thousand, I shall never forget the thrill of that line "in a play with John Drew." All the world was in chaos, war had just been declared, but that was insignificant when compared to this summons that

51

Mommy had just received. It was then about ten o'clock; I called Mommy from bed, with my friends clamoring for supper, and told her she was to play with John Drew, the most beloved actor of our time and a great star. Grandpa Brown was phoning to the station for reservations, Graddy Hayes trying to appease the appetites of my guests while Mommy and I packed grips. Here is a strange thing about this. Neither Mommy nor I doubted that she would be engaged. We instinctively knew she would play the part. When we arrived in New York at seven o'clock (we had been up and dressed in the train from five o'clock), we went immediately to a hotel. We just dropped our bags and rushed out and walked the streets until eleven. It was Mommy's suggestion that we go right to the neighborhood of the Empire Theatre so that when eleven o'clock came we'd be right there.

I forgot to tell you that we occupied one berth coming from Washington and I'm positive neither of us slept a wink. Mommy had never seen Mr. Drew. As a matter of fact, she had only seen stock performances up to that time, so I had to tell her about all the plays I had seen him in. As he had always been one of my idols, I had seen him in every play he had brought to Washington. As I told Mommy the dramatic plots of many of his plays, her excitement mounted. At last she was going to be in a play that told a story from beginning to end. She wouldn't make her entrance to a music cue. She would *belong* to the story.

Promptly on the dot of eleven, I asked a tall, smiling, colored man, who was standing by the elevator just off the lobby, where I would find Mr. Frohman's office. He laughed and said, "Step right in the elevator and I'll take you to Mr. Hayman's office. He's the man you want to see." I was beginning to get a little frightened and Mommy held my hand with such a grip as I never believed she could. Mommy was fourteen but looked ten, and when I opened the door marked "Alf. Hayman, Private" I honestly thought it was the largest room I had ever seen and that my legs wouldn't hold out to reach the desk where Mr. Hayman sat. I'm sure Mommy was just as frightened, but she told me afterward that she only held back because I was shaking. She honestly believed this.

We had been so accustomed to a courteous and joyous welcome in the years with Mr. Fields that we were a bit frightened by Mr. Hayman's gruff, "Well, what do you want?" He didn't suggest our sitting down, so I clung to the end of his desk. Mommy never moved from my side and never took her eyes from his. He asked me what she had done, and to this day I don't know what I said to him. He explained that the play required a child, in the first act, who must look enough like the leading lady to be her grown-up. Then he said, "Is that clear?" Well, Miss Jessie Glendening was the leading lady and she had played in the Columbia Stock with Mommy. People used to remark the resemblance. They had the same coloring and the same ash-blonde hair, so she suggested Mommy for the part. Mr.

Hayman took Mommy's hand and drew her toward him and I don't know whether I was holding Mommy up or she held me, but I do know that when I let go of her I collapsed in the chair, uninvited. He took off her hat and asked her if she could act. She answered straightforwardly, "Yes." She added nothing to this.

If I hadn't been so nervous and so wanting her to be engaged, I probably would have ruined everything by babbling about how clever she was. Again, Mommy's guardian angel stood by her and made me mute. It turned out that Mr. Hayman knew all about Mommy or he never would have brought us from Washington. He was deeply impressed by her simplicity, he told me afterward. Then he took her hand and led us to the door, saying in the nicest way, "Now you go to the stage where Mr. Drew is rehearsing and tell him you are his new leading lady." Mommy made her little curtsy as she was leaving him, just as she had when he first took her hand, and both times the expression on his face was almost comical with pleasure. It was as if he couldn't believe she was real. I learned later that Mr. Drew had seen dozens of experienced stage children but had found all of them too "stagey" looking. He insisted that he must find a child who looked as if she could grow into the cultured and lovely woman whom he would fall in love with afterward. When we got to the stage of the Empire Theatre, Mr. Hayman had already phoned down to Mr. Drew. He said, "This child has been sent from heaven." In him she was to add another power to further her career.

They were deep in rehearsal when we got there, so I had time to take off Mommy's coat and hat and fluff up her ribbon bow which she wore tied on top of her long straight hair. Her dress was a simple little gingham one made by hand by Aunt Mamie. After the rehearsal Miss Glendening introduced us to all the cast and Mommy very sedately curtsied to each one. If Mommy hadn't been so tiny this would have seemed silly, for she was fourteen then, but in the convent all the pupils curtsied to the nuns and Mommy just naturally did it to everyone.

She was given her part to read for Mr. Drew and the director, whose name escapes me now, and while she made no attempt to put any expression in her voice, Mr. Drew was pleased. He told me afterward, it was her voice which he thought was the sweetest child's voice he had ever heard. From then on he always called her "Childy."

Mommy was told to remain after rehearsal, as Mr. Frohman wanted to hear her read the part to him. Mr. Drew and Mommy were standing in the center of the empty stage and I was standing over at the side by the door leading into the orchestra. A little round man with the kindest face pushed past me and went toward Mr. Drew and Mommy, and I heard Mr. Drew say, "C.F., I want you to meet my leading lady, Helen Hayes." This was Mr. Charles Frohman, considered the finest producer of that time, who had under his management such great stars as Miss Maude Adams, Miss Ethel Barrymore, Miss Billie Burke, Mr. William Gillette and Mr. John Drew.

He shook hands with Mommy and said, "How do you like your part?"

Mommy said, "I think I am going to like it very much."

Mr. Drew left them then and there was no one left but Mr. Frohman, the director, Mommy and me. Mommy was half way through the reading when Miss Billie Burke, the most dazzlingly beautiful young girl, rushed to Mr. Frohman saying, "How are you, darling?" He answered, "I am fine, Billie dear, but do you mind waiting while this young lady finishes reading this part? She is going to be John's new leading lady in *The Prodigal Husband*." Miss Burke said, turning to Mommy, "I am sorry I interrupted. Please go on."

This thrill, I was afraid, would be too much for Mommy but she finished reading "brilliantly."

I am sure I heard at least a dozen times before we reached our hotel, "Mr. Frohman called me young lady and *Miss Billie Burke* apologized to me for interrupting!" Mommy said, "Isn't the theatre the most wonderful place in the world?" Mommy was told to report at ten o'clock the next morning for rehearsal, and this is a good time to tell you that neither Mommy nor I slept more than a few hours that whole week. We were too excited and thrilled. Mommy was letter perfect her second day of rehearsal. It wasn't a terribly long part and Mommy was a very quick study.

All my love,

Grandma

MARY DARLING, One day we arrived for rehearsal and saw "C.F.," as Mr. Frohman was lovingly called, seated at a table with the director. By this time Mommy had reached the forehead-tapping stage and since C.F. had never seen her rehearse before, or at least I thought he hadn't, I feared a repetition of the Fields' director incident, but undoubtedly in a more polite way, possibly by just taking the part from her without giving her a chance to explain this idiosyncrasy.

In the middle of a very touching crying scene C.F. got up and said, "Look, little one, this is the way to do it." Then with the strangest grunts, gestures and incoherencies and with hardly one intelligible word he went through this scene with Mr. Drew while Mommy stood in front of them. Since I couldn't see her face I could only imagine the incomprehensible fright in her eyes. C.F. finished and said, "Do you understand what I mean?" and she said, "Yes, sir. I do." She asked Mr. Drew if he minded going back to her entrance and he, thinking no doubt that she wanted time to collect herself, said, "Certainly, Childy," and whispered to her, "You are going to be wonderful." Well, she reached the crying scene, and threw herself on Mr. Drew's chest and became quite hysterically frightened. When the scene was over the applause from all the cast and C.F. in particular was most gratifying.

When we got home I said to her, "What do you suppose Mr. Frohman meant, for certainly you didn't understand that pantomiming?" She said, "You forget, Mother, I've been brought up on inarticulateness, and demonstrations. Don't you know when you and Graddy Hayes would be clearing up after supper, Father would be reading and I'd be doing my lessons at the kitchen table, you two would be telling a simple story about some happening. The story teller would begin setting the scene by putting a vegetable dish here for the woman in the story, a stew pan where the street car was, a chair where the man was, then the performance would be finished off with the weirdest facial expressions and gestures. Just the same I would get a clear vision of the real scene." I still maintain she had to have a vivid imagination to be able to see what she did in C.F.'s performance.

In my next letter I'll tell you about that wonderful opening with John Drew at the Empire Theatre. I don't think any other opening afterward gave me the thrill that did.

All my love, dear,

Grandma

MARY DARLING, The night of the opening at the Empire Theatre of *The Prodigal Husband* came around, and while I knew Mommy would be grand, I was frightened for her. You see, children have no conscious fear, but now she was fourteen, this was her first big dramatic part and she had been impressed by the rest of the cast with the importance of this opening. I was afraid she might have stage fright, for at this period I had it myself in no small degree. She shared a dressing room with Miss Carlisle. I could see that she was horribly nervous, for she couldn't seem to get her make-up on and I, who had no other outlet for my nervousness, kept up a running fire of chatter, with constant admonitions, from both Miss Carlisle and Mommy, to keep quiet.

At last, to get me out of the room, Mommy said, "Now, Mother, come on. We'll stand in the wings and watch Mr. Drew." She didn't make her entrance for some time after the curtain rose, but she wanted to hear Mr. Drew's reception. When he did make his entrance it was minutes before the audience permitted him to go on with his scene. Such deafening applause I had never heard before. The theatre was packed with the socially prominent. Since the opening night of *Old Dutch* when Diamond Jim Brady occupied a box with Lillian Russell, I had never seen so many jewels. Mommy, whose cold and clammy hand was holding mine, said, "It must be wonderful to earn applause like that."

As the time drew near for Mommy's entrance my stomach began to feel queerer and queerer. Mommy said, "You won't leave the wings, Mother. I want to see you there." I promised and intended to stick it out, but she had to stand for a second just inside the door, and in that second there was a burst of applause from, I'm sure, her friends of the Lew Fields' days. It was too much for me. I knew I couldn't make the dressing room, so I dashed to a "flat" that was leaning well away from the wall. There in the dark sat little C.F., rocking back and forth like a Billikin. I put my hand over my mouth and muttered, "I'm going to be sick." He said, "I know just how you feel." I turned away and gave up everything in a corner. After all, I kept my promise. I didn't leave the wings. Mommy was exquisite and heartbreaking in her scenes with Mr. Drew, and when the curtain descended on them seated on the floor playing with toys, the applause was equal to Mr. Drew's reception. In those days curtain calls were taken between acts, and after two or three bows Mr. Drew insisted on Mommy taking them alone. We lost track of the number, for the audience knew she was through in that act. She begged me to let her stay till the play was over, but Mr. Drew forestalled that by saying, "Now, take the childy home at once and get her to bed. Tomorrow she will be famous." Mommy didn't understand what Mr. Drew meant by "tomorrow" because I had never let Mommy read a criticism. I had seen too much importance placed on one man's opinion by much older and wiser heads than hers. I told her always when she had been especially good and we agreed when she wasn't so good. It was one of our happy, sleepless nights.

One of the first things I asked Mommy, as we were going home, was if she had been frightened or nervous and she said quite simply, "No, I forgot everything but being

Simone." She never heard the applause at all when she made her entrance, and this "deafness" is still noticeable on opening nights. The next morning I read all the criticisms to myself, and Mommy was acclaimed. Most of the critics thought she was ten or eleven, and two spoke of her strong resemblance to Maude Adams in voice, looks and simplicity of acting. These gave rise to a strange rumor about Mommy's parentage, which I'll tell you of later. That night when we went to the dressing room, Mr. Drew called to Mommy and asked if she had seen the criticisms. She said, "Mother doesn't like me to read them."

He was quite cross with me, said she should read them to be encouraged. I said that she was fourteen and had managed very nicely without that sort of encouragement. However, he insisted on her taking them, but I saw to it that she didn't read them. I told her they were all most kind to her. As we were leaving her room he said, "I put a surprise for you on your dressing table, Childy," and just as we reached the door he called, "It's candy."

Mommy would carry the opened box to Mr. Drew and he would help himself most generously. They went through this ritual before every performance after that, and they were always peppermint chocolates.

All my love,

Grandma

P.S.—The season with Mr. Drew, I would say, was the

real foundation of Mommy's dramatic career. With him she learned the real importance of understanding and belief in one's part in the play.

Grandma

MARY DARLING, One day just before the opening we were going home from rehearsal and saw C.F. coming toward us on Broadway. By this time I was getting very cocky about Mommy, for the cast and director were always saying such grand things about her. I was all for stopping to speak to C.F. just to hear him say something nice when Mommy grabbed my hand and said, "Don't stop him, Mother. He won't remember us. He's an awfully busy man." She dreaded one of my incoherent explanations of who we were, for in those days I was in a rather hysterical state over her undoubted success. We looked away quickly, but in the sweetest way he stopped in front of us and took Mommy's hand and said, "I am hearing fine things about you and I watch you every day from way up in the gallery. You speak very distinctly. Always remember the man in the gallery pays to hear too." Lotta, a famous soubrette of gold-rush days, paid her the same compliment and gave her the same advice some years later.

All my love, dear,

Grandma

M$_{\text{ARY}}$ DARLING, *The Prodigal Husband* wasn't a success in New York, so after eight weeks at the Empire plans were made for a road tour. C.F. had a young Swedish actress, Martha Hedman, under contract and she too was in a play at the Lyceum that was not a success and was to close outright about the same time we were to go on tour. One day Mr. Hayman sent for Mommy and me to come to his office and he told me to take Mommy, after her scene with Mr. Drew, to the Lyceum to watch Miss Hedman and get her accent, as she would go on tour as Simone grown up instead of Jessie Glendening. C.F. had no play ready for Miss Hedman, so a place had to be made for her. Well, that night as we were leaving the theatre and as Mommy stopped to say good night to Mr. Drew, he said, as he did every night, "Good night, Childy. You are going right straight home, aren't you?" Always before, and I might say regretfully, Mommy would answer, "Yes, Mr. Drew." This night she was almost too excited to answer but managed to say, "Oh, no! We are going to watch Miss Hedman act." Mr. Drew called me in and said, "What's this I hear about your taking the childy to a play this hour of the night?" I explained and truly I thought he was going to have a stroke. He walked to his phone and called Mr. Hayman and in our presence said, "The childy is not going to imitate anyone. Let Martha imitate the childy. This is final and I'm sending her home to bed, where she belongs."

This was the only time during Mommy's association with

Mr. Drew that she resented his interference for her good. She had been looking forward with such keen anticipation to being part of a night audience. I took her to the matinee afterward but it wasn't the same. Mr. Drew told Mommy the next night that she must never let anyone change her voice or method of acting. He had that same true devotion and sincere admiration for her that she inspired in all great artists and still does. I have just remembered that it was Gustave Von Seifertitz who was Mommy's director with Mr. Drew. He was a great German director, but his accent was so thick it was almost impossible for me to understand him, but Mommy seemed to grasp his meaning immediately.

All my love,

Grandma

MARY DARLING, This letter will be about our "road" tour with Mr. Drew. I was surprised at the one-, two- and three-night stands that this great artist played. I know now that he was also a grand trouper and wanted to give the small towns a chance to see good companies and the best acting. Few stars in those days were as particular about changes in cast when they went on tour as Mr. Drew was. If there had to be a change, the replacement, he insisted, must be just as good as the actor leaving had been. In many cases they got inferior actors because they were depending on the star's name to draw to the box office. This was a fatal error, for it was this very cheapening of companies for the hinterland that ruined the "road" as a theatrical "gold mine." I once read an article in which Sarah Bernhardt said that no play could stand on an individual performance and therefore each part, no matter how small, should be played as well as the star role. I think she meant, too, that the story and play should be well balanced to make a perfect whole.

Katharine Cornell, Alfred Lunt and Lynn Fontanne, George M. Cohan and Mommy have done more in this period to restore the prestige of the theatre on the "road" than any other artists.

Their "road" productions are just the same or just as good as the New York ones. Mommy never forgot this lesson she learned from Mr. Drew.

The day we left New York for our first one-night stand in a small town in upper New York State there was a florist at the station. As each lady of the company arrived to board the train she was handed an enormous bouquet of violets, except Mommy, who was given tiny pink rosebuds. These were from Mr. Drew who was the most gallant gentleman throughout the entire tour.

We arrived late Sunday afternoon in a terrific snowstorm. Miss Carlisle, Miss Rose Winter, Miss Helen Collier, who was the general understudy, Mommy and I hired a sleigh at the station and were driven to the only hotel in town.

Mr. Drew, of course, was welcome, but they would have none of us. We were "show folks." We asked the clerk if there was any other hotel in the town and were told that there was a "tavern" up the street that might take us in. So out we went, bag and baggage, found our sleigh waiting, for the driver expected us to be turned away and counted on a double set of fares. He took us to what was frankly a saloon. I protested we couldn't go in there, but the driver said, "This is all right, ladies. They've got private rooms upstairs. Besides there ain't any place else you can get in. Whoa," said he to his horse. So there was nothing for us to do but pile out. My only thought at this moment was one of gratitude that Grandpa Brown was too far away ever to hear of my taking Mommy into a "saloon" on a Sunday afternoon.

The proprietor, who was bartender and waiter, gave us three of the largest keys I have ever seen and said, "One is a very large room, so you will have to double up." Miss Collier said she would take the room with Mommy and me. We had to carry our bags to our rooms ourselves. "Mine host" could not leave the bar.

The room was enormous and pitch dark. After stumbling about I found a small electric bulb suspended from the ceiling in a corner of the room where it had no reason for being. There were two large double iron beds, but it was so dark where they were we could not see whether they were clean or not. In a far corner were wash bowl and pitcher, and they, too, were enormous. There was just one chair in the room which out of respect for my age was mine exclusively during that night's stay.

The other two ladies came in shortly after we got settled and each said her room was worse than ours and couldn't they stay with us until supper time. Mommy was delighted, for there would be "shop talk" and she was just as happy in that barren room as if she were in a palace, for, said she, "We are trouping with Mr. Drew."

Fumes of beer kept coming up to us, so we four ladies decided we would send down for some to lighten our spirits, since we could not lighten the room. There was not a bell in the place, so one of us called down the stairs and asked if we couldn't have some beer sent up. The proprietor came up and said he would have to have our washstand pitcher. He returned with it flowing over with nectar, and the price was ten cents.

The next day Mr. Drew took us for a sleigh ride. He didn't ask us if we were comfortable and we didn't mention our accommodations. There seemed to be a tacit understanding that you accepted conditions as you found them without complaints. All this went to make up a good trouper and show what stern stuff actors were made of.

When we got to the theatre that night we found there were no doors on the dressing rooms, but Mr. Drew had sent out for sheets to be hung over the openings. There were tin basins covered with ice to wash in, and I am sure there wasn't a lavatory in the place.

I wondered what Mommy would think of trouping now,

having just left the beautiful Empire Theatre with its exquisitely appointed dressing room. But she said that she would not change places with a queen.

Good night, dear, and pleasant dreams,

Grandma

M<small>ARY</small> <small>DEAR</small>, One of the many lovely things that Mr. Drew did every day when it was possible, was to have a big open car brought to our hotel and all the ladies of the company would be driven to a country club as Mr. Drew's guests. He had entrée to all the clubs everywhere. We would have tea, then drive back in time for dinner and the theatre.

One of Mr. Drew's peculiarities was that he never ate dinner before the performance. He took this time to rest. After the play he would go into the dining room for the meal which he had ordered in advance. A fresh bottle of Haig and Haig was always a part of this dinner. We were in many towns where Mommy and I would have friends, and as Mr. Drew never failed to order me to take Mommy right straight to the hotel and to bed, I was compelled to entertain our friends in our room. One night some friends of mine living in Pittsburgh insisted that I have supper with them in the hotel restaurant. They had heard Mr. Drew was having supper there with his niece, Miss Ethel Barrymore, who was playing in *The Twelve-Pound Look* in

William Gillette and Helen Hayes in *Dear Brutus*

vaudeville. My friends wanted a "close-up" of the celebri-ties. I hired a maid in the hotel to sit outside our bedroom door to "guard" Mommy.

Mr. Drew came into the dining room but spoke very coolly to me. After a little while he came to our table and asked, "Where is Childy?" I told him I had left Mommy in the care of a maid. He went back to the table, but kept watching me. Finally, he could stand it no longer. He came to the table and said, "Mrs. Brown, are you sure you can trust this strange maid?"

I knew he wanted me to go to Mommy, so I told him I was just going up. My friends were furious and accused me of lying about Mommy's age and said that I was passing her off as much younger than her fourteen years. Mommy was too proud of being in her teens for me to try to con-ceal her true age. You will feel the same some day, dear.

My love,

Grandma

P.S.—One Sunday night in a small town that had sort of blue laws, no place of business was open, and as the hotel dining room was closed when we arrived, three or four of us began looking for a place to eat. We asked everyone we met, but they were mostly home-bodies and knew nothing of restaurants. Finally, we met a man who directed us to a lunch wagon near the railroad tracks. When we got there, who do you think was seated at the counter, eating steak and country fried potatoes, but Mr. Drew and Miss Hedman? He jumped down and with a great flourish said, "I am so glad you could come to dinner," meanwhile helping each lady to a stool. He was a grand person to know.

Grandma

M<small>ARY</small> <small>SWEET</small>, After I left you at Dwight School the other day and we had been talking about your lessons, especially your French, I remembered Mommy's French "conversations" with Mr. Drew when we were touring.

Whenever possible, Mr. Drew had a drawing room on the train and he would send his valet for Mommy to come there and discuss her lessons, which the nuns sent her by mail, and have a little French "conversation." Now his French accent was very strange, or at least it was to Mommy. Half the time she could not understand what he said. The valet became a "bird of ill omen," for she dreaded those "talks," because Mr. Drew would look so reproachful when she couldn't answer him immediately in French. When he would send for her she very cunningly would take along her English literature lesson, hoping he would confine himself to what she knew would be safe.

He gave her a beautifully illustrated book, *Jeanne d'Arc* in French, and she could read it splendidly to him. But she was convinced she had not been taught to speak French correctly, for Mr. Drew could do no wrong.

Mommy is saving her *Jeanne d'Arc* with Mr. Drew's autograph in it for you.

My love,

Grandma

P.S.—Apropos of this gift of *Jeanne d'Arc* to Mommy, I want to tell you an incident with John Barrymore years later. As a matter of fact, you were about six years old when John Barrymore came out to Nyack to see your papa. Mommy had never met him and to tell you the real truth wasn't very keen to meet him, for as I have told you before she was always at a disadvantage when she first met people because of her shyness. Then, too, she was a bit apprehensive because of John Barrymore's reputation for impatience with people who didn't catch his interest right off.

Because of Mommy's shyness they weren't getting on very well, and, as a matter of fact, Mr. Barrymore began to eliminate her from his conversation entirely. Now, whether Papa was aware of this or whether he wanted really to show you off, he left the room and returned a minute later with you by the hand to introduce you to John Barrymore, the greatest Hamlet of our time. Mommy told me he nearly frightened the life out of you by exclaiming, "My God! she is a Boutet de Monvel drawing." Then he turned to Papa and said, "Perhaps you don't know de Monvel, but you should, for he has designed your child for you."

Mommy went to the bookshelf that holds her greatest treasures (the treasures that will be yours some day), the

71

books personally autographed to her by Booth Tarkington, William Allen White, Maxwell Anderson, Sir James M. Barrie, and last, but not least, Mrs. Franklin Delano Roosevelt, and oh! so many others whose names I can't recall. From this shelf she took a book and handed it to Mr. Barrymore. "Is this what you mean?" she asked. It was a copy of *Jeanne d'Arc* illustrated by Boutet de Monvel. Mr. Barrymore became very excited and began quickly turning the pages, exclaiming meanwhile, "You see! You see, she is in every one of these pictures! Lord! What memories this book brings back to me! My Uncle Jack (that was John Drew) used to read this to us when we were kids."

Mommy with very studied nonchalance said to him, "Look at the first page." He turned to it and there read "To Helen from John Drew, 1915." John Barrymore and Mommy found a common bond, and from then on the week-end went swimmingly.

You see, darling, even at that early age you and John Drew helped Mommy over a very difficult spot.

Love,

Grandma

MARY, MY SWEET, C.F. decided he would revive *Rosemary* with Mr. Drew for the balance of the season, since *The Prodigal Husband* was no more successful on tour than it had been in New York. That reminds me how angry Mommy used to get at the audience on that tour. She felt that any play that had Mr. Drew as a star should be more appreciated. Mr. Drew closed *The Prodigal Husband* in Washington, D. C., for, said Mr. Drew to Mommy, "I want to deliver you to your own home." This was in the year 1915, and that was the year the German submarine sank the *Lusitania* and dear C.F. was one of her passengers on his last "beautiful adventure" as he said just before the ship went down. Only a few of her passengers were saved and C.F. was not among them.

C.F. was another important factor in Mommy's career, though the association had been so brief.

When Mommy left Mr. Fields I thought her heart would break, but as time went on I expected her to accept partings as a natural thing that was happening all the time in the theatre, but she cried nearly all night after she said good-bye to Mr. Drew. From now on, she said the next morning, she would play only "grown-up" parts. She was fifteen the next October but she still looked no more than ten or twelve.

All my love, dear,

Grandma

Mary darling, Mommy returned to the Sacred Heart Convent, after closing with Mr. Drew, where she specialized in English. Just before school closed that summer there was a debate held over the practicability of the Panama Canal and whether the United States would receive as much financial return as it cost her to build it. Mommy took the affirmative and a young lady in a class much higher than Mommy's took the negative side. Mommy came home with the prize, a beautiful bound volume of Tennyson's poems.

Before Mommy got home the Mother Superior called me up and begged me to consider sending Mommy to college to study law. She said it was amazing to the judges, one of whom was Joseph Tumulty, then private secretary to President Wilson, that one so young could delve so deeply into the subject and argue so convincingly. I was told afterward that they could hardly see her for the reference books in front of her. Well, bearing in mind what the old actors had said years before about the precariousness of the theatrical business and also having seen a play in which the most popular star, John Drew, had to close in mid-season, I talked very seriously to Mommy that night about college. She said, "Mother, I don't know any more about the Panama Canal than you do. I studied it like a part and then gave a performance. The reference books were props. Please let me stay in the theatre." That was that! I never mentioned college to her again. We both concentrated on the

74

theatre from then on. She was graduated from Sacred Heart with honors that spring and said she would not go back for the academic course we had first planned. She read all the published plays we could find. A book of George Bernard Shaw's plays was given to her, and after reading his *Caesar and Cleopatra* she said to me, "Some day I'm going to play Cleopatra!" I asked, "Shakespeare's?" She answered, "No. Shaw's."

All my love,

Grandma

Mary DARLING, Now, we will go back to that summer. A Mr. Poli had stock companies all over the country, and since the Columbia Players were no more, he had organized a company in Washington. Most of the old favorites from the Columbia Players had been engaged for the Poli stock, among them A. H. Van Buren, leading man, and Edwin Curtis, a director. They immediately spoke to Mommy about joining the company. She was delighted but insisted she wanted to play ingenue roles. No more "child parts" for her. They didn't know what to do, for she didn't look more than a day over twelve, but since she was a big draw in Washington they decided to give her a trial. When a play was popular in one stock company they would send it to another town for the next week, so for that reason they sent a play called *The Woman* to Washington for their opening bill. There was nothing in that play for Mommy but the part of a Polish slavey girl of indefinite age. She had one line to say: "Good evening."

I got an idea that if she could say that in Polish it would at least make her noticed in her home town for her first grown-up part. I was told that the head of the Hepner Beauty Parlor was a Pole, but I didn't feel as if we could take up his time having him teach Mommy how to say "Good evening" in Polish. Mommy said, "Couldn't you have your hair done there and while he is working on you he could repeat it several times and I would learn that way?" It cost me five dollars, but I thought it money well spent. All week of the rehearsal Mommy said "Doubravitcha" and made her exit. The director thought it was wonderful. At home she said it over and over again. On opening night I was standing in the first entrance waiting for at least a big gasp from the audience when Washington's "favorite daughter" should speak in this foreign tongue, but to my utter demoralization and Mommy's too, she said, "Good evening" without even an accent. To her credit, she said it in Polish at every performance after that, but the critics didn't mention her as being in the cast.

A week or two later the director of the stock company thought he would give Mommy a chance at the ingenue part in a play called *Kick In*. Mommy was supposed to be very sophisticated and had to light and smoke a cigarette during the play and also cross her legs. Neither of these

76

things had she been taught to do by her teachers, so Mommy thought she ought to study the cigarette business at home. I will never forget Grandpa Brown's face when he saw her. To see Mommy with a cigarette in her "baby" mouth was just the last straw and "it was time we both put this stage truck out of our heads once and for all. What other iniquity would she be expected to learn?"

For the next couple of days Mommy and I would sneak into her bedroom, but we didn't dare practice with a lighted cigarette for fear he would smell the smoke. When we thought she had mastered putting it in her mouth and puffing serenely, we decided the real smoking could be done at rehearsals. That was the funniest sight you have ever seen —Mommy, whose feet barely touched the floor when she was seated in an ordinary chair, holding the cigarette as if she expected it to go off, coughing and spitting, but still trying to act nonchalant and sophisticated.

At the same time she was trying to cross her legs, which refused to stay crossed since she couldn't reach the floor firmly enough to support them. It was just too much for the director who, after three days' rehearsal, took the part away from Mommy, saying, "Never mind, Helen, I'll have a better grown-up part for you soon." A few weeks later he gave Mommy the ingenue part in another play. He wanted to use her if possible, but it was no use. Although she was fifteen she still looked only ten or twelve. I could see Mommy was baffled, so as we were going home I said, "This is the day of the wise-cracking girl, but soon there will come along a play that will have a part which you will fit perfectly." I didn't fool her a bit, for she answered, "I guess I'll have to have more experience." I never knew whether she meant "life" or the stage.

Good night, darling,

Grandma

P.S.—I hope, my sweet, you are enjoying reading my letters as much as I do writing them. Mommy was always such fun for me and I'd like to make her as clear to you as she is to me.

Love,

Grandma

MARY DARLING, Mommy had an unforgettable experience one afternoon while she was playing at the Poli Theatre. Fritz Kreisler, the greatest violinist of our time, had been disabled in the War and had been sent back to Austria. He planned to come to America and give a series of concerts for the benefit of his beloved country, and Washington was the first city he came to on this tour.

Seats were sold weeks in advance and at enormous prices, so the stock company decided they would all listen from the balcony which was outside the dressing room. As early as Mommy and I got there the house was already jammed with people. From the orchestra to the last row in the top-most gallery one could see nothing but faces. Boxes were filled and about fifty people occupied seats on the very large stage. The President and Mrs. Wilson and party, completely surrounded by secret service men, entered his flag-draped box. The entire house arose as one and applauded President Wilson deafeningly, for whether they all agreed with his policies or not he was still our President and we were not yet in the War.

Mommy and I were standing with the rest of the cast on the narrow balcony waiting to see Mr. Kreisler make his appearance on the stage. He was already about fifteen minutes late. Suddenly, there was a frightening commotion behind the President's box. The audience fearing that the President was in danger began making strange cries and yelling unintelligible words. Mommy and I with one thought grabbed each other's hand and dashed down to the first entrance of the stage, just in time to see Mr. Kreisler, white as a sheet, stagger on.

The audience seeing him so white, apparently so weak, thought he was still ill from his wounds. Whereupon they began to applaud and yell the most vociferous welcome to him.

Now this is what happened. Mr. Kreisler, having been met at the station by the Poli manager, was taken through the front of the theatre, and as the only entrance to the stage was directly behind the President's box, he was being hustled back there as fast as he could be. He was whispering orders to his accompanist in German, and the secret service men, not being able to see him in the dark, assumed him to be a German spy with designs on the life of the President. They surrounded him with drawn pistols.

It took only a second for an explanation, but is it any wonder he was white and shaking when he got on the stage? However, he was quiet and composed when he began to play a minute later.

Mommy and I remained in the first entrance, since Mommy could see Mr. Kreisler perfectly and I could see him over her head.

After the first half of his program, when the audience finally let him leave the stage for a brief rest, he came off the first entrance, and, seeing Mommy standing there, chucked her under the chin and walked to the star's dressing room which had been put at his disposal. A minute or so later he came over to Mommy. Leaning down to her, he said, "Would you like me to play 'Poor Butterfly' for you?" Mommy just stared and nodded her head. He stood there and played very softly for Mommy the most popular ballad of that time—"Poor Butterfly." (The lyric was by John Golden.)

All my love,

Grandma

Mᴀʀʏ sᴡᴇᴇᴛ, A few weeks after Mommy had been "put in her place" the director sent again for her, this time for a ten-year-old girl in a play called *The Dummy*. A bit timidly I asked her what she wanted me to say to him. She answered, "Why, that I'll be glad to play it." And she did, with lots of joking about a fifteen-year-old looking more like ten years than she did like seventeen, which was the age of the ingenue that she couldn't play. She didn't like it much, but the ladies in the .company told her looking younger than her years would be a blessing some day. She made such a hit in this part (remember, it was her home town) that a stock company in Baltimore engaged her to play it the following week. We commuted nightly by trolley and I contracted muscular rheumatism, but in spite of my agony I had to stand in the wings so I could tell Mommy whether she "pounded" a line too much. This was an expression she picked up from the company and she loved to appear like an old-timer.

She played a very lovely part later on that summer of a sweet girl of fifteen, and this was the part that the play scout from New York saw her in and suggested her to George Tyler for *Pollyanna*. In the meantime, a New York producer was preparing a road company of *Fair and Warmer*. He sent for Mommy to come to Philadelphia to give him a reading of the leading part. There were more sleepless nights, and days of putting on her eighteen-year-old cousin's clothes, dressing her hair so she would look older and otherwise driving Grandpa Brown distracted. We didn't dare leave Washington in the regalia which she planned to wear when she met Mr. Bragdon.

I had to take a room in a hotel so she could change. We were to be at the Forrest Theatre that afternocn and when we spoke to Mr. Bragdon his astonishment at Mommy's appearance was most eloquent. He handed Mommy the part and as she began to read it her nose began to bleed. It bled and bled, and I was so frightened I asked him if we could go to the hotel to see a doctor, and we would come back later. Her nose stopped bleeding almost immediately after we got in the cab and when we arrived at the hotel there was a message from Mr. Bragdon, saying, he "was sorry but Miss Hayes was not the type." Mommy became resigned to playing child parts the rest of her life.

Good night. Sweet dreams.

Grandma

MARY DARLING, Mommy and I returned home after this ignominious experience and, as I said in my last letter, she was resigned to play child parts. Her one wish, however, was that some manager would send for her soon to play anything.

She was beginning to be a little difficult when she received a wire from Mr. Alf Hayman reading, "Report at my office tomorrow morning for a part with Mr. William Gillette!" More excitement in the Hayes-Brown menage!

Then began the wondering. "Is it a child or an ingenue?" "How shall I dress?" Finally Mommy suggested that I pack the high-heeled slippers that I had bought for the *Fair and Warmer* trial. These slippers, too, had been kept a secret from Grandpa Brown.

When Mommy was preparing to go to see Mr. Hayman she decided she would play safe. She would wear her hair down in case it was a child part but would also wear the high-heeled slippers if it was an ingenue he wanted.

Now I wish I could describe this effect as we walked down Broadway, Mommy teetering on the high heels with her long hair flowing down her back. From the waist up she was a little girl. From the waist down she was a girl of no uncertain sophistication. No wonder people stared. I was quite embarrassed, but not Mommy. One way or another she was going to get that part.

Mr. Hayman's greeting was most cordial but a little surprised. Mommy hadn't grown two inches since he had seen her with Mr. Drew. He explained the part was that of a grown young lady, so he told us to go down to Miss Ethel Barrymore's dressing room (she was playing at the Empire then) and Mommy was to put her hair up on her head. Afterward, she was to go out on the stage where Mr. Gillette was rehearsing. When the stage-door man unlocked Miss Barrymore's dressing-room door, Mommy all but made an obeisance, as if entering a sanctuary. She had never seen

Miss Barrymore act but had heard that she was the Queen of the American Theatre, the world Mommy loved.

After the door was closed Mommy stood in the middle of this room as if in a trance. Now, she had been in it many times when Mr. Drew occupied it, but this was different. This was a great actress's room. Now it was full of lovely feminine things—beautiful curtains, a chaise-longue with exquisite covers of silk and lace piled high with lovely pillows.

I began pulling aside curtains to see the gowns, but Mommy was horrified at my daring to do such a thing. It was sacrilege! But she didn't scorn to peep herself. I said at last, "We had better get started if you are going to dress your hair for Mr. Gillette." Then I looked under the cloth on the dressing table which was covering Miss Barrymore's make-up and started to help myself to hairpins. You see, we had neglected to bring any, but again Mommy said, "Please don't touch anything in this room, Mother. Just let me have your hairpins."

I have always had a great mop of hair, but I gave Mommy all my hairpins except one. I hoped, with the assistance of a high-crowned hat, my hair might stay up.

Meanwhile, Mommy was trying to get her hair into a sort of pompadour. This was done by "ratting" and rolling it in front, then piling the straight back hair on the top of that. Now, this was no work of art when it was finished. "But we mustn't keep Mr. Gillette waiting any longer," said Mommy.

84

Elsie Mackaye, Helen Hayes, Alfred Lunt, Glenn Hunter and Mary Boland in *Clarence*

In spite of the fact that by this time my hair was refusing to be confined by one hairpin and was half way down my back, we walked out together to meet Mr. Gillette on the stage.

His astonishment when he saw these two strange apparitions is indescribable, but he was as gentle as he could be when he said to Mommy, "I hear you are a great actress, but I am afraid I am too tall to play opposite you. I'll have a grand part for you some day, I'm sure."

We went up to tell Mr. Hayman and he was furious with Mr. Gillette, apparently. He said, "Why, Helen Hayes can play Lady Macbeth if she wanted to right now."

We said good-bye to Mr. Hayman, but Mommy wasn't unhappy because both Mr. Hayman and Mr. Gillette had expressed confidence in her ability and she *knew* that they would send for her some day.

All my love,

Grandma

M<small>ARY</small> <small>DARLING</small>, It was during this period of "irksome idleness" that Chamberlain Brown, whose scout had seen Mommy in the play I mentioned in one of my other letters, sent for her to come to New York for the lead in *Pollyanna*.

Mommy, who had never read or heard of *Pollyanna*, said, "I guess it's another child's part," but she just couldn't resist that word "lead." Then, too, as there were no more parts for her with the stock company, she had come to the conclusion she would never be sent for again. I really believe if a manager of a number three *Uncle Tom's Cabin* company had sent for her to play Topsy she would have ordered her trunk packed just the same, and have gone gladly to be in her beloved theatre.

Still being financed by Grandpa Brown we made our plans, Mommy and I, to live so cheaply we could remain in New York until something turned up. This was the way I was reasoning, but Mommy, with her old optimism, was sure she would get the part.

I took Mommy immediately to see Mr. Brown, the agent, and he sent us at once to Mr. George Tyler, whose office was in the Amsterdam Theatre Building. The moment we entered his office and saw his jovial face and were greeted with "And here's my Western Pollyanna," we were certain of another happy engagement.

It turned out that Miss Patricia Collinge, who had played the part the year before in New York, would star in the play throughout the East. Mommy would head the cast in the Far West and the Deep South. We went back to Mr. Brown's office to sign the contract for one hundred dollars a week and started rehearsals at once under Frederick Stanhope's direction.

Rehearsals were most happy for Mommy because Pat Collinge ran in frequently to help with bits of business that

Mommy never would have thought of. Mr. Stanhope was such fun, too, and after a few rehearsals was quite satisfied that the part was in safe hands.

By the time the play was ready to open in Rochester Mommy had grown very attached to Mr. Tyler. He would drop around during rehearsals and always encourage Mommy so much by his confidence in her ability. He said to her one day before we left town, "You are going to go very far, little lady, and I am expecting wonderful things will be said of you during this tour. Don't let them turn your head!"

When we started on tour we really looked like part of a circus, what with "Sodom" and "Gomorrah," the puppy and kitten of the first act which Mommy insisted on caring for herself. The property man took care of the grown-up "Sodom" and "Gomorrah."

Mr. Tyler said he would try to get to the opening if he possibly could, but he was casting other plays and had to remain in town. Mr. Stanhope held the dress rehearsal at the hotel in Rochester that night, and I was dubious about the success of the play, watching it without scenery. You see, the theatre charged so frightfully for its Sunday-night use and the stage crew charged double wages for their time. However, Mr. Stanhope said, "It's going to be great and you will pack them in wherever you go." The next night Mommy was pretty nervous, for she hadn't slept all the night before. There was no sign of this during the play, and she was truly lovely. The critics were wonderful about her performance and from then on it was the same story everywhere.

Good night. All my love,

Grandma

MARY, MY SWEET, I am afraid my geography of Mommy's tour in *Pollyanna* is going to be terribly jumbled as far as the incidents are concerned, but you won't care though whether they happened in Kalamazoo or Keokuk, so I will tell them to you.

There were three couples in the company, none of them young, but all living happily together since their marriage many years before. Because we carried considerable scenery and baggage, the railroad gave us our own coach to travel in. To many of the company this was the best engagement they had had for years, and this mode of travel was sheer luxury.

Mommy would dash from one to the other to hear one say, "Now in my day we only had a coach with immigrants who carried all their meals on the trains." "Many times we sat up in stations all night in order to catch a train early enough to make the next town. We even rode in a freight train," another would tell her. Still another would top this story by saying, "Why, many a time we would be caught in a blizzard, our train switched to a siding and we never would make the next town."

I would sit listening with half an ear to all these tales, quite confident this would never happen to us, and Mommy listening with ears and eyes agape wishing that such "adventures" could occur again. Mommy was just sixteen.

Pollyanna played three nights and a matinee in Rochester to packed houses, and Mr. Stanhope, who was to remain with us until after Albany, wired Mr. Tyler daily that Mommy was better and better at each performance.

George M. Cohan was to start his road tour, in one of his New York successes, the night after Mommy would close in Rochester, and at dinner Mr. Stanhope spoke to Mr. Cohan, who was seated alone across the dining room. Mommy couldn't take her eyes off him, nor could she eat her dinner. Finally, Mr. Stanhope said to Mommy, "Would you like to meet Cohan?" Mommy said, "Oh, yes. Mr. Cohan is my favorite actor." Mr. Stanhope took her to the table and I watched from ours, wondering just how Mommy would accept this introduction. You see, I knew Mr. Cohan was the only great star Mommy had seen from an orchestra seat up to this time.

Mr. Cohan stood up, held out his hand. And what do you think Mommy did? She reverted to her convent days and made a curtsy! She was truly awed by this meeting. When she returned to the table she was so embarrassed by this "slip" that she was quite sure Mr. Cohan would think she was just a "kid" and not an "adult" of sixteen. This feeling didn't last long, for she was in the same class with Mr. Cohan. They were both "trouping."

My dearest love and kisses,

Grandma

M ARY DEAR, Mr. Tyler came to Albany to see a performance, and he too said, "That child has a great feeling for the theatre and I predict a big future for her." Mommy was so happy that he had come all the way to Albany to see for himself that what the critics and Mr. Stanhope said wasn't prejudice in her favor. Another thing, she wanted him to see her as the grown-up Pollyanna, for she was afraid that he, too, looked upon her as a child. She started on her long tour quite content to face any hardship because Mr. Tyler promised her an ingenue part when she returned to New York.

With this tour, too, there were few week stands, and oh! the midnight jumps to make the next town in sleepers that were so cold we frequently piled our coats on top of us. Then, there were early morning risings, sometimes before the sun was up, and Mommy was close "to death" on many of these occasions because her enthusiasm was unlimited. The rest of us would be dead for sleep and sometimes half frozen, but she would rave about this "beautiful sunrise" or "that range of mountains peeping above the clouds" until I felt I could smother her.

Mommy played one night in a small town in Montana, whose name escapes me now. As was our custom, we went to the theatre almost immediately on arriving. The manager of the theatre met us in the lobby with an enormous ten-gallon hat on and "trigger" heel boots. He said to Mommy, "I hope your show's good, young lady, because the theatre's practically sold out to cow-hands just in from a round-up and a big pay-off, and if they don't like your show, they just start shooting through the ceiling." Whether he was joking or not we never knew.

Mommy looked out of a little peep hole in the curtain and saw that the theatre was jammed with the hardest-looking, tobacco-chewing, peanut-cracking lot of men you could imagine. Some kept their hats on and all wore chaps.

Mommy was terrified, for she knew how innocuous *Pollyanna* was. She said afterward she never knew how she got through that performance.

During the second act Mommy kept hearing the strangest sounds out front in the audience that she thought were "boos." She began to wish the act over as quickly as possible. Then, during the climax of the second act, she began to dread the end, for Pollyanna is carried on, having had both legs broken, crying hysterically, "*I am glad I am alive! I am glad I am alive!*"

Now this is a pretty big pill for anyone to swallow, even the most sentimental, but when the curtain descended on that act there was very little applause. However, those strange noises which had bothered Mommy during the act were ten times louder, and when she looked through the little peep hole she saw the entire house, almost to a man, blowing their noses like trumpets to hide their tears.

When we left the theatre that night we saw many horses hitched outside of what we supposed were saloons, and Mommy wanted to run all the way to the hotel, for, as she said, "Those cowboys may be drinking, and if they begin to realize they paid their money to see almost a Sunday School play they may begin shooting and I want to be in bed when that happens." We never heard a shot.

All my love, sweet,

Grandma

M<small>ARY</small> DARLING, Mommy's first leading part on tour taught her that "the play's the thing" as Shakespeare wrote. Here she was absolutely unknown, yet it was one triumphant tour from beginning to end. Everybody knew the story of *Pollyanna*.

Long before the play would reach the town, ministers from their pulpits advised their congregation to see *Pollyanna*. In many towns the manager of the theatre would have photos taken of the hundreds of people storming the box office for seats.

No matter how late we would be in reaching a town for a performance, the audience would wait. Frequently Mommy had to go on without any make-up except her Pollyanna wig and little gingham dress. I always thought she looked more the character of the undernourished Pollyanna at these times.

We were getting farther west all the time and therefore farther away from home and news of home. You see, this was before there was such a thing as air mail. Mommy never missed any news because she was having the most thrilling experience acting the lead in a play which was meeting with such tremendous success. Many of the critics on this tour would speak of Mommy as the "star" of *Pollyanna* and rarely spoke of her youth. Now you can see how this helped Mommy to "think grown-up" and how happy it made her to be considered "a lady of vast experience."

The farther west we got, the harder traveling became and I was afraid the strain might break down the splendid health Mommy had started out with.

She seldom complained of colds or illness, so when she wakened one morning in a small Mid-Western town and couldn't speak I was thoroughly frightened. I sent for a doctor immediately and he diagnosed it as laryngitis. He said, "I'll work on her all day, but she mustn't go on the stage tonight."

Mommy shook her head up and down most emphatically and with such fright in her eyes, but I couldn't understand this. The doctor asked me if she had an understudy and I replied, "Of course she has." "That settles it, young lady. You stay right in this bed." He gave her a couple of treatments and left, saying he would return later and give her some treatments before bedtime.

He was no sooner out of the room than she attempted to tell me she was going on that night or die trying.

I got very cross with her, accused her of behaving like a child and said, "You know Mary Fowler can go on for one night." With tears in her eyes she whispered, "That's just it. She is so pretty and I saw her rehearsing the part one day and she was awfully good. Maybe she will be better than I and Mr. Tyler won't give me that ingenue part."

When the doctor came again I asked him if he would go to the theatre with us and give her treatments throughout the play in her dressing room as I was quite sure she would be more ill if she remained in bed. Under protest he agreed to do this.

When we got to the theatre I told the stage manager to have the understudy ready in case Mommy couldn't get through the play. Now, here is the extraordinary thing about this whole incident: The doctor and I stood in the wings, he to spray her throat when she came off, and I to encourage her. She whispered as she made her first entrance, "I'll be all right."

We all waited for her first speech with grave doubts that she would be heard over the footlights, but her voice rang out clarion-like throughout that scene. After each exit she would lose her voice, only to regain it the moment she

94

went on the stage again. She never spoke as loud again as she had in her opening speech—just spoke in her natural voice.

She explained to the doctor and me afterward that she was straining her voice, in the opening speech, so she could be heard. That is why it had sounded so loud. She said, "I was as surprised as you were when I heard it."

I asked her, when we were alone, why, since her voice was so bad, she wouldn't give her understudy a chance. She said, "It wasn't jealousy or that I didn't want to give Mary a chance, but fear of my position made me want to go on. There are so many people to take your place as well and sometimes better."

Good night, my dear. Love,

Grandma

P.S.—I forgot to tell you Mommy explained the regaining of her voice when she would be on the stage by saying, "I guess I became Pollyanna then." I know the little country doctor believed he had accomplished a miracle.

Grandma

MARY DARLING, Mommy celebrated her seventeenth birthday in Fort Keogh, Montana, where she spent part of the day at the Fort watching them break in horses to be

95

sent "over there" for our boys in France. Mommy welcomed with joy each birthday, for she had the strangest notions about her "advancing" years and that was that she grew in height in proportion to each year. Then, too, with each year, whether it was the style or not, Mommy insisted on dropping her skirts an inch or two—anything to make her look older.

This birthday, however, she wasn't so gay, for by the time we reached Fort Keogh, she had already visited Army and Navy hospitals where many of our boys had been returned from France shell-shocked, maimed and crippled. Pollyanna became a sort of evangelist. Committees would meet us at stations and ask Mommy if she would bring "her message of gladness to the boys."

Now, as I told you before, Mommy had no parlor tricks, so she took to reading up on all the funny stories and jokes she could find and would tell a different one to each boy as she came to his cot or chair. Some of these stories and jokes were moss-grown, but Mommy didn't know it and was quite happy that she was doing her bit, and furthermore all this required "acting."

I always noticed, though, after a visit to a hospital, Mommy's second-act closing speech after she has had both legs broken was less convincing. She had seen too many who had no reason for being "glad."

All my love,

Grandma

Mary darling, When Mommy reached Los Angeles she couldn't wait to be taken to Hollywood and the studios. The Hollywood of 1917 was nothing like the Hollywood of today. There were no huge stages as they have now, but great long sheds on which pieces of scenery would be set and the most horrible Klieg lights that all but blinded you ten feet away.

Mommy was introduced to Bill Hart, the great star of Western movies, and was photographed with him, and then, happiness supreme! they asked her to play a scene and, if it was good they promised they would send for her and give her a contract. This was at the Fox Studios.

Mommy played Los Angeles for two weeks and kept hoping that a letter with the "Fox Studios" printed in the corner would come, but it never came, and this really spoiled her impression of California.

Before we left Los Angeles Mommy sent her route for the next three weeks to Fox Studios, and for the next three weeks we were all made miserable by her "wonderings" and, "Oh, I wish I hadn't worn that dress and hat when they made the test. They made me look so young."

If the letter had come, she would have refused an offer, I am sure, for even in those days the movies hadn't the glamor that the stage had for Mommy and still has.

Love and kisses, dear,

Grandma

M<small>ARY</small> <small>DEAR</small>, *Pollyanna* was to play Biloxi, Mississippi, one night and we were so late in arriving that we only had time to feed "Sodom" and "Gomorrah" and rush down to the dining room in the hotel to have our own supper, then rush to the theatre.

It was my custom when we were as late as this to read all the mail while Mommy made up. This night there was a very fat letter from Grandpa Brown, but that was because it also included a long enclosure from Mr. Hayman for Mommy.

I wish I could remember every word of his letter, but it was so long ago. I'll do my best to give you the gist of it, for it was the most important communication Mommy had ever received. This I do remember: It started, "Dear little Great Actress." Then it went on, "Where are you? We want you most terribly for the greatest part an actress ever had in a play by Sir James Barrie, starring William Gillette. How long are you to be under Mr. Tyler's management? Let me hear from you at once!!! Alf. Hayman."

Well, Mommy practically had to be prompted throughout the entire performance after that; she was so excited. After the play a telegram was given to Mommy. It had been there several days, but as a wire may contain bad news it is never given to an actor before the play. You see, it might spoil the performance. The good news in Mr. Hayman's letter affected Mommy badly enough, for in her excitement she cut out a whole scene. The wire was from the

Packard Agency, saying about the same thing Mr. Hayman's letter had.

Since it would cost an awful lot to send a wire saying all Mommy wanted to say to Mr. Tyler she decided to write him, enclosing the letter and wire, but said, "I'll send it special delivery. That will hurry it." There was no use telling her it would only hurry it on the New York end and that it would still take from six to eight days to reach Mr. Tyler. However, I was just as stupid as she was, for if I had wired Mr. Hayman to get in touch with Mr. Tyler all Mommy's agonizing suspense and my mental torture would have been over and we would still have Mr. Hayman's letter for your collection.

I shall just quote Mr. Tyler's answer to Mommy's letter:

Helen dear,

Will you kindly write Mrs. Packard about one line and tell her that I said for her to go to the·devil? And if any other agents write you send them each a copy of the letter you sent to Miss Humbert. I expect you to remain with me for the next fifteen years. You are going to be well taken care of next season with an increase in salary, and you are going to have a play all your own (I hope before the year is out). Don't ask me what it is going to be, for I don't know myself—but it *is* going to be, if I live. Anyhow, when the season is over, we will have a long chat, which is so much better than to discuss such matters by correspondence. Of course, you can work in pictures if you wish, but I don't think it wise for you to do so. Your future is as-

99

sured, and I promise you shan't want for money. So why do that which is likely to result in a great deal of injury both to your health and to your artistic possibilities, simply in order to increase your income? Anyhow, don't do anything of any kind until after you have talked with me, will you, dear?

With lots of love,

Yours as ever,
(Signed) G. C. T.

Mommy must have anticipated she would be sent a contract to do a picture for Fox, but as I told you before, she never heard from them again.

All my love, dear,

Grandma

Mary sweet, At this point in Mommy's career she wanted to play every part that was offered to her, so that when she received Mr. Tyler's letter with its indefinite promise she was terribly upset. Mr. Hayman had, from the beginning of his association with Mommy, shown himself such a partisan that she thought he knew better what she could do than Mr. Tyler who had only seen her one night in *Pollyanna*. Then, too, the prospects of playing in a Barrie play, with such a star as Mr. Gillette who would take all the responsibility of the play, filled her with a great hope that Mr. Tyler would let her accept this offer.

That Mr. Tyler was promising her a play of her own didn't make her as happy as you would expect. She knew she "must learn to crawl before she could walk." Her idea of a play of her own was that she would have to do a sort of monologue and carry the whole burden alone.

She wrote Mr. Hayman a beautifully sad but grateful letter, saying that Mr. Tyler expected to have a play for her the next season, but she didn't tell him to "go to the devil." The next Saturday afternoon there was one hundred and fifty dollars in Mommy's envelope, and Mr. St. John, her manager on tour, said that Mr. Tyler wanted her to have a drawing room on all-night jumps whenever possible. I shall never forget our first drawing room. Mommy and I just managed to restrain ourselves until after the porter had put our bags on the rack, our hats in paper bags and a pillow for each of us, then quietly closed the door, when we both fell onto the seats and burst into hysterical laughter. The idea of Mommy and me getting a drawing room all to ourselves without having to pay for it was far beyond all our dreams of luxury. Indeed, indeed, the theatre was a glorious world.

All my love,

Grandma

P.S.—The balance of Mommy's season with *Pollyanna* through the South was uneventful but tremendously interesting to her, and during this time Mr. Tyler wrote of having a wonderful part for her in Booth Tarkington's *Penrod*.

She and Paul Kelly were to be the "love interest"!!! That was a "grown-up" part.

Grandma

MARY DARLING, Again Mommy went through a sad parting, for she had become so attached to everyone in the *Pollyanna* company, but it had its compensations.

She would return to Washington, D. C., a very much traveled "young lady." No one would speak of her as a child again. She was seventeen and had been a most successful leading lady for nine months and was to be a full-fledged ingenue in the fall in New York.

When she had exhausted the subject of her travels, she began to get restless. So I decided at Mr. Tyler's suggestion to find a quiet place in the mountains where no one knew her as an actress and she could live a simple life out of doors. I found such a place way up in the Alleghenies. It was just a farm house and had only a few guests.

At first Mommy spent her days in raking hay and riding dray horses and studying the part of Margaret in *Penrod*, which Mr. Tyler had sent to her in Washington. I tried to leave the script at home but found Mommy had packed it herself. The more she got in the spirit of Margaret the more impossible Helen Hayes Brown became. Finally, about the middle of August I decided we were wasting both time and money because Mommy spent her days in our room telling me how she was going to play Margaret. We went back to Washington.

I discussed our future with Grandpa Brown, made him see that New York must be Mommy's home from then on. In other words, I burned our bridges.

We found a darling little apartment on the fifth floor of a house on West Forty-ninth Street which had previously been occupied by John Charles Thomas. Because Mommy was such a hero-worshiper, I was afraid that this atmosphere might give her an operatic complex, but, after all, Mommy knew her limitations. Shortly after we got settled rehearsals of *Penrod* began and Mommy was in her seventh heaven again.

All my love,

Grandma

MARY DARLING, This is going to be a very long letter because it is going to be devoted almost exclusively to stories of the little colored boy who played the part of Vermin in *Penrod*. He was about eight years old and I am sure he had never been out of Harlem in his life. I don't know how Mr. Tyler ever found him, but he was brought to the Globe Theatre the first day of rehearsal by his grandmother, a real old-time Southern darkey. From that first day, discipline flew out of the stage door. No one could count on Vermin. His grandmother was told to see that he was there for his cues, but the theatre being strange to her, she was inclined to watch the play and other actors and forget to watch Vermin.

He was like a flea, here and there and everywhere but the place he should be. The poor stage manager spent his time running up and down Broadway looking for him.

Vermin had a script, but his grandmother held on to that so Vermin never noticed that everyone else was repeating the same thing over every day at the rehearsals.

After being forcibly dragged back by the stage manager, he would run on the stage and say anything that popped into his head. The other children, Andrew Lawlor, Penrod; Richard Ross, Sam; Helen Chandler, Marjorie; Herman, another little colored boy, would just go to pieces and the whole rehearsal would develop into a conglomerate mess.

Mr. Tyler would have gotten rid of him, but Mr. Tarkington insisted he was his dream Vermin and was quite sure that when the novelty of being on the stage wore off Vermin would settle down to the seriousness of his work. Sad to relate, he never did, and to the last night that *Penrod* played in New York he never stopped his pranks and never ceased to be the most adorable little monkey you have ever heard of.

Penrod was to open in Atlantic City for one week before coming to New York. We had a grand cast: Dudley Digges,

Katherine Emmett, John Davidson, Paul Kelly and Mommy, besides the children already mentioned.

The dress rehearsal was called for Sunday morning at eleven o'clock. Everybody concerned reported promptly, except Mr. Tarkington and Vermin. The stage was set for the first scene, everyone was made up and dressed, but nothing could be done until those two showed up. Mr. Tyler had a call put in to Mr. Tarkington's hotel and was told he had left for the Apollo Theatre more than an hour ago. Vermin's grandmother declared that Vermin had come into the theatre with her. We all decided that she, seeing the stage set for the first time and being intrigued by this, forgot all about Vermin, and of course he took advantage and fled to the boardwalk to see the sights of this wonderland.

As every minute a stage crew gives of their time on Sunday means double pay, Mr. Tyler was getting into a terrible state over the cost of this delay. Finally, Vermin walked on the stage, bursting with excitement, jingling a lot of coins and suffering horribly from an overdose of ice-cream cones and salt-water taffy. Mr. Tarkington came down the aisle to Mr. Tyler, chuckling like a bad boy who had been on a lark.

It seems he had started out to take his constitutional on the boardwalk and saw Vermin surrounded by a number of people who had been watching the sand carvers. He got close enough to hear Vermin holding forth about what he was doing down there. He was an "actor," an assistant of a "detecativ." These people, Mr. Tarkington said, were in convulsions and instead of throwing the coins intended for the sand carvers they were giving them to Vermin to buy the ice cream cones or taffy. The poor sand carvers must have had meager gleanings that morning.

After Vermin would come out of the ice cream or taffy place, Mr. Tarkington said, he would make for another group of sand-carving watchers, with Mr. Tarkington close by having the time of his life. This kept up until they reached the Apollo Theatre, when Mr. Tarkington realized there was work waiting for both of them and steered Vermin into the theatre.

When the children asked Vermin how he had gotten all this money, he said, "I didn't do nuthin' for it. I just told 'em I was an actor."

Penrod opened that Monday night in Atlantic City to a crowded theatre and as everyone constituted himself as guardian to see that Vermin got on and told him each time he made an entrance what to say, it was a fairly smooth first-night performance.

If he couldn't remember every line he would resort to a strange gibberish which the other children had been told to ignore and to go on with their next line.

When the play was over that night everyone breathed a sigh of relief, for the suspense to them throughout was terrible. They just could not guess Vermin.

The second night, because Vermin had been so good the

first night, the cast was lulled into a sense of security about him. They were sure it was playing to an audience that would chasten him and make him conscious of his responsibilities. That was their mistake.

Now, there was a scene in the second act when Penrod called his "able assistants" around him—Sam, Herman and Vermin—to give them their orders about following the "villain." Penrod blew his police whistle and Sam and Herman responded. Vermin was supposed to crawl through the hedge on all fours *head first*. Instead, he crawled backward until he reached Penrod and the center of the stage. He stood up, turned around and the whole theatre rocked with laughter. He had taken a bag of flour into the hedge with him and covered his entire face with it!

The effect on the other three boys was devastating. Not one line of their parts could one of them speak, but it didn't matter, for the audience could not pull themselves together at the sight of two black eyes shining out of that white face under that black woolly head. Vermin was surely enjoying the effect this make-up was having on his playfellows by grinning from ear to ear, jumping up and down like a monkey and leaving an island of flour on the stage wherever he stepped.

Now, all of the white children had been in the theatre for two or three years and knew its code "The Play Must Go On!" but even if the theatre had tumbled about their ears they could not stop laughing at Vermin. I think Andrew Lawlor, who was twelve then, really suffered, for all we heard him say, while the audience was shrieking, was, "Oh! oh!" in a voice of real agony.

Now, the adults of the cast might have saved the situation if they, too, hadn't been hysterical. Vermin was finally gotten off the stage and the play went on from there, but in that one scene he "stole the show."

It is a well-known fact in the theatre that there is always a terrible "let-down" in everyone's performance on the second night, but I think this one went on record as the worst that had ever been seen.

Vermin's grandmother was always threatening to "bash" his head against the wall, but as far as we could find out she never punished him in any way. She adored him.

Mommy was so happy playing Margaret, though it was hardly a real ingenue part—it was really one of the first flapper parts that was written in a play at that time.

Mr. Tyler took *Penrod* into the Globe Theatre, which had always been a musical-comedy house and therefore too large for an intimate little play like *Penrod*. It made no money there. Mr. Tyler decided to move it to the smallest theatre then in New York, the Punch and Judy.

By this time Mommy decided there was too much laughing at one Master Vermin's pranks by the cast, particularly the children, so she began to train herself and steel herself against "breaking up." She knew eventually her performance would suffer if she didn't learn to control laughing at him. It was awfully hard at first, but she finally conquered her desire to laugh, and it was several years later before she succumbed to this failing again. I'll tell you about that when I reach the play in which it happened.

You know, dear, the audience resents an actor's having a private joke, since they have paid their money either to be entertained or amused.

All my love, dear,

Grandma

M<small>ARY</small> <small>DEAR</small>, *Penrod* had been playing about a month at the Punch and Judy when an epidemic of infantile paralysis broke out in New York City and the health authorities ordered schools, and all places of amusement catering to children, closed at once. This order went out on Thursday, and on Friday a list of the theatres and plays closing on Saturday night was in all the papers. *Penrod* was one of them. On Saturday afternoon, when we arrived at the theatre for the final matinee, there was a special-delivery letter from Mr. Hayman asking Mommy to come to see him in his office after the matinee that day.

Mommy knew it was about *Dear Brutus*, for there had been frequent mention in the newspapers that the Frohman management had been unable to secure a Margaret for that play, which it had hoped to produce in the fall.

We went down to see Mr. Hayman and he told Mommy he understood or had learned that *Penrod* would not reopen and that Mr. Tyler hadn't another play for Mommy for this season. Then he gave Mommy the part of Margaret to take home to read. I explained to him that we would have to see Mr. Tyler first. He said, "By all means." He was always so fair in his dealings with us. On our way to Mr. Tyler's office Mommy read the part of Margaret and was entranced with the beauty of it.

Then she began to worry for fear Mr. Tyler wouldn't let her play it. I said, "Since he hasn't a part for you, I see no reason why you shouldn't tell him that you want to play this, and play it." Mommy said, "No. If he doesn't wish me to play it, back it goes to Mr. Hayman and he, I suppose, will never send for me again." She argued, "Mr. Tyler has been mighty good to me and I just can't fail him." Mommy's sense of loyalty was much greater than mine, for she had no contract with Mr. Tyler. I reminded her of this, but she said, "Don't you remember, Mother, that when I joined *Penrod* Mr. Tyler said, 'A contract won't be necessary between us any more. My word is sufficient.'"

After Mommy told Mr. Tyler what Mr. Hayman had said he called Mr. Hayman on the phone and said he would like to read the script of *Dear Brutus* so he could judge whether it would be wise for him to lend Mommy for the play. The script was sent over by a messenger at once. Mr. Tyler read it that night and phoned Mr. Hayman that Mommy could play it for three hundred dollars a week. That was one hundred and fifty dollars more than she had gotten with *Penrod*. Again, Mommy began to worry. "No part was worth that much and Mr. Hayman would surely get someone else." Well, he did take Mommy at that fabulous salary and she signed the contract that afternoon.

Mr. Hayman said to Mommy as he saw us to the door, "I'd have waited until doomsday if necessary so that you could play this part. I think Sir James Barrie had you in mind when he wrote it."

All my love, dear,

Grandma

Mary dear, This is just a little personal story about Mommy and how I wanted her to begin *looking* like a successful actress. She had no jewelry except a little narrow gold bracelet which Santa Claus had brought her when she was six years old. She had no particular vanity about clothes except when they made her look older. I was going to change all that. So months before her eighteenth birthday I began setting my heart on a real pearl, set simply in a narrow platinum ring for Mommy's tiny hand. I went from jeweler to jeweler only to find the pearl I wanted would cost between four hundred and five hundred dollars. After *Penrod* closed we went home for a short visit and then began my campaign to get Grandpa Brown to buy Mommy the ring.

I'd start talking about the ring before Mommy would be up in the morning and continue the subject after she had gone to bed. I didn't want her to know anything about it. It was to be a surprise. He began to weaken when I pointed out that all the young actresses in New York wore beautiful jewelry and what an impression of success it created. The fatal moment came when he asked how much a "thing" like that would cost. I knew I couldn't just blurt out four hundred dollars to a man who never failed to ask when he would get a bill from the convent, "Is all this education necessary for a girl in her walk of life?" There was only one thing to do. I did it. I tossed the amount quite casually over my shoulder and left the room. I heard a frightful oath and then mutterings about "these highfalutin ideas." When I finally went back into the room he said, "Does it have to be a real pearl?" We compromised. He paid half and I paid half.

Mommy loved her ring but I spent my time from her eighteenth birthday asking her whenever she came in if she had her pearl. It was stolen from her years later at a house party in San Sebastian, Spain.

She wasn't careless, but she never placed a material value on anything.

All my love, dear,

Grandma

Mary darling, When Mommy started rehearsals as Margaret in *Dear Brutus* I thought that with more than ten years' experience behind her all she would have to do was learn the part as directed. I shortly came to the conclusion she couldn't live long enough to know all there was to know about this art of acting.

First of all, Mommy spoke with a decided Southern accent, but as mine was a bit thick too, I hadn't noticed this. Mr. Iden Paine, an Englishman, was her director and kept constantly correcting her diction. Finally he said, "Listen to the others." As three-fourths of the cast were English and in speaking clipped their words very short sometimes, Mommy didn't see how she could improve her speech by listening to them. After three or four days' rehearsal the corrections became so constant that Mommy decided Mr. Paine didn't like her and she thought she ought to give up the part.

After she had come to this decision we left the theatre to go to Mr. Tyler and tell him all about it. We hadn't gone half a block up Broadway when Mommy began to cry. People began to stare at Mommy, then glare at me as if I was responsible for her tears. I suggested we go into a drug store at Broadway and Forty-second Street and she could go into a telephone booth and have her "cry out" there. She did, while I waited outside, with as heavy a heart as she had.

We arrived at Mr. Tyler's office with no sign of the

agony Mommy had gone through in that phone booth except two very red eyes and a most terribly red nose. Mommy told Mr. Tyler her troubles and he said, "You are not going to give the part up but you are going to try to overcome this accent you have. This part will make you."

The next day I asked Mr. Paine what Mommy could do about her accent and he suggested that she read Shakespeare's sonnets aloud. We bought a copy on our way home that day and for days and days and nights and nights we had sonnets instead of conversation. It was surprising how quickly Mommy's diction improved, and soon Mr. Paine was complimenting her on her understanding and interpretation of Margaret. He had been so conscious of her accent up to this time he hadn't noticed how much soul she was putting into the part. From then until *Dear Brutus* opened Mommy worked like a Trojan and was gloriously happy.

My love and kisses,

Grandma

P.S.—This was the cast for *Dear Brutus:* William Gillette, Miss Hilda Spong, Miss Elizabeth Risdon, Miss Marie Wainwright, Miss Violet Kemble Cooper, Miss Myrtle Tannehill, John Brewer, Sam Sothern (E. H. Sothern's brother), Grant Stewart, Louis Calvert, and Mommy.

Grandma

Mary sweet, Mr. Gillette didn't approve of Mr. Paine's direction of Mommy, so he suggested that I bring her to Mr. Hayman's office upstairs in the Empire Theatre Building at eight o'clock every night and they would rehearse their own scene in their way. This was the last week of the rehearsal in New York. This was a tremendous help to Mommy, for he gave her free rein to play the entire scene as if he were her real father.

He was a bit "wicked" about these secret rehearsals, for he told Mommy that they both would follow Mr. Paine's directions during the daily rehearsal and forget them completely on the opening night. This was Mr. Gillette's own little joke.

Since no one else was concerned in this scene but Mr. Gillette and Mommy it was easy to keep the secret. "Laughing John" who took us up in the elevator at night, was the only one who knew of them, and he never told. Every once in a while at the daily rehearsals Mommy would forget and do something that Mr. Gillette and she had put in of their own the night before. Mr. Paine would immediately correct Mommy and say, "This is the way I want it done." One night Mr. Gillette said, "You see, he wants you to play it like a British girl and that will take all your individuality away. That is why we must keep these rehearsals our own secret."

What a surprised man Mr. Paine must have been on the opening night when he saw that scene! He certainly

couldn't have recognized one bit of his direction in it.
Much love, dear,

Grandma

P.S.—There was a piece of business in this scene in which Margaret tells her Dream Daddy that "The nicest time in a young girl's life is the year she puts up her hair." Then Margaret runs to a pool, looks at her reflection, meanwhile telling Daddy to keep his eyes closed. She then pins her hair up on her head, dances downstage and says, "Look, Daddy."

Mommy's hair was down to her waist, but it was as straight as a poker, so it was not as pretty a picture as Mommy felt it should be. Nothing would do to correct this fault, she insisted, but a permanent wave, which she had done before the opening. Mommy certainly was getting on.

P.P.S.—On November 11, 1918, *Dear Brutus* was in the midst of rehearsal when the most terrible din arose outside of the theatre. People were screaming, sirens and horns were blowing. Bedlam had broken loose. Every one of the cast rushed to the street to find all New York City gone mad.

The Armistice had been signed!!!

The whole cast broke up and began running in every direction but to the theatre. Mommy grabbed my hand and we never stopped running until we reached St. Patrick's Cathedral. It was crowded to the doors, but Mommy made

116

Helen Hayes and Kenneth MacKenna in *What Every Woman Knows*

a genuflection and whispered a little prayer and dashed out again to me. This was one of the most glorious days in the world and Mommy was part of it.

Love,

Grandma

Mary darling, As the opening date of *Dear Brutus* drew near (it was to open December 11, 1918, in Atlantic City) Mommy began to worry about the mixed performance she might give. You see, by this time she wasn't sure which were the right directions, Mr. Gillette's or Mr. Paine's. I could see she was very confused in her own mind, so I advised her to play it in her own way, which was the way Mr. Gillette had let her do it at the night rehearsals. I didn't expect her to follow my advice, but I didn't know what else to tell her.

It was bitter cold that opening night in Atlantic City and the audience was almost as cold to the play. It wasn't clear to them. It wasn't a very smooth performance, and to me Mommy seemed to be hopping about a great deal unnecessarily and was giving a composite performance of Mr. Paine's and Mr. Gillette's directions.

After the performance Mr. Hayman and all the cast congratulated Mommy—all except Mr. Paine, and he had such a list of "don'ts" for her that she was thrown into a state,

117

for she knew he was right. Her performance wasn't good.

Mr. Gillette asked us to wait until he removed his make-up, and we three would walk back to the hotel and talk over their performance. Mommy said, "Mother and I had better go alone, Mr. Gillette, for I want to take a long walk to clear my mind of the faults in my performance and I won't let even Mother speak a word." This I knew wouldn't be so. I knew she was suffering mentally, for she had let Mr. Hayman and Mr. Gillette down and would have an outlet before she went to bed. We had no sooner gotten on the boardwalk than Mommy began, "What was the matter with me, Mother? Why did I say that line in that unconvincing way? What do you suppose happened to me? Did I play it like that at the dress rehearsal?" We must have walked for two or three hours and the whys and what-she-shouldn't-have-dones never stopped. I think Mommy would have walked all night, but my feet were hurting and I was awfully cold. Besides, I couldn't see we were getting anywhere. I persuaded her, after we had passed our hotel several times, to go in and we could talk it over comfortably in our room. When we entered the lobby Mr. Gillette rose from a chair and said, "I have been waiting for you, 'Dream Daughter,' to give you a message from Mr. Hayman. He said to tell you he was prouder than ever of his great little leading lady." Mr. Gillette knew better than I did the best medicine for Mommy's troubled mind.

Good night, dear,

Grandma

Mary sweet, *Dear Brutus* played all that week in Atlantic City with daily rehearsals. Whether Mr. Hayman or Mr. Gillette, or both, told Mr. Paine to let Mommy alone, he only told her where her position should be and she kept getting better at each performance. By the time they reached Washington, where they were to play a week before going to New York, Mommy was giving an exquisitely poignant characterization of the Dream Daughter. I could hardly sleep a wink that Monday night and I am sure Mommy didn't, for the audience had been very enthusiastic. I felt that the criticisms would be wonderful the next day. Well, "A prophet is truly without honor in his home," for, while the critics were nice to Mommy, they were not enthusiastic.

Mommy took it splendidly. She said, "I guess I was too nervous to convince them." I tried to assure her there was no sign of this noticeable to me where I stood watching her from the wings. She said, "You couldn't have seen me at the pool, then? I couldn't find the hairpins where I had hidden them for what seemed like an hour and my hands were so cold clammy and shook so much that I nearly dropped the pins when I did find them." I had noticed that she said a lot of "Now don't look, Daddys" but I thought she was just taking a bit more time for her hair. You see, the pool was way upstage and so I could only see Mr. Gillette, who was seated downstage at his easel. She said, "Margaret is a great part and I will play it as it should be played before I reach New York." Gillette was so wonderful that week. He sensed that she was worried, so he would send his valet with notes to Mommy's dressing room, saying he had something very important to talk to her about, and would she stop at his room before the second act? It was never anything important and he would never mention the play. He would have a funny little toy or novelty that he had bought during the day for her, or he would tell her of some awful mishap he had had when he first went on the stage. By the time the curtain would go up on the second act, their act, they would make their entrance in gales of real laughter. By Saturday night, Mommy's performance was truly beautiful. She was sorry the critics couldn't see her in the play again for Grandpa Brown's sake.

My next letter will be about another glorious opening at the Empire Theatre.

Loads of love and kisses,

Grandma

P.S.—I want to tell you of the dressing room arrangements for the cast of *Dear Brutus* at the Empire Theatre, for I have a reason' for doing this which you will understand in my next letter. Mr. Gillette, of course, had the Star dressing room; Miss Spong had the one next to his, where Mommy had dressed when she was with Mr. Drew. These two were on the first floor; Miss Kemble Cooper, Miss Wainwright and Sam Sothern on the second floor; Miss Tannehill, Miss Risdon and Mr. Brewer on the third floor; Grant Stewart, Louis Calvert and Mommy on the fourth floor. Mommy's was an enormous one all to herself.

Just before the curtain went up on the opening night Mommy received this letter from Mr. Gillette:

Dream of My Life:
   It is important that I come up at once. It will be impossible for me to play the second act unless you let me come—for my mind would be distracted and harassed. It must be *at rest*. Make it so by saying to the Japanese one that I may come for a moment. I am relying on you for this.
                    Your Hallucination Daddy

He climbed those four flights of stairs just to tell Mommy she would be magnificent.
                              Grandma

MARY DARLING, Mommy and I were at the Empire Theatre at seven-thirty o'clock on December 23, 1918. Mommy was dressed and made up though she didn't go on for her scene until almost ten o'clock. She wanted to be in the wings from the moment the curtain went up to hear everybody's reception. Three or four of the cast had been in recent hits so they, as well as Mr. Gillette, all got tumultuous applause.

After the first act, Mommy and I remained in the wings, her clammy hand and my clammy hand clasped closely together. I even walked over with her while she hid her hairpins by the pool preparatory to the hair-dressing scene. Mr. Gillette joined us at the "upper left," where they would make their entrance into the Dream Forest. When the signal came for the curtain to rise Mommy's head went up like a race horse that hears the starting gong. She followed her Dream Daddy, laughing, dancing with a reed to her mouth. I thought I would faint as I ran from "upper left" to "lower right," where Mommy asked me to stand so I could both see and hear how she was doing. She was exquisite, and when the curtain came down as she was screaming "I don't want to be a might-have-been" the applause was deafening. I didn't count the number of curtain calls Mr. Gillette and she took, but they seemed unending. I ran to Mommy's dressing room, so no one would see me crying, but Mr. Gillette brought Mommy upstairs to her room as if she was a queen and she noticed my tears. She said, "You are crying, Mother," and I hastened to say, "They are tears of joy—you have come into your own tonight."

After Mr. Gillette left us I asked Mommy if she had been frightened at any time during the scene. She said, "Not for a moment, for wasn't I playing the best part a girl ever had and I was playing it the best I knew how." The next day she was acclaimed the greatest young actress of her age in New York City.

All my love,

Grandma

MARY DARLING, When I was looking in the attic in your home for some old photographs the other day, I came across a number of New York newspaper criticisms that appeared the day after the opening of *Dear Brutus*. They were worn because Mommy and I had read and re-read them so many times when the play first opened, and too, they are quite yellow after twenty-one years of knocking about. I know you will only be interested in what they said about Mommy, so I shall just quote you excerpts from the best-known critics then:

Alan Dale, *New York American*—
"The real attraction of the performance was Miss Helen Hayes, who, as the young girl, was one of the surprises of the season. Here we are simply starving for ingenues and obliged to use mature actresses for the purpose, and this exquisite little girl steps in and carries away all the honors of a 'star' performance."

John Corbin, *New York Times*—
"Mr. Gillette has never been more humanly gracious and delicately real; and he is admirably seconded by Helen Hayes whose little Margaret is a wonderful blending of dream beauty and girlish actuality."

Miss Dorothy Parker, *Vanity Fair*—
"The ladies' cup goes to Helen Hayes, who does an exquisite bit of acting. Hers is one of those roles that could be overdone without a struggle, yet she never

once skips over into the kittenish, never once grows too exuberantly sweet—and when you think how easily she could have ruined the whole thing, her work seems little short of marvelous."

Burns Mantle, *Evening Mail*—
"It is exquisitely acted by Mr. Gillette and Helen Hayes, an alluring little actress, who thus gets her first New York chance, and makes much of it. She has the fairy grace, the wistful, childish charm of the Barrie dream children and a nice skill in projecting it and her personal success was quite complete."

Heywood Broun, *New York Tribune*—
"Miss Helen Hayes, who is not yet eighteen, and these are the official George Tyler figures, played the daughter, and Miss Hayes is as eager as Christmas morning and as dazzling as Christmas night. It may be that nobody will ever call her the great Miss Hayes, but if not she will have to grow out of an amazing equipment of natural charm and technical skill. She was on top of the tree last night."

By this time Mommy was reading all her criticisms and truly, as Mr. Broun said, she was sitting on top of the Christmas tree.

All my love, dear,

Grandma

P.S.—Darling, a few days after *Dear Brutus* opened in New York, Mr. Hayman sent for Mommy and me to come to his office. Mommy immediately became worried but not I, for after reading those beautiful notices I was sure this summons meant an increase in salary, but it didn't. He began warning me not to allow Mommy to be seen in too many public places—restaurants or motion-picture theatres. Then, in order to impress us with the importance of enveloping her in an aura of aloofness and mystery he told us how "C.F." hadn't permitted Maude Adams to eat a meal in a public restaurant. When on tour she had all her meals in her hotel suite. This reminded me of an experience Mommy and I had one day when Mommy was playing *Pollyanna*. I think it was in St. Louis. Mommy had played the first three nights and Miss Adams was to appear for the balance of the week. We were just leaving the hotel for our next jump when Miss Adams arrived. Mommy had never seen Miss Adams on or off the stage, but I whispered to her who it was, so she turned like a flash and followed close on Miss Adams' heels to the elevator, only to have the elevator boy say "I'll be down directly" and close the door in Mommy's face. You see, no one was permitted to ride in the same elevator with Miss Adams.

Well, when Mr. Hayman laid down these rules for Mommy who was just coming out of her shell, so to speak, I protested that it was too late, that Mommy loved to eat in restaurants and adored motion pictures, and all work and no play and not being allowed to rub elbows with her fellow men would certainly make her pretty dull. "Furthermore," said I, "that may affect a star's standing with the public, but, remember, Helen is a long way from being a star."

Then he told us of a "horrible" example of this public-appearance menace. He said that when Miss Ethel Barry-more first became a star she was seen several times at parties, after a play, in restaurants, that it took the Frohman management a full year to restore the illusion about Miss Barrymore. He explained that the public wouldn't pay to see their stars if they could see them any time for nothing.

I promised to do my best not to cheapen Mommy, but since she had few diversions outside of her work I made up my mind that I would certainly not restrict her to the extent that he had ordered. I had to keep reassuring Mommy that I had no intention of burying myself, much less her. I was sure Mr. Hayman was wrong about the public's desire for their favorites to be put on another plane from their everyday lives. I, myself, would have been more loyal to Miss Adams and have loved her longer if I could have known her better.

Thank goodness, Mommy was old enough to do what she wanted to, and it was her mingling with all sorts of people that has helped her depict and understand all sorts of characters she has played on the stage.

Love,

Grandma

Mary darling, Life was very gay and happy for Mommy these days, especially when she was at the theatre. Because the fireman in making his rounds at every performance never came above the third floor, all the cast would foregather in Mommy's dressing room to smoke during the intermissions.

Mommy loved these times, for now she was eighteen and wasn't just limited to the fairly nice stories of the theatre. She heard some of the most harrowing experiences many of them had had, especially in the English provinces. Sometimes the experiences they would tell of wouldn't be so bad. Then Mommy would feel she could mention some of her "terrible experiences" traveling through the West. They would listen attentively while she told her tales, but compared to theirs her stories sounded like picnics. After awhile she took to exaggerating them unconsciously. At first I wondered where I was when these "frightful things" happened. Then I realized Mommy was exercising her imagination and I never questioned her story.

As usual, Mommy and I would be at the theatre before anyone else. She would be dressed, made up and downstairs when the curtain went up on the first act. Then, before the curtain came down on that act, she would dash up her four flights of stairs to be in her "salon" when the smokers arrived. Mr. Gillette began to notice that she never came down for the second act until it was almost time to go on. When the play first opened Mr. Gillette asked Mommy why she spent all of the first act and the intermission down in the wings, and she told him she liked to get into the "atmosphere." One night he stopped her, as they made their exit and she was about to dash upstairs, and said, "My dear, have you decided that you have absorbed all the atmosphere necessary for a good performance? You don't spend so much time down on the stage, and I miss you." Mommy said, "Oh, no! I am still in the atmosphere of the theatre." Then Mommy explained about the smokers and the fabulous stories they told. Mr. Gillette said, "Though I am not eligible to be a member of your smokers' club (he didn't use tobacco), couldn't I come up too and contribute some fabulous stories?" Mommy said that everyone would be delighted to have him. "Maybe Mr. Gillette will make us too self-conscious and there won't be any more fun," she said afterward.

A couple of nights later, just before the first act, Mr. Gillette's valet brought up Mr. Gillette's personal card on which was written "Listen, Vanishing Dream! I hope you will let me come in and see you some time this evening. Say yes! W.G."

This began a series of notes written on scraps of paper, telegraph blanks and Hotel Plaza stationery, where Mr. Gillette lived when in town. Then Mommy would send down word that everyone would be happy to see him, and they truly were. He would come bouncing up those iron stairs with the most amazing agility for one in his sixties.

Mr. Gillette's stories were funny ones and didn't tax Mommy's imagination. After that he joined the circle regularly.

All my love, dear,

Grandma

MARY SWEET, One day early in May, Mr. Tyler sent for Mommy to start rehearsals with his repertory company which was to have six weeks in Washington, D. C., during June and July. There was a marvelous company gathered on the New Amsterdam Theatre stage—Miss Emily Stevens, Miss Fania Marinoff, Miss Josephine Hall, Sidney Toler, Alfred Lunt, Glenn Hunter and Harry Mestayer.

We had heard that Miss Stevens was one of the wittiest women of that time, but that her wit was of the acid variety. This frightened Mommy terribly, because everyone had always been so careful of her feelings, even when joking, that she had no clever retorts ready in case one of these barbed witticisms should be directed at her. We had been told Miss Stevens spared no one. Well, Mommy found her terribly witty but charmingly so, and became so fascinated by her that she followed Miss Stevens about almost to the point of annoyance. That first day was just a reading of the play, *On the Hiring Line*, written by Mr. and Mrs. Harvey O'Higgins, which would open the repertory season in Washington. All through the reading I kept worrying about Mommy leaving *Dear Brutus*. I feared we were making a terrible mistake. I asked Mr. Tyler when I should give Mommy's two weeks' notice of leaving. He said there was plenty of time, that the middle of May would be time enough. He also told us to say nothing until Mommy did give her written notice. He said Mr. Hayman understood that Mommy had only been loaned to them until he, Mr. Tyler, had a play to put her in and that her leaving wouldn't disturb them, as *Dear Brutus* was probably going to close anyway. I told Mr. Tyler that Mr. Gillette hoped Mommy could go on tour with them next season and that I thought it would be valuable to her inasmuch as she practically shared honors with Mr. Gillette. He answered, "The experience she will get in playing these different roles will be more valuable than going on tour in a part that she has already squeezed dry." I was thinking of the friends she would make in playing this beautiful part throughout the country.

That night Mommy told Mr. Gillette, for, she said, "I think he should know at once, because if I tell him now it won't be necessary to write that horrid notice to Mr. Hayman." I said, "Since you feel so badly about leaving, why do you? You have no contract with Mr. Tyler." Mommy insisted that Mr. Tyler was looking way ahead for her and she had promised to stay under his management.

We had many discussions and several heated arguments,

for my loyalty went to the Frohman management, which I felt we both knew so well by this time and I also felt would do as much for her as Mr. Tyler.

Mr. Gillette went to see Mr. Tyler to try to persuade him to let Mommy stay another season with them but Mr. Tyler was adamant ("his plans were made").

All my love, dear,

Grandma

MARY DARLING, Mommy was having such a good time at these rehearsals that the pain of leaving *Dear Brutus* was growing less and less. Each day when she would arrive for the rehearsal someone of the company would be repeating and chuckling over some *bon mot* of Miss Stevens which she had made as the ladies walked home together. One day as we got to the stage door, Mommy said, "Do you mind, Mother, if I go to lunch and walk home with the ladies of the company? Miss Stevens is such fun and it might sharpen my sense of humor, the lack of which Mr. Tyler is always deploring." I was just as well pleased to go home, for my heart was still heavy about her leaving *Dear Brutus*. After a day or two I noticed Mommy had a very strained manner in talking. She seemed to be striving to make the most trivial thing sound funny.

Just a couple of nights before she was to close with *Dear Brutus* she said to me with a far-away look in her eyes, "You know, Mother, I'd rather be a great wit than anything else in the world." She had never been funnier than at that moment. I said, "My dear, wits are born, not made. You stick to the thing you do best and that is acting."

All my love,

Grandma

P.S.—I do think, Mary dear, that I forgot to tell you Mommy was still hoping to get into motion pictures and she told Miss Stevens of this ambition. Miss Stevens was very clever in her advice, for she laughed Mommy out of the idea by saying, "Well, Helen, there is this much to be said for the movies: They are most democratic. For instance, the first week I went into them I was Miss Stevens. The second week I was Emily and after that I was just Stevens. Another thing, my dear, if you do go out to Hollywood don't ever do a picture in which there is a baby, a dog or a railroad train. You are sunk before you get started." From then on Mommy never talked of going into pictures. I blessed Miss Stevens for that.

Grandma

Mary darling, The Saturday night that Mommy was to close she asked me to put her hairpins by the pool, for, she said, "If I talk to Mr. Gillette before I go on I will be too miserable to give a good performance." As I crossed

Helen Hayes in *Coquette*, with Charles Waldron

the stage to the pool I saw Mr. Gillette pacing up and down with a dreadful scowl on his face. I tried to get upstairs without being seen by him, but he had been waiting for Mommy and pounced on me. He asked me why Mommy hadn't come down, and I, in a moment of confusion, said she was so unhappy at leaving that she couldn't bear to talk to anyone before she went on. He immediately accused me of conspiring with Mr. Tyler to ruin her career. He said, "What did George Tyler do for her?" I said, "He has been very kind to her always." Said he, "In what way have we failed to be kind to her?" Well, I was cornered, and since I was innocent I said the only thing that popped into my head, and that was what Mommy had said to me, "Mr. Tyler raised her salary on tour without being asked and furnished us a drawing room whenever possible." He said, "You should be very happy. You have sold Helen for a couple of Pullman tickets." I had brought this on my own head, so I could only make an ignominious retreat and I never told Mommy for days afterward, when we could both laugh over the fool reasons I had given for her leaving.

All my love, dear,

Grandma

P.S.—Mommy and I left on the midnight train for Washington with very heavy hearts. I wanted to tell Mr. Gillette we were paying for our own sleepers this time, but he wouldn't even say good-bye to me.

Grandma

Mary darling, Mommy's part in On the Hiring Line was the usual flapper, with no demands on her acting ability. She was satisfied, for there was a lot to learn from watching and working with those fine artists. The season opened June 2, 1919, at the National Theatre in Washington, D. C. The reviews were excellent, but business was bad all week. Mr. Tyler was sure that the next week's play, A Young Man's Fancy, which he thought was a grand one, would certainly bring them to the box office. There was no part in this second week's play for Mommy, but as the idea was to put her in the other plays which were to follow, we didn't at all mind this week of rest at home with the family.

At that opening night of A Young Man's Fancy there wasn't a handful of people in the house, and the reviews next day were not conducive to any better business. Mr. Tyler posted notice that the company would close that Saturday night, and Mommy had only played one small part. I think I said to Mommy, "I told you so."

I felt sorry for Mr. Tyler, for he had gone to a tremendous outlay. There were enormous salaries, except Mommy's, but we were home and we didn't mind a reduction. There were elaborate scenery, gowns, and, of course, options on all the plays. Mr. Tyler took it very philosophically but blamed Washington's bad taste.

Much love,

Grandma

P.S.—Alfred Lunt and Miss Lynn Fontanne were co-starred in A Young Man's Fancy, and it was at the rehearsals of this play that these two people met and their romance began.

Grandma

MARY DARLING, After the failure of the repertory company in Washington, Mr. Tyler told Mommy that Booth Tarkington was writing a play for Alfred Lunt called Clarence. He said there was a grand part in it for Mommy and that he hoped to try it out in Atlantic City for one week some time in July.

About the middle of June Mr. Tarkington presented to Mr. Tyler an almost perfect script, and he, Mr. Tyler, started casting at once, and this is the cast Clarence had when it opened the last week in July: Miss Mary Boland, Miss Phoebe Foster, Miss Susanne Westford, Miss Rea Martin, Alfred Lunt, Glenn Hunter, John Flood, Barlow Borland and Mommy. It was a grand play and everyone had a gay time at rehearsals. No wonder then when it opened in Atlantic City it was an instantaneous hit. Mommy hated that week to come to an end. However, Mommy and I had planned to go to Lake Placid for a month direct from Atlantic City and then return to Washington when rehearsals would be called for Clarence in the fall.

While we were at Placid storm clouds were gathering in the ranks of the Actors' Equity. Some of the members were opposed to the threatened affiliation with the American Federation of Labor and they formed an organization known as the Fidelity League.

Now, at this time Mommy knew nothing about the Actors' Equity. So when Mr. Tyler wrote her to have nothing to do with the affair and to remain away from New York until the trouble blew over, she naturally wrote him that she would be guided by anything he would advise.

All that summer there were meetings and threats of walk-outs and strikes by all the Equity members. Finally, Mr. Tyler wrote Mommy to come back to New York and join the Fidelity League, which she did. The Equity joined the union and a general strike was ordered. Then Mommy's Gethsemane began.

Nearly all the actors Mommy had worked with (not the stars) belonged to Equity, and they began to importune Mommy to leave the "Fidos" and join Equity. Mommy, having given her word to Mr. Tyler, refused, with her heart just breaking, for she felt such a renegade. She held out against the pleadings of such actors as Miss Ethel Barrymore, Miss Mary Boland, Mr. Francis Wilson and Mr. Ralph Morgan for three years.

I'll tell you of her capitulation in another letter.

All my love, dear,

Grandma

MARY SWEET, The Actors' Equity finally won their demands after they joined the American Federation of Labor.

Mr. Tyler called the first rehearsal of *Clarence* with the same cast he had in Atlantic City, with this one change, Miss Elsie Mackaye instead of Miss Foster, all members of Equity except Mommy. They were all so happy at being back to work and in this grand play again that all differences were forgotten.

Alfred Lunt had forgotten the little he had learned about the saxophone since the "try-out." He had many moments during the play when his playing on this instrument bore an important part, so he practiced it during rehearsals whenever possible. It was pretty awful, for there was one very high note which he just couldn't control and that would toot out in a certain passage at the most unexpected moment. He kept the company in a constant state of hilarity with his jokes about that one note. He said that it was the spirit of Adelina Patti coming back for another "farewell performance." Every once in awhile he would say, "Patti's in again" and there were moments when no one could collect himself to go on with the rehearsal. Mommy's part, Cora, was that of a brat flapper who was always telling tales on her adolescent brother, played by Glenn Hunter.

Though Mommy hadn't a brother she had two cousins— sister and brother—who were fine examples for her characterization. It was easy then for her to express by different inflections contempt, cynical tolerance and sarcasm when speaking to her brother in the play. Glenn Hunter, too, helped tremendously in making her scene seem most convincing, for he showed such an utter contempt for this younger sister who was trying to act grown-up and who had a terrible "crush" on Clarence that the entire company would be convulsed during this scene. I will tell you about the opening night of Clarence in New York in my next letter.

Love,

Grandma

Mary darling, The opening of Clarence at the Hudson Theatre on September 20, 1919, made theatrical history. Now, in the play, Clarence was supposed to be a discharged soldier from the World War. Before the War he had, as a student, made an extensive study of the coleoptera (beetle). After he returned to America he had to get work at once in order to pursue his studies, so he applied to the "Wheelers" for a position as handyman, which they gave him. Out of this arose the most hilarious complications, and it just struck the right note for a recently war-torn public. After the last-act curtain the audience began yelling, applauding and stamping their feet. When the first call came and the curtain went up the entire house was standing, and they remained that way up to about twenty-five curtain calls. At first, the audience tore their programs up and were throwing them like confetti. When the program supply was exhausted the men in the audience began throwing their hats in the air and the women threw their handkerchiefs. It was as wildly exciting as Armistice Day. Many men went home bareheaded or with the wrong hat that night, but all went with a new lease on life because of that play. Next day *Clarence* was hailed as the great American comedy of all time.

All my love,

Grandma

P.S.—The reviews, without exception, next day were so glowing for everyone and so much better for Mommy than they had been ever before that she practically bought out the entire supply of our neighborhood newsdealer. The entire *Clarence* company settled down for a two-years' residence at the Hudson Theatre.

Love,

Grandma

Mary sweet, I want to tell you how praise and constant pointing out the perfections of certain pieces of business nearly ruined Mommy's performance after she had been playing Cora for three months.

Mr. Tyler, because he was so happy over the success of *Clarence*, took to coming to the theatre and sitting in Mommy's dressing room. They would be discussing his plans for her for the next season when suddenly, without being called or even hearing any word from the stage, Mommy would dart from the room and dash down the iron stairs and walk on the stage just as her cue came. She didn't realize it then, but it was a mechanical sense that told her when she should be down for her entrance. One matinee, though, she suddenly left the room and dashed down to and on the stage, thereby cutting out a long scene between Miss Mackay and Alfred Lunt. Mr. Tyler stopped his visits after that.

This mechanical thing was insidious. It crept upon her until there was no spontaneity left in her performance. No one in the cast noticed it. One night, the scene in which Cora's father, after a particularly bitter scene between brother and sister and in the presence of Cora's latest crush, Clarence, tells her to "go to her room and wash her face." Cora made her exit, saying with the most awful contempt and humiliation, "Wash my face. Wash my face. Wash my face."

This was the famous line that used to, in the parlance of the theatre, "bring the house down." It was always seconds before the applause died down sufficiently for the next scene to go on. This particular night there was the most horrible silence, both in front and in back of the footlights. Immediately, each actor concerned in the scene thought he had done something, unconsciously of course, that had spoiled the exit. When the curtain came down on that act, each one asked the other if he had moved or spoken too soon. No one blamed Mommy, and she didn't know what had happened to her.

The next performance and several after that she made her exit in complete silence as far as the audience was concerned. The whole cast was heartsick for Mommy because her distress was painful to watch. One night, Miss Boland said to Mommy just before Mommy made her first entrance, "Helen, I have just remembered that what has happened to you happened to me some years ago in a play with Mr. Drew. I had been made conscious of my comedy. Just forget you have one funny line or scene, and it will come back to you and be spontaneous again." Mommy said to me that night after the play, "I am going to a dramatic school to learn how to act!" This frightened me terribly, for my experience with dramatic teachers had been too much waving of arms, elocution and extreme affectation. I immediately began arguing against this notion, reminding her what C.F., Mr. Drew and Mr. Gillette had warned her against, that was: "Never allow anyone to change your natural gift." Finally, she asked me to come down and watch her scene. I went down at the next performance to my old place at the first entrance, where I was always to be found on her opening nights. I found her straining her voice, "pounding" her lines and otherwise overplaying every piece of business that had been pointed out as being so wonderful by both critics and friends. I told her of these faults, but unfortunately I had no suggestions to make for correcting them.

Mommy was kept so busy trying to eliminate all the wrong things she had drifted into doing that she forgot all about being funny in the play, and one glorious night to the joy of the whole cast she made her exit to the usual roars of laughter and a tremendous round of applause.

She never lost that beautiful exit again, thanks to Miss Boland.

To this day, Mommy will not allow anyone to tell her that a gesture is particularly good or that a piece of business is clever for fear of becoming conscious of them.

My love,

Grandma

P.S.—During the run of *Clarence* Miss Fontanne and Alfred Lunt were in the throes of their great romance. As a matter of fact, theirs was love at first sight. Alfred had such naïveté and was so gentle and sweet to all the ladies in the cast that each one of them felt a certain possessiveness for him. I, being my age, was probably the only one who didn't resent Miss Fontanne. Mommy, who all this time was carrying a secret passion in her heart for Alfred, was the most resentful. My heart used to ache for Lynn when she had to run that gauntlet of spiteful faces and their remarks about her "pursuing him." I thought because Lynn carried her head so high she was indifferent to anyone's opinion of her, but she told Mommy long after she and Alfred were married that she suffered acutely in that walk to Alfred's dressing room.

Grandma

M<small>ARY</small> <small>SWEET</small>, About the middle of the run of *Clarence* in New York Mr. Tyler told Mommy that Edward Childs Carpenter was adapting Mary Roberts Rinehart's sub-deb *Bab* diaries for her and she would leave *Clarence* as soon as Mr. Carpenter finished the play. Again Mommy was rebellious, for she was so happy with this play and company and at that time would have been satisfied to go on playing Cora forever.

Mr. Tyler insisted Mommy mustn't be content to stand still and that he would not stop advancing her until she was at the top of the ladder. In the meantime he had gathered together a grand cast for *Bab* and soon they were rehearsing like mad. Mommy was to remain with *Clarence* until the Saturday night preceding the opening of *Bab* at Taunton, Mass.

The night Mommy closed in *Clarence* even the weather was upset, for a terrific snowstorm was raging. The theatre was jammed just the same with a typical *Clarence* audience, gay, happy and prepared to love every minute of the play. The cast and stage crew, however, were in very low spirits at Mommy's leaving, but there was something so exhilarating in that *Clarence* comedy and the gales of laughter it evoked that even Mommy forgot her sadness while she was on the stage.

After the final curtain, which Mommy was anticipating with her usual agony at parting, the company and stage crew surrounded her while Alfred Lunt presented her with a silver loving cup on which each member of the cast had inscribed his name. Alfred made a beautiful speech, telling Mommy how sorry they all were to see her go. Then the stage carpenter stepped up and, on behalf of the entire crew, gave Mommy the largest bouquet of violets I had ever seen. There was not a name missing, not even the doormen. Also, on the card was written, "We will miss you, Miss Hayes." At this moment Mommy was no older than Cora, for she was crying like a baby and not a pretty one either. Her make-up was all over her face in blotches and the mascara was running down her cheeks in black rivulets. All she could cry was, "I don't want to leave. I don't want to leave."

Mr. Tyler's ears must have burned that night, for the company felt very bitter toward him and said quite openly, "He has no right to take Helen out of the play."

It was well after twelve o'clock when Mommy got her face clean and had gathered up her numerous gifts and packages to start for home. When we got out of the theatre the storm was raging more fiercely than when we had first gotten there. Mommy's tears were still falling and almost freezing as they fell, for she hadn't a free hand with which to wipe them away. I hailed taxi after taxi, but for some reason they just wouldn't stop for us. We walked blocks and I was half frozen before a cab finally took us in, but Mommy seemed oblivious of everything with her heart breaking at leaving her beloved *Clarence* company.

I am afraid Mommy was becoming a fickle jade, for by the next Saturday night she was as happy as a lark in her new role of Bab.

Good night and sweet dreams,

Grandma

P.S.—In reaching this stage in Mommy's career, you know, "where the brook and river meet," I realize that up to this time she was very emotional and easily moved to tears. Your great-grandfather used to say, "The Hayeses could keen at the drop of a hat." Like all clowns, Mommy too wanted to play tragedy. Since she was much too young for a tragic role in the theatre she turned it on in her private life at the slightest provocation. Those first nineteen years were her most lachrymose.

Grandma

Mary darling, *Bab* opened in Taunton, Mass., February 13, 1920, and Mommy could have papered the four walls of her dressing room with the telegrams of good wishes she received. They came from actors whom she had worked with as far back as the Lew Fields' days. Many were from total strangers who only knew her across the footlights but had followed her career from the *Dear Brutus* days. We were both so touched by all this that the Hayes-Browns had a perfect orgy of keening that night.

The audience adored the play and Mommy, and for the three nights and one matinee she was in Taunton there wasn't a seat to be had. Mommy was bubbling over with happiness and could hardly wait to get to Boston for new worlds to conquer.

Love,

Grandma

P.S.—This was the cast in *Bab*: Tom Powers, leading man, Miss Percy Haswell, Robert Hudson, Miss Lillian Ross, Miss Katherine Alexander, Miss Helen Gurney, Sam Edwards, Arthur Eldred, Stephen Davis and James Kearney.

Grandma

M<small>ARY</small> <small>SWEET</small>, On February 16, 1920, Mommy opened her memorable engagement in *Bab* at the Hollis Street Theatre in Boston, Mass. Memorable, not only to Mommy, who had her first attack of love during this engagement, but to a number of Harvard juniors, sophomores and even seniors, who developed severe cases of puppy love for an actress. Mommy played at the Hollis eight weeks, and she had the most thrilling time of her whole life because of these students. I must explain this. Though Mommy was then nineteen, she hadn't met many young men. There were only a few in the companies she had been with and those had no more experience than she had. For this reason she cultivated the older actors, for they could tell her things that had happened in the theatre before she was born. During the Boston engagement she was used for more initiations in fraternities than most girls of her age are. Here are just two initiations in which Mommy was asked to share.

One matinee day the stage-door man of the Hollis Theatre came to the dressing room and said, "There is a young boy at the door who wants to see Miss Hayes' maid." Mommy had no maid then, so I said I would talk with him. I found a tall stout blond boy with cow-licks all over his head. He was aghast when he saw me, but managed to stammer, "I have been sent to get a pair of Miss Hayes' corsets before I can be initiated in the fraternity." I tried to put him at his ease as I said with a friendly smile, "I am sorry, but Miss Hayes hasn't started to wear them yet.

Would mine do?" You could have lighted a match with his flaming face as he turned and fled.

Mommy and I were leaving the theatre after a matinee one day and as we stepped to the sidewalk that was crowded with girls and boys waiting to see the actors come out, a tall, lanky young man was all but thrown at Mommy by two much older young men. He fell on his knees at Mommy's feet, shouting in a very loud voice, "I have the honor to beg your hand in marriage." Then he added as he struggled to his feet, "I don't mean this, but I had to do it for the fraternity." He, too, fled as he was followed by the derisive laughter of the crowd, but he had earned his initiation. Mommy was the most amazed person until she realized it was another fraternity joke and then she said, "He might have given me a chance to refuse him."

Mommy was learning that she could have a lot of fun outside of the theatre, too.

Much love,

Grandma

Mary, my sweet, I want to tell you how Mommy became Bab, the sub-deb, on and off the stage.

Two days after she opened in Boston she found at the theatre several bids for a dance that one of the senior clubs of Harvard was giving the next week at the Copley-Plaza, where we were stopping. This caused great agitation in

Mommy's mind not only because it was her first big dance, but it meant the choosing and buying of her first real evening dress. This took first an awful lot of consideration, then many cancellations because Mommy changed her mind hourly about the color. Finally I got embarrassed at calling up shops to say we had decided that was not "exactly" the sort of dress Miss Hayes wanted. I told her if she didn't make up her mind at once and stick to it she wouldn't have time to get the dress for the dance. Her indecision was caused mainly by the fact that she was trying to find a frock that had some sophistication about it, but they weren't making that type of gown for one as tiny as Mommy.

We rushed out to make a tour of the shops that we hadn't been in before, and Mommy ended by buying the most exquisite and most angelic white chiffon gown; but she bought brilliant red satin slippers with extremely high heels to give a touch of devilishness to her otherwise modest outfit. She also bought that day a darling little cream velvet cape and a tiny, white, lace fan.

When we got to the theatre the night of the dance there were a number of corsages. Each of her "crushes" had remembered her.

Her performance that night was like a great big bubble that she never let touch the ground. She was so happy. After the play she insisted on carrying all the bouquets to the hotel, so she could try each one on her dress and wear the one that looked the best.

I'll never forget Mommy that night. She must have put her hair up and taken it down a dozen times before she was satisfied. I had been dressed so long I was wishing I could undress and go to bed. When she was at last ready to go down, she insisted, though we weren't going out of doors, on carrying her cape over one arm, and her small evening bag and her fan in the other hand.

Her hair was piled high in a shower of curls (it was another permanent wave). She pinned a single purple orchid on her shoulder, and with her face aglow and eyes shining she looked like a butterfly that had just burst from its chrysalis.

That was a happy night for me, too. You see, Mommy had never shown any interest in the young boys she had met before and I began to fear she might be one of those women "wedded" to her career, and I didn't want that to happen to her.

All my fears were put to rest when we went up to bed at four o'clock that morning, for while Mommy was a bit of a bedraggled butterfly she was decidedly a social one.

I spent the balance of the morning picking up notes that were pushed under the door, first being preceded by a good loud knock. They were mostly requests for luncheons, teas and after-theatre suppers, all of which she wanted to accept. I only had to remind her then that her work would suffer if she plunged into a whirl of gaiety that she hadn't been accustomed to. She decided that day to send her regrets for nearly all after-theatre affairs.

Mommy made many real friends among the Junior League girls, too, so whenever she takes the company to Boston now it is like Old Home Week for her.

Much love,

Grandma

M ARY DEAR, I suddenly realized one day that the luncheon and tea engagements were not an altogether good idea for the students either. You see, in order to take Mommy out at those hours during the day they had to miss a number of classes. One student was Alan Rinehart, son of the author of the *Bab* diaries, who boasted he had seen the play more than twenty-five times. Some of these were matinees when he should have been attending classes. He was most endearing but he would dramatize this puppy love of his until you would have thought his the one great love of all time. I think he was just eighteen. He didn't quite ring true to Mommy, for he had told her when she first met him that he was going to be a writer, so she thought this would be the love story he would write some day.

One professor at Harvard told me Mommy had disrupted his classes, and the art teacher there said there were seven heads of Helen Hayes submitted to him for criticism in one day. Mommy fell heir to two of them later.

I told both of them the same thing: that it was Bab the actress and not the girl that was the cause of it all.

I didn't worry about Mommy's being seriously affected by this "rushing" because there is safety in numbers, and, besides, when anyone of these suitors invited Mommy to luncheon or tea she always answered, "Oh, yes. *Mother* and I would love it." Now you can't be very much in love with a man and want your mother around, too.

Much love, dear,

Grandma

P.S.—This is a little advice I want to give you, dear: When you are nineteen and are invited out by a young man, don't insist on Mommy going along. You know the old saying, "Two's company, three's a crowd," and while you may not consider Mommy a crowd, you will make it awkward for her with the young man.

Grandma

Mary darling, I must tell you about the day Mommy first met Lotta Crabtree, the best-known soubrette of the "Forty-niners."

The manager of the Hollis Theatre told Mommy that Lotta had reserved two seats in the balcony for that afternoon. Mommy, knowing that Lotta was famous and not knowing that she was rich, thought she couldn't afford the orchestra, so she asked the manager to see that Lotta had better seats. He said to Mommy, "She comes to see every new play and will never sit anywhere but in the balcony." He also told Mommy that if Lotta liked her performance she would come backstage and tell her so.

Well, just before the last curtain I put the kettle on and made some bread and butter sandwiches, so we could all be comfortable and friendly over a cup of tea and that Lotta then might wax reminiscent about those "gold rush" days. This would be something that none of the old-timers that Mommy had been associated with could tell her about.

William Seymour, Mommy's manager, was one of those old-timers but he had never met Lotta, so I asked him to come in and have a cup of tea with us.

Lotta came back, and if her face hadn't been so wrinkled I'd have thought her as young as Mommy. She was no taller than Mommy and had bright yellow hair in curls around her face. She had on a delicate lavender silk dress with lace ruffles all over it and a girlish hat with a wreath of pink and blue flowers on it. She carried a lemon-colored broadcloth coat with a large ermine scarf. She herself was as gay as her outfit. Mr. Seymour said he couldn't wait for tea, so he followed Lotta in and Mommy introduced them. Mr. Seymour said, "Miss Lotta, I have admired you for years. My mother took me to see you when I was a little boy." Well, Lotta looked at his white hair and said, "That was my mother you went to see." He understood the implication and fairly fled from the room.

I was afraid that this passage at arms would spoil Mommy's visit with her, for there was an unmistakable glint in Lotta's eye when she turned to me and said, "It is astonishing the number of old people I meet today whose parents brought them, by the hand, to see me when I was twenty." Mommy was inwardly convulsed, but was busily pouring tea for all of us and she didn't make the mistake of pressing Lotta into a chair.

Lotta sat down and said to Mommy, "Now let's talk about you. First, I want to say you are a born comedienne. You have three great qualities, first, speaking distinctly so the man in the balcony and gallery can understand every word you say. People go to those seats because they can't afford to go anywhere else and I go in the balcony because that is where the true lover of the theatre will be found. Second, you have a beautiful natural speaking voice, and last, but most important, you are a good listener." Turning to me she said, "Where did she learn this grand sense of comedy?" I replied, "You said she was a born comedienne and then, too, she is Irish." As she was leaving she invited us to have tea with her some day. Mommy went alone a week later, hoping Lotta would tell her something of her youth in the theatre. She found Lotta did not live in the past but knew every great happening, every new invention of this day. She avoided all mention of shop that afternoon.

All my love, dear,

Grandma

MARY SWEET, Mommy had been having such a good time in Boston and had been entertained so wonderfully by people she had never known before this engagement that she decided to give a supper dance at the Copley-Plaza and invite all the girls and boys she had met, and also those parents who lived in Boston for me, so I wouldn't get bored. That list kept growing by leaps and bounds until I called Mommy's attention to what that number would cost. She hadn't sent out invitations yet, but there wasn't a name she wanted to cross off. She got a very practical idea, and that was she would have the supper (I think there were sixty to be invited) on the night the Copley-Plaza had its Saturday-night dance. She wouldn't have to hire an orchestra and yet they could all dance just the same. It worked out beautifully and Mommy didn't receive one regret.

Now this was Mommy's first big party of her own, and there wasn't a guest who had as good a time as she had. She danced every dance and never seemed to tire. This was during Prohibition, so there were no drinks served. A few of the boys would disappear between dances and return a few minutes later a little glassy-eyed. Alan Rinehart was one of them and when each time he returned to find Mommy dancing with somebody else he would sit by me brooding. When he went out again I told Mommy to wait until he returned and give him that next dance and to try to see if she couldn't keep him near her for the balance of the night. He was pathetically young. He was so surprised

155

to find Mommy not dancing that he just sat down without a word. Mommy said, "Alan, I have saved this dance for you." Now, I want to describe him so you can see how funny they looked on the floor. He was at least six feet tall, very thin, with dark eyes and hair. He was really very handsome. Mommy's head just came to about the second button of his vest, and as he swung her around in the dance her feet left the floor entirely. It looked like an apache dance, for he seemed to be swinging her by the neck.

The captain who had charge of these Saturday-night dances came over to that crowded floor, touched Alan on the shoulder and said, "You can't dance that way here, Mr. Rinehart." One of the other boys rescued Mommy and danced off with her, leaving Alan to get off the floor so embarrassed and humiliated that my heart ached for him. He came over to me, apologized and begged to be excused and said he would go back to Cambridge. Mommy didn't refer to the incident until we got to our room, where she found a note under the door from Alan. He started it this way (Mommy read the first part aloud): "Helen dear, I was drunk at the ball tonight." She didn't get any farther, for I almost died laughing, and she said, "You see, Alan just can't stop writing a romance story around himself. All he had was one glass of port." She told me after she finished reading his letter to herself that he had written: "I just cannot bear to see you in another man's arms." Mommy said, "He must have eyes in the back of his head, for his eyes were turned from the dance floor all the time he was in the room." Just the same, she looked a bit like "the cat that has swallowed the canary," for pretended or not, it read well.

All my love, dear,

Grandma

P.S.—A week or so later, Mommy got a note from Alan, asking if she would take a walk on the Common with him, as he was going home to Sewickley, Penn., and wanted to say good-bye to her. Mommy went to meet him in the hotel lobby and was gone about two hours. I wasn't at all worried, for I reckoned it would take every bit that long for Mommy to give Alan—"the little boy" to her—one of her grown-up lectures. When she came in she was bursting with merriment. She said, "Well, I have just received my first proposal of marriage. At least I think Alan was proposing. He asked me to go to Peru with him." Then she told me that they walked around the Common until she knew every blade of grass and until her tongue was hanging out with thirst. She asked him to buy her a glass of soda. But he said he only had fifteen cents, ten of which was for carfare back to Cambridge. He bought her a five-cent bar of Hershey's chocolate though, which he helped her eat, while he urged her to flee with him to Peru. Thirst drove them both home.

Love,

Grandma

157

Mary darling, I think I ought to tell you about some of the things that happened to Mommy while playing *Bab*. You know I wrote you how she was always trying to improve her performances. She never made any radical change in her scenes with others, but when she was entirely alone on the stage, she would often try something different. I watched her always from the wings so that I could tell her whether it was a good or bad change.

Now, in the role of Bab, Mommy was so gay and happy all the time that she rarely walked on the stage. Her feet didn't seem to touch the ground. In consequence, she had a hard time keeping her equilibrium. She seemed to be slipping and sliding every step she took. I cautioned her not to go flying around so much, but she said, "This is the way I feel the part." One night as she was running across the stage to make an exit before Miss Haswell, her "stage mother" could see her, she slipped and fell flat on her face. She was up immediately and, turning to her mother, said, "Well, I won't get married this year," and ran off to the wildest laughter and applause she had ever gotten in the play. People came again and again not so much for the play as it was to see what changes Mommy would make in her performance. So Mommy knew that there were many of them and some of her erstwhile suitors out front who knew it was an accident, but Mommy just thought of it as an excellent piece of business, under the circumstances, but she never actually fell again. I am sure any other girl of

Mommy's age would have been terribly embarrassed at such a catastrophe.

I was waiting for her after the act and grimly said, "Now, you will pay attention to my warning." She said, "I can't play Bab any other way, and if I ever fall again I shall remember to say that line. It saved that situation beautifully."

Good night, dear,

Grandma

M**ARY** **SWEET**, Mommy had been playing Bab for about six or eight weeks and in this time many private schools had given theatre parties for their pupils. Most of these were satisfied just to come to the play and a few days later she would receive a number of fan letters as a result. One matinee a note was brought back to Mommy from the teacher of a dramatic class in a school in or near Boston, asking Mommy if she would address a few remarks to her class after the matinee. Mommy sent back word she would be happy to. Now, while her dressing room at the Hollis was enormous it was hardly large enough to accommodate a class of about fifty girls ranging from the age of twelve to fifteen. In one corner of the room, dark, red brocade curtains hid the wash basin, so I fled there without being seen. Mommy wanted to talk to the class on the stage, when she saw the size of it, but half were already in the room and they were all determined to get into a star's dressing room or die in the attempt.

The teacher in a very pedantic manner said to Mommy, "Now, Miss Hayes, won't you tell my class just how hard you have to study and work to attain the position you have in the theatre today?" I hardly breathed in my hiding place, waiting for Mommy's answer to this poser. I had never doubted Mommy's veracity before, but that day I decided she had inherited something else besides Graddy Hayes' vivid imagination, and that was to lie convincingly. This is what she said, "I had to, and still do, get up early, take physical and breathing exercises and then an hour of French, then off to school for the study of English and musical accomplishments. At night, I study the various female roles in Shakespeare's plays."

She hadn't taken a moment's exercise since the Lew Fields Hess Sisters days, and as for her French, I don't think she had looked in a French book since her experience with Mr. Drew and their French conversations. Shakespeare she had never studied except when it came up in her classes, for she was scared to death of him.

She considered this fabulous story an excellent exit speech, for she said, "I have to say good-bye now, so I can get a little rest for my evening's strenuous performance."

When they had gone and Mommy closed the door, I came out from behind the curtains. I couldn't speak. Mommy said, "I know what you are thinking, but if you had seen the look of justified satisfaction on that teacher's face you would have known I had answered her as she hoped I would. Besides, she gave me my cue when she said, 'Tell my pupils how hard et cetera, et cetera.' It was just another performance I had to give." I couldn't help feeling sorry for that class, for I could see how Helen Hayes and her hard work would be held over them as a beautiful example of what constant application would do for them. And now, Mary dear, I want to say if ever anyone had a red plush carpet for her, metaphorically speaking, it was Mommy. Mr. Tyler once said, "She is the most extraordinary person. She never makes a mistake in her reaction to a line or a thought, but she doesn't know why she doesn't. It is an unerring instinct."

All my love, dear,

Grandma

P.S.—I promised you in one of my early letters to tell you a funny happening about Mommy's noise phobia. There was a scene in *Bab* in which Mommy had to run and hide in a closet holding a revolver in her hand. While hidden, Bab is supposed to sneeze, and the revolver goes off. Tom Powers, who is on the stage, rushes to the closet door, and on opening it Bab staggers out, coughing, with a smoking revolver in her hand.

Because Mommy couldn't stand noise the property man stood just outside the range of the audience with a revolver and one extra in case the other missed fire. When Mommy got in the closet she would hand her revolver to the property man to be shot off while she stuffed her fingers in both ears, so she wouldn't hear the report. Then he would thrust the smoking revolver into her hand as the closet door was pulled open. One night she sneezed but there was no report. Her revolver was stuck. A second later he pulled the trigger of the spare revolver, which was twice the size of the one Bab carried into the closet. Mommy grabbed that one because it was smoking and in the confusion the property man pulled the trigger of Bab's gun, and as Mommy had taken her fingers out of her ears, this second report, loud as a cannon to Mommy, catapulted her onto the stage white as chalk through her make-up. The audience saw the difference in the size of the revolvers and burst into shrieks of laughter. Mommy said afterward, "That is the most blood-thirsty audience I ever expect to play before. Couldn't they see I was genuinely frightened?"

Tom Powers had to support her through the whole scene. A week or two later *Bab* closed in Boston, but since it was going to play around New England within commuting distance of Boston, the partings weren't as bad as they might have been.

Love,

Grandma

MARY SWEET, The following Monday night after *Bab* closed in Boston it opened in Newport, R. I. Mommy was terribly excited at spending three whole days at a resort where American "royalty" spent their summers. She hired a car the minute we got there and told the driver to take us to where the beautiful homes were. Mommy would ask him whose home that was and at mention of each name Mommy would sigh with such awe that the driver decided to give up all accuracy and mention nearly every name in the Social Register as summer residents. Finally he pointed out a vast place, completely shut off from even a glimpse of the house and gardens by a very high iron fence, as Mrs. John Jacob Astor's summer home. Mommy began to laugh, and when I asked her what she was laughing at she said, "Mother, if anyone had told you ten years ago when we were living in that little apartment on Chapin Street in Washington that you and I would be riding around in Newport in a big car some day, would you have believed him?"

From Newport *Bab* played several New England cities, one of them Northampton, Mass., the home of Smith College. It was Commencement Week and the little town was crowded with parents and friends of the students who had come for the exercises. One of the girls at Smith had been in Miss Hawke's dancing class at the same time Mommy was there, and her parents and I had become great friends. She was Dorothy Hogan, daughter of Frank J.

Hogan, the lawyer who today is President of the Bar Association. Through Dorothy Mommy was invited to the Junior Prom, a privilege accorded few girls outside of the college.

Another honor accorded Mommy that week was an invitation to lunch with the Dean of Smith College. It seemed to me I had never seen so many lovely girls as I saw strolling about the campus and in and out of the stores on the main street, always in groups. They all seemed so carefree, it was hard to believe they were studying the most profound subjects in the various classes. Mommy spoke of the life-long friends college girls made, and I reminded her that she had been given the opportunity to go to college once. I asked her if she wished she had (I knew she didn't) but wanted to hear her answer. She said, "It wouldn't have worked out for me so well. I am not the studious kind. Then, too, after spending Father's money I would still end in the theatre and would have missed all these wonderful experiences, and not to have known all the really great and wonderful people of the theatre is more than I can bear to think of. Let's drop the subject."

After playing a few more cities in New England, we came to that great but frightening night when Mommy's name went up in electric lights for the first time.

Good night, dear,

Grandma

Ronald Colman and Helen Hayes in *Arrowsmith*

MARY DEAR, When we arrived in Springfield, Mass., Mommy and I went directly to the stage entrance of the Court Square Theatre. When we got to Mommy's dressing room (and we were a good hour too early) the manager came back and told Mommy he wanted to take her across the square to show her something. We went through the front of the house and he took us to the middle of the park directly opposite the theatre. Then he said, "Now, turn around and look." There across the front of the marquee in letters about three feet high was the announcement:

THE COURT SQUARE THEATRE

BAB

WITH HELEN HAYES

Mommy fell weakly on a bench and she told the manager that she would like to stay there for a while and admire her "beautiful name." He left us and we both just stared and stared. Mommy said, "Did you think my name was as beautiful as that until you saw it spelled out in 'diamonds'?"

The next night the manager brought a photograph that he had taken of the sign. As he handed it to Mommy he said, "Well, young lady, you are made now. Your name is up in electric lights." Mommy astounded me with her answer, which was, "My job has just begun. I will have to work mighty hard to keep my name there." She had just turned nineteen and I got a little frightened at the great responsibility that would be hers from then on.

All my love, dear,

Grandma

P.S.—Mommy had three wonderful days in Springfield, playing to packed houses as usual. New England had claimed her as its own. We saw very little of the town, for Mommy spent most of the time in the park looking at her name.

Grandma

MARY SWEET, *Bab* closed for the season in Springfield on May 23, 1920. The beautiful name came down, but Mommy didn't mind, for Mr. Tyler promised her when she opened in New York the following October, her name would be up again for her twentieth-birthday present. Mommy said to me after reading Mr. Tyler's letter, "I hope we open at a theatre that has a marquee." When we got back to New York Mr. Tyler suggested that Mommy had better go to some quiet mountain or lake resort so she could get a good rest before the start of her long and arduous season in *Bab*. We went home to Washington for a short visit to Grandpa Brown, whose chest had become so expanded through pride in Mommy that he was going around looking like a pouter pigeon. He would have burst, no doubt, if he had had some of the great thrills I had because of Mommy. I even wondered how I kept my head, and I suspect now I didn't always because I, too, was awfully proud of her.

When we returned to New York Mommy said, "We must find a place for the summer where the sub-debs of the Bab variety go with their parents. They may take me in as one of their own and speak freely."

I heard of a wonderful place at Loon Lake, New York, but we were also told it was frightfully expensive. This gave me pause, for while Mommy had been receiving three hundred dollars a week during the *Bab* engagement we had been living quite extravagantly in Boston and Mommy had done a great deal of expensive entertaining on her own there. She had bought a few clothes but they were winter ones and her greatest extravagance had been a nutria fur coat. However, from a description of Loon Lake House Mommy decided it was just the place for her to go. Mommy also decided on taking as her guest Rea Martin, who had played with her in *Clarence*. For, said Mommy, "If I can't stand the sub-deb line of talk I can always fall back on Rea, who speaks my language."

I wrote to Mrs. Chase, who owned hundreds of acres of ground and also Loon Lake House and who, we were told, was sort of eccentric. I told her the accommodations we wanted and the number in our party and asked her rates, explaining that I wanted the very lowest. By return mail, I received the most cordial letter, quoting terms much less than we had expected. However, my friend told me there was a catch in it. If, after we got there, Mrs. Chase didn't take an immediate fancy to us she would find a good and unbreakable reason for getting us out.

Then came the awful problem of summer clothes, when Rea had the bright idea that she and Mommy go over to Mr. Tyler's theatrical wardrobe and pick out the least used gowns from different productions and they could be purchased at half or less. With Mr. Tyler's permission, they went in and wasted a lot of time trying on gowns that they couldn't possibly repair or alter, but just for the fun of putting on a dress that Viola Allen or Eleanor Robson had once worn in a play. They came home with two huge boxes filled to overflowing with sport, afternoon and dinner frocks two or three years old. They worked diligently, and both being slight, it was easy to make most of the frocks fit perfectly. They were not Paquin creations when they got through, but with the girls' youth and freshness they would pass.

I cautioned both Rea and Mommy under no circumstances to mention the theatre, for I hadn't any wish to make that long trip in vain. I wasn't worried about Mommy talking shop, but that little Irish Rea, who had gotten so much fun out of being an actress, I knew would have to be watched all the time. It wasn't Rea who exposed Mommy, but I'll tell you about that in my next letter.

All my love,

Grandma

M<small>ARY</small> <small>DARLING</small>, We three, Mommy, Rea and I, left on a very late train for Loon Lake, very excited at the prospects of a gay time with young people who weren't so advanced as the girls and boys Mommy had known in Boston, and, by the way, her most particular suitor came on from Bar Harbor to say good-bye to Mommy. While Mommy was on the back of the train, having her first amorous parting, Rea and I were sitting in our berths discovering that the prospects of gay young people weren't so promising.

There were two very aristocratic, elderly ladies, obviously sisters, with a Pekinese which one of them had smuggled into her berth. They were most garrulous, and when Rea and I heard one caution the porter to be sure to call them a full hour before we reached Loon Lake we both looked at each other with apprehension. I am going to tell you right now those two ladies turned out to be a godsend to all of us. They were more fun and had more intelligence than all the other guests at Loon Lake House put together. They became two of our dearest friends. After the train started to move Mommy came rushing down the aisle and threw herself down on her berth with her face buried in her pillow to stifle her sobs. She was going through another "emotional parting." She lay there so long without undressing that I went to her and found her with the pillow soaking wet, and from it she raised a very swollen face to cry, "Oh, my heart is broken. I will never see him again!" I tried to tell her that her heart had been "broken" at other partings, but it is very hard to be convincing when you have to whisper to keep from disturbing other passengers.

Mommy threw what she thought would be a bomb at my placidity. She said, "This is different. He kissed me!" I answered, "I had hoped he would." I learned long afterward it was on her ear she received her first kiss, because when he leaned down to give her this chaste salute her ear was the only thing visible. Her face was buried in his shirt front.

We arrived at Loon Lake Station and were driven for miles to our hotel, which was almost on the edge of a lake and was an old log shooting lodge that had been added to and converted into this beautiful hotel. Our hostess greeted us standing very erect behind her desk in the main lounge.

I must describe Mrs. Chase to you. She was a very aristocratic-looking, tall, thin woman. This particular morning she had a long purple chiffon veil, such as lady motorists wore in those days, draped over her head and around her neck. She changed these veils daily and usually in the evening wore a light-colored one under which wisps of putty-colored hair were sometimes visible. There was no gaiety in her face nor was it unkind-looking. Just sort of peaceful.

We were taken to our rooms, and while they were cheery, I could understand why we had gotten them at the reduced rate. We were on the wrong side of the house. Not a glimmer of the lake could we see. There was no sign of youth about, either. Rea and I were forcing ourselves to joke about everything so far we had seen but Mommy was still being a Duse. I was almost hoping Mrs. Chase wouldn't like us and we could go somewhere else, so I suggested we shouldn't unpack until after luncheon. I forgot to tell you that, besides the two elderly ladies I have already mentioned, there were three other guests who came on the same train we did, an elderly couple and a middle-aged man who looked as if he had jaundice. Rea, trying to make Mommy laugh, said, "I saw him first and he is mine." We sat in our rooms until lunch time was announced and as we had freshened ourselves and changed our clothes we looked less like mourners than when we arrived. When we went to the desk to have our table assigned and as we waited for Mrs. Chase to appear, we noticed the jaundiced man pacing up and down the front porch with his luggage piled high in front of him. I whispered to Rea, "Our luggage will be there when we get out from lunch." Mrs. Chase came out and took us to her head waiter and mentioned a table which overlooked the lake.

The dining room was filled with the guests, people young and old and mostly young. We were served the most delicious food I have ever had before or since in this country or in Europe. We were told by a guest who had been coming there since Mr. and Mrs. Chase had first opened the hunting lodge that Mrs. Chase never sat down to a full meal because she tasted every dish that was prepared for breakfast, luncheon and dinner before those meals were announced. She was undoubtedly a gourmet.

Just as we were finishing dessert the captain told me Mrs. Chase wished to see us at the desk before we went to our room. A cold chill ran over me, for by this time Mommy was responding to the cordial faces all around and was looking forward to a gay summer. I told the girls to meet me in the lounge after they finished their coffee. I just had to get the suspense over. Mommy guessed by my face that I was anticipating something unpleasant and insisted on going with me. Out we three marched to the desk and Mrs. Chase. She smiled and said, "I have had your luggage moved to another suite and I want this child to occupy the sun-porch leading off from your room. I think she is a little pale. We must get her nicely tanned and plump before she leaves." I thanked her and we walked sedately to the elevator, neither daring to look at the other for fear of bursting out laughing, the relief was so great. We were taken to a very large room, exquisitely furnished with twin beds, a bath leading off from this, and when we went on the sun-porch they were putting up a bed for Mommy and a dressing table for her own use. Her room was practically over the lake. Before going downstairs to thank Mrs. Chase again, I said, "This is going to cost us more than we counted on, so we will just have to curtail our stay." Before we could say a word to Mrs. Chase she said, "I forgot to tell you this suite will be at the same rate as the other."

A week or so later after Mommy had gotten acquainted

with the other people they asked her what her "drag" was with "Old Chase." Certainly Mommy had impressed Mrs. Chase most favorably, for she was constantly giving Mommy privileges that no other guest was allowed or giving extras gratis that other guests had to pay for.

Then began Mommy's first lessons in sub-debry.

All my love, dear,

Grandma

Mary darling, At first Mommy couldn't seem to reach the inner circle of the sub-debs and there were at least fifteen of these around fifteen and sixteen years of age. If we walked up to a group as they were talking they immediately thought of something they had to do elsewhere. I decided it was because I was with Mommy and Rea that they wouldn't loosen up, but Mommy declared it was her fault. She said they talked in initials, and when she showed her ignorance they considered her a sort of an old maid. I asked her what she meant by initials and she said that one day she walked up to a group of girls who were discussing another girl who was not present and Mommy was told she was a "D.C.B." Interpreted later, Mommy learned that the girl was a "dark corner baby." Mommy decided she was too old to learn another language.

One day at lunch our table suddenly seemed to have be-

173

come the focal point for every eye in the dining room. Later, at the hairdresser's, I learned why. In an adjoining booth I heard one of the little ladies who had come on the train with us tell her operator that the famous young actress, Helen Hayes, was a guest in the hotel and that she had thought her face and voice were familiar, but she couldn't place them. Someone had received a copy of *Vanity Fair* that day, she continued, and there was a full-page photo of Helen Hayes who was registered under the name of Helen Brown. I could hardly wait for my hair to dry to hurry out to tell Mommy to be prepared for the great exposé.

When I found Mommy she was surrounded by the entire sub-deb and adolescent colony. If it hadn't been that Rea was on the outer edge and being ignored by the group, I would never have guessed that it was Mommy who was suddenly so popular. I decided they had all been shown the magazine and there was only Mrs. Chase to worry about. I called Mommy and she came to me with the most mystified look on her face. As we were going into the hotel boys and girls began to call. "Remember I have got a bid for you tonight. Save a dance for me." When we got into the lobby, Mommy and Rea said in one voice, "What do you suppose has happened to that bunch of kids?" "Why, some of them didn't finish their lunch to get to me and one boy asked me to go out on the lake with him in his motor launch when the moon was up." I said, "Didn't any of them tell you about your picture in *Vanity Fair?*" Mommy said, "That is the explanation. Not a soul said a word about the theatre to me and I am supposed to think they love me suddenly for myself, alone. They are smart in more ways than one."

We three put ourselves out to contact Mrs. Chase that afternoon to get the suspense over with, but she never referred to it in any way, then or ever. She either didn't know about it or she understood. She was a very tactful hostess. From then on Mommy was taken to the bosoms of these "sophisticates" and "she learned about sub-debs from them."

Much love,

Grandma

P.S.—I forgot to tell you, dear, that at first Mommy and the "one love of her life" corresponded almost daily for about three weeks. Then his letters came less and less frequently. I don't know whether she was writing him any more often, but when days would go by and there wouldn't be a letter from him for her, I wondered if it would make any difference to her. It apparently didn't, for she stopped even mentioning his name long before the summer was over. It wasn't because she had found another male interesting, for there were only two that were her age at Loon Lake and mentally they were five years younger. I forgot, also, to tell you Mommy didn't go on the lake that night with the young man who owned the launch. Just as she went to get her wrap to go with him one of the sub-debs told her confidentially she would have to be an "N.B." (necking baby) if she went out with him. Mommy decided that she would only end up with a wretched headache trying to define these initials all evening, a language which he would undoubtedly use. So Mommy used me as her excuse to get out of the sail.

Grandma

M ARY SWEET, When *Bab* opened at the Park Theatre there was not only a marquee where Mommy's name would shine, but there was Central Park across the way. She would have needed binoculars to see her name if she had occupied a bench in the Park. We would stand at the feet of Columbus, whose statue stood in the middle of the Circle, to admire it.

To go back to the New York opening of *Bab*, October 18, 1920, because it had been such a hit in Boston and everywhere in New England, everyone concerned expected nothing short of a year's run in New York. As far as I could tell from where I was standing in the wings that opening-night audience was as enthusiastic as any Mommy had played before with the exception of *Clarence*. There were the usual number of telegrams of good wishes and this time Mommy got more flowers than ever before, for wasn't she a featured player, now? And, oh, these dear friends who just say nice things and at the time I am sure they mean them, but one should get their opinions after the reviews come out, for then they always see the same fault in you or the play that the critics have pointed out! That night we had to take a taxi home because of the flowers. When we got to the apartment at Gramercy Park the meter registered enough to pay for the taxi outright. I said to Mommy when we got in, "We take no more taxis from that distance." Mommy, who had no sense of money at all, said, "Please don't start being so penurious, Mother."

We went to bed that night quite sure that *Bab* and Mommy were a success. I had ordered all the morning papers sent in bright and early, but we were awake and up before they were delivered. Mommy said, "Give me Heywood Broun first." I opened to Alan Dale in the *American* and he was marvelous. I looked at Mommy, who had not said a word from the moment she started to read, and she was as white as a sheet. She just handed me the paper, and I was shocked to read that Mr. Broun chastised Mommy for an unconvincing performance, pounding lines, hammering comedy and playing so "cutely" throughout the whole play. "Cute," a word Mommy particularly abhorred! This from the critic who had put Mommy as a golden star on the top of a Christmas tree a few years before! In my secret soul I knew he was right in part, but I blamed Mommy for ever studying the real sub-debs at Loon Lake. She had played them too literally for the stage.

Most of the other critics were wonderful to her. Some

liked the play, some didn't think it worthy of Mommy, but Mr. Broun's review made the greatest impression, with the consequence that her second night's performance was so underplayed you would have thought her walking in her sleep. Another thing that depressed her was the small attendance after such good reviews on the whole. She didn't realize that the number of people scattered over the Park would have jammed a smaller theatre.

We had a long talk that night. I said, "You were right when you said the first time your name went up in electric lights 'my job has just begun, etc, etc.' From now on the public expects more of you."

I didn't feel that I could tell her then that her performance wasn't anything like she had given in Boston. I told her to forget good, bad and indifferent criticisms and analyze her own performance. Another thing I told her was to forget everything that the sub-debs did that summer that she thought was like Bab. I reminded her of what Mr. Fields had said about her comedy, which was unconscious and unstressed.

My next letter, darling, will be a sort of lecture but I hope an enlightening one for you in whatever medium you may express yourself.

Good night, dear,

Grandma

MARY SWEET, I guess this letter could be called "Grandma's Lecture" but I am going to try to make it pleasant. After Mommy's adverse reviews in *Bab* (she got three or four) she would lie awake nights worrying about her performance and wondering how to go about correcting her faults. I worried, too. Besides I felt so helpless, for to me Mommy was just as good as she had always been. Mother's blindness, I guess.

We had moved to the Great Northern Hotel on Fifty-seventh Street, and Miss Ruth Chatterton and her mother, who had been friends of ours since the old Columbia Players days in Washington, lived on West Fifty-fifth Street. We visited them often, so it was the most natural thing in the world for Mommy to discuss her acting problem with Ruth, another actress. Ruth immediately said, "There is nothing the matter with your ability, but you haven't any technique." Now, Mommy wouldn't have known this word if she fell over it, so she asked Ruth how she could acquire this and where. Ruth told Mommy of Miss Frances Robinson-Duff, a great dramatic teacher here in New York. Mommy asked Ruth to make an appointment for her right away. She wanted to lose no time in getting "technique." Miss Duff said she would see Mommy the next day.

I spent another sleepless night, for my idea of dramatic teachers was that they spoiled your naturalness and spontaneity.

Miss Duff, who had watched Mommy from the *Dear*

Brutus days and had known all along where the trouble lay, gave Mommy two lessons a week at her studio, but spent many nights watching Mommy's performances. She never made Mommy self-conscious of either faults or perfections, but as she said to me once, "I cannot create that great gift Helen has, but I can free her channels of expression." So subtly did Miss Duff bring this about and so quickly that in less than six weeks people were remarking how Mommy was growing in her art. We were too close to it to realize the change. Under Miss Duff Mommy learned breath control too, for one of the criticisms that used to hurt Mommy was that she seemed to work so hard. Mommy wasn't conscious of working hard, but since she did not know how to place her voice she seemed constantly to be under a strain. That, too, I had never noticed.

I have told you all this to prove a point, dear, and that is that no matter what God-given gift you have you must have help to learn how to use it. Above all things, have confidence in your teacher, or get another. This lecture is for you, primarily, dear, for from your very first drawing and the little stories you made up at the age of seven to tell me, I felt an artistic career would be yours too. I don't think it will be acting, but I am sure it will be in something more lasting. Whatever it is, study it first.

All my love, sweet,

Grandma

Mary, Queen of Scots

MARY DARLING, After Mommy had been playing *Bab* at the Park about a month, she said to me, "Would you feel terribly hurt, Mother, if I got a maid? I would want you to be at all the performances just the same, but I don't like you to be waiting on me and to be so confined." I told her that thought had been in my mind for a long time but I didn't want her to know I was getting a little tired being with her so much and not getting to see a play at night. We had a good laugh after this exchange of secret thoughts.

And just another word of advice, Mary sweet: be frank with Mommy always. She is most understanding and you will find mothers aren't as easily hurt as you think.

Now, the engaging of a maid by a Hayes-Brown was the most important step Mommy had taken, not only because it gave her a feeling of professional success, but because she figured it would help her in her work. She decided she would get a good French maid, one who not only spoke perfectly in that language, but would be willing to speak it all the time to Mommy. Mommy asked one of the nuns at the Dominican Academy where she had gone years before, and the nun suggested the Jeanne d'Arc Home for French Girls on 14th Street in New York City. She cautioned Mommy to get one who came from Tours, France, if possible, for there they spoke pure French.

The next day I called up the Mother Superior at the Home and she said she had only one girl from Tours, but that she was an excellent professional maid, had been with a very wealthy, socially prominent lady just recently. This information was a bit discouraging, for I was afraid she might expect us to live luxuriously, and, too, I had never had anything in the way of a servant except a cook who had to do everything around the house besides. So I was uncertain about the duties of a personal maid.

The girl reported at the apartment in about an hour, gave said apartment a very supercilious look, and when I informed her that it was as a theatre personal maid we would want her, a look of fear came into her eyes and she said in the most frightful, broken English, "I have never worked for anyone in the theatre before. I have only worked for ladies." I was sorry Mommy wasn't there to hear *that*. I asked the girl if she would agree to try it for a week, and she said she would. Then she said, "Is mademoiselle a star?" I said, "Certainly," and for the first time I felt the name in electric lights had justified itself.

I asked her what her name was and was quite sure that I hadn't understood her when she said, "Marthe Bastard." I asked her to write it on a piece of paper, so I wouldn't forget it when Miss Hayes came in. There was no mistaking that *last* name! I told her to be at the theatre at 7:30 that night, so I could instruct her in her duties. When Mommy came in I told her she had a gem of a maid, spoke very little English, could understand a lot and was a beautiful seamstress. Then I handed Mommy her card, and she said, "How does she pronounce her last name?" I answered, "Just the way it is written."

When she came to the dressing room Mommy tried to be very "grand." Both Mommy and I gave the funniest performances that night. I would tell Marthe while Mommy was on the stage just what change of dress, stockings and shoes would be made in the next scene. Then, when Mommy would come up, I would rush over to her, take her dress off, even hang it up, while Marthe knelt down to put her stockings on. Mommy would grab these out of Marthe's hands and put them on herself. Before the evening was over Marthe was handing things to Mommy and me and would step back as we worked. During the evening Marthe said she thought she would leave the Jeanne d'Arc Home, as they didn't like the girls to be out so late. Then, too, the nuns didn't like the idea of her working for an actress. You can get a sort of idea how that French girl had intimidated me, but if it hadn't been that I thought she would eventually be good for Mommy, I would have sent her packing then and there. I just didn't like her manner, but she hadn't aroused my Irish yet.

She then said, "I'll have my mail sent to the theatre. How do I write it?" I told her. Then I began to see what the men would do with that last name when they saw it on an envelope in the company mail box!

I almost decided to get rid of her when she said in French as we were about to leave, "Shall I go down to mademoiselle's car with her?" Mommy said in English, "I have no car." "Then a taxi for mademoiselle?" Mommy, with fire in her eyes by this time, said, "We take a street car home." We were treated to another French shrug as we left the room. We were half way to the door when Mommy said, "I can't let her get away with that." She went back, with me trailing behind to see how Mommy would handle her. Mommy said, when she got into the room, in her most cutting, "leading lady" manner, "Marthe, I wish you to be here at seven every night and two on matinee days. See that my clothes are in perfect order and are cleaned, and lay out everything I use during the performance." Mommy turned and swept out of the room. A very meek "Oui, Mademoiselle" followed us. When we got out I said to Mommy, "That was a grand performance you gave and I think you have turned the tables on Marthe." Mommy said, "I'll never do that again. It has taken too much out of me. I am still trembling." We both realized we had started off on the wrong foot with her by not ordering her to do everything. From then on I left the entire handling of Marthe to Mommy, for she was a better actress in and out of the dressing room than I was.

All my love, dear,

Grandma

P.S.—I told Mommy about Marthe having her mail addressed to the theatre with the danger of ribald remarks being made by the stage hands to Marthe when they saw her name. Mommy said, "I'll suggest to her that she change it, at least the last two letters." I said, "Why don't you tell her what it means in English?" Mommy said, "It means the same in French." We went to bed a trifle exhausted after our first experience with a personal maid.

The next night Mommy very carefully explained to Marthe that her last name, because of its definition as given in the dictionary, might occasion her, Marthe, a little embarrassment if a low-minded person made a joke of it. Mommy suggested the name "Baston," since it would sound, when pronounced quickly, almost the same as Marthe's own name, yet when written would not cause any comment. Marthe took the suggestion quite philosophically by saying, "You can change my name if you wish, though I see no harm in it, for is it not in the dictionary?"

Marthe stayed with Mommy two years. One night she informed me she was going on the stage the following week with "a real French lady." I didn't even bother to ask whether she meant "real French" or "real lady," but I was curious to know what she expected to do. She said she was to appear in a sketch with a star as a *couturière*. I asked her what she had to say and she said, "I do not speak. I pin up a very beautiful gown on the star." Ol' Debbil Theatre had gotten Marthe!

Grandma

Mary sweet, Business at the Park kept getting worse and worse. Salaries were cut and it seemed that they weren't even earning those. Mr. Tyler, since the season was still young, thought *Bab* would do better on tour, so again we packed up and started off gaily enough, everyone hoping the business of our New England tour might be repeated in the West.

One of the cities on our way out was Cleveland and *Bab* was booked to open the new Ohio Theatre. It wasn't quite finished when we got there, at least backstage wasn't. The front of the house, or orchestra, was most luxurious, and all Cleveland society turned out for the new theatre as well as for the play. Mommy was so anxious to be as good as possible and as beautiful as the new house. All went well until the second act, which took place in the sitting room of the Archibald home. The theatre furnished the stage with a beautiful bright red carpet. When the curtain went up on that act Clinton Beresford, played by Arthur Eldred, and Bab were discovered upstage near a window. He was arguing with her and she turned downstage to avoid answering him. She was met by a huge wave of red carpet almost hiding her from the audience. When the curtain went up it either created a draught under the carpet or the carpet had been put down too loosely. Arthur followed Mommy down, lifting his legs over these red billows. He would squash them down in front only to have them rise up behind him again, practically burying Mommy.

The audience was screaming and Mommy was laughing so she couldn't speak her lines. Every time Arthur turned upstage he would yell at Mommy, over the screams in the audience, "Pull yourself together. Pull yourself together," which only made Mommy worse. The tears and mascara were running down her face. She was anything but beautiful. From then on both cast and audience were delirious. The audience laughed in and out of turn, and most of the cast was hysterical, for they didn't know what might happen any moment backstage. After the play that night Arthur read Mommy a long lecture about carrying on no matter what went wrong. You see, he had been in the War. Mommy said she knew he was right but hoped she wouldn't be put to such a test again. I don't think she ever was.

All my love, dear,

Grandma

P.S.—This is just a little story, Mary dear, to tell you of Mommy's last appearance as a professional entertainer. Tom Powers had been an ace flyer in the World War, and as I said before, Arthur Eldred was an ex-soldier of the British Army. Tom had been entertaining wounded soldiers in the hospitals all along the route. He had a fund of good stories which he told to them, frequently in dialect. Then, too, he was a grand monologist.

About three weeks before we were to play in Toronto, Tom received a wire from one of the officers of the Canadian Air Force, asking if he and the *Bab* company would entertain the wounded soldiers one afternoon while *Bab* was there. Tom put it up to the company and Mommy, forgetting her previous fiascos at entertaining, said, of course, they would all do something. Then she began worrying. She couldn't dance, sing, recite or tell stories. As usual, she told her troubles to all the company and crew, too.

Stephen Davis, fifteen years old, who played Eddie Perkins in *Bab*, suggested that he and Mommy sing "Whispering" with cuddlings and gestures. He thought the soldiers would like that. The boy was clever. He had a secret crush on Mommy and here was his chance. They rehearsed and rehearsed strolling "à la Floradora," Stephen with his arms around Mommy and she with her head thrown back against his chest. It was very "cute" and might have been entertaining enough if Mommy could have remembered that she wasn't really supposed to "whisper" and if Stephen hadn't gotten self-conscious about his cuddling when he had an audience. They were screamingly funny because they were so pathetically serious. Instead of applause they got shrieks of laughter. Mommy vowed she would engage and pay for professional entertainers after that. She was cured. Mommy was still learning what not to do.

Love,

Grandma

Mary dear, Mommy finally reached Chicago, I think some time in the latter part of March, and again Mr. Tyler hoped *Bab* would catch on. It hadn't packed them in anywhere, though the business wasn't bad. Well, as usual, Mommy was claimed as Chicago's own, and while critics considered the play light they and the public just adored Mommy, especially the young people. Mommy began having a glorious time and one of the grandest things that happened there was the renewal of the old friendship with Irene Castle, who had become Mrs. Frederick McLaughlin. Most of their conversation was about Vernon, and he really lived again to them.

Because the Blackstone Theatre was out of the beaten track, it only drew what was called the carriage trade. So in a short time the matinees were the only performances doing big business.

Almost at the end of the run, Mommy had one of the most terrible experiences that could happen to anyone. One night Sam Edwards, Bab's father, had a long scene with Mommy alone. When he made his entrance Mommy noticed his face was almost purple and he walked very slowly to Mommy muttering in a whisper, "What do I say?" Mommy gave him his cue and he repeated it. Mommy answered him. Again, he said, "What do I say?" She gave him his cue again, and again she answered him. Then he stared at her with almost unseeing eyes and she realized something dreadful was happening. She remembered what

Alfred Lunt had done with Glenn in *Clarence* when Glenn was hysterical, so she kept saying, "I know what you want to say, Father. I know what you want me to do, Father," and kept saying his lines loudly, each time hoping someone in the wings would hear her. Suddenly, Sam clutched his heart with one hand, threw his whole weight on Mommy and said, "My God!" and slumped. Mommy held him close and said quite shrilly, "Father, I'll take you to your room," and it was then that Tom Powers realized something was wrong and rushed on and said, "Mr. Archibald, let me take you to your room."

They laid him down in the wings. An ambulance was called, but he was gone before he reached the hospital. Mommy "carried on," not knowing how seriously ill Sam was.

She had scene after scene with different members of the cast. This was one time she could not leave the stage until the final curtain. She played that entire act seated. Her legs refused to hold her up. Every once in awhile the correct line was interjected until the final curtain came down on the most mystifying play an audience could have seen.

Tom Powers was wonderful. He told Mommy they had taken Sam to the hospital, and that Sam's only concern was that he couldn't remember his line and that he had distressed the "little lady." Mommy didn't know until after the funeral that he was dead. As I have said before, actors are grand people!

Love,

Grandma

Mary sweet, *Bab* closed in Chicago after a two-months'
run, and Mr. Tyler told Mommy it was time she traveled
abroad and saw some of the beauties of the Old World.
This gave Mommy something to look forward to, so she
didn't leave Chicago with the regrets she might have. Then,
too, she was thoroughly tired of *Bab*.

Percy Hammond, considered one of the greatest drama
critics in the country, was coming to the *New York Tribune*
Dramatic Department. He was on our train and joined a
number of the cast in Mommy's drawing room. Someone
produced a pair of dice and Mr. Hammond began teaching
Mommy and Miriam Collins, who had played *Bab's* sister,
all the expressions in a crap game. "Read 'em and weep"
was their favorite. Heretofore Mr. Hammond had only
written criticisms in the Chicago paper, but now he was
to have his own drama column, and he was frankly terrified. It was a very funny situation. Here was one of the
great drama critics held in abject fear by all actors having
the same fear of how he would be accepted in New York.
Since he would not only have to criticize, but discuss the
theatre in his column, he wanted an original title for it.
Every once in awhile he would ask for an idea. By this time
they were all pals together, so when he had interrupted the
game again to ask everyone to concentrate on a name for
his column, Miriam Collins, who was a great wit, suggested
"Read It and Weep."

When we stepped off the train all the actors bade Mr.

Hammond good-bye most regretfully. From now on he would be someone to fear again. By the mere dash of his pen he could chop off their heads in their next play. He wasn't always kind to Mommy in his reviews, but I expect that's the way he felt·about her performance. Fortunately, that one trip of equal comradeship kept her from being seriously affected by his criticism.

All my love,

Grandma

MARY DEAR, When we returned to New York after *Bab's* closing, we went at once to see Mr. Tyler, who told us that Mr. Bradford had made reservations on the *Olympic*, sailing late in July. The *Olympic* was one of the largest liners afloat at that time and its rates were higher than those of smaller vessels, so I asked how much the tickets were, and when he told me the amount I almost fainted, and so did Mommy.

She had been saving all during the *Bab* run so she would have a nice nest egg to spend on her vacation. These fares alone looked as if they would gobble up the entire nest.

When Mommy demurred at spending so much just for passage, that look came into Mr. Tyler's eyes that always debarred any argument, and he said to Mommy, "I am building you up to stardom and stars are expected by the public to do everything on a grand scale. I am spending money to do this, getting the best authors to write plays for you, so you must do your share to live up to it." Mommy in a weak voice said, "I just don't know how to live that grandly." She meant on the money she had earned so far, but he misunderstood and said, "I'll send you Eleanor Robson's press book and you will know how a star lives." Mommy said, "But, Mr. Tyler, I haven't, nor has Mother, the clothes to go with the rest of the steamer luxuries." His answer to this was we could buy real French gowns in Paris and much cheaper than we could buy them in America. Mommy gave up any further discussion of our finances, as they only irritated all of us and still didn't make our bank balance any larger.

Mr. Tyler then said he was leaving shortly for Europe, but would meet us with a car on our arrival at Cherbourg. As we were leaving Mommy said, "Now, don't forget to send me Miss Robson's press book before you go, for I don't want to embarrass you when we arrive." With that we fled. Sarcasm was another thing Mommy couldn't live up to, and I never could understand why she indulged in it, for she always suffered so.

Dearest love,

Grandma

P.S.—This is what Mommy learned from Miss Robson's press book:

Miss Robson never wore a pair of gloves after the first cleaning. They were discarded. She kept one hundred pairs in reserve.

Miss Robson never wore a pair of slippers more than two weeks because they would begin to lose their shape.

This was in the "Anna Held Milk Bath Era" when the press agents' brains ran wild with the most fantastic stories about their stars. We decided that these extravagances of Miss Robson's were also figments of a press agent's mind. Though Mommy half believed these stories she cut her wardrobe-buying down for this trip.

Grandma

MARY DARLING, We sailed away the second week in July just a little frightened. We knew nothing about ship etiquette and we were both so anxious not to appear too much like "greenhorns." Mommy worried a little about what was the correct thing to wear aboard ship and how to keep her limited wardrobe from being noticed. This ignorance had disastrous results the second day out.

Everyone from the captain down and an awful lot of the passengers knew Mommy was an actress by the first meal. I suspected Mr. Bradford, for he had arranged for our table and deck chairs. Our second day out the chief engineer asked Mommy if she would like to inspect the engine room, not with the usual group, but as his guest. He told her to invite whomever she wished to go along.

Mommy had purchased a beautiful white sport outfit and white sport coat and hat in Chicago. This was for her first morning aboard; she thought it was nautical-looking. She gathered two or three of the Harvard boys who were aboard ship and whom she knew, and met the engineer a few minutes later. I had refused to go, for I had been riding so long behind engines that I wanted none of them on a pleasure trip. Mommy was gone about ten minutes when our stewardess came to me and said my daughter wanted me in our cabin. When I got there what had been "Phoebe Snow" a few minutes before was black oil from the nape of her neck to the hem of her coat. Face, hands and shoes were a sight. I burst out laughing and asked her what had happened. It seems that she was in the vanguard of the group and skipped down the highly polished steps in her usual bouncing-ball way, slipped on the last one and landed flat on her back in a puddle of oil. She was furious with herself, for she said, "With my scarcity of changes I should have known better than to wear this when I was going down into the bowels of a ship." That outfit was practically lost on shipboard, for though it was cleaned it showed decided marks of the oil.

The night of the ship's concert Mommy was approached to contribute either a scene from one of her plays or to sing and dance. Before Mommy could consent, for I knew

195

she would then ask me afterward to get her out of it, I
said, "She has worked so hard all winter that it is out of
the question for her to get up anything at such short notice.
She will contribute five dollars to the fund." The master
of ceremonies, who was a female impersonator, said, "Better still, Miss Hayes, have you a photo of yourself? We
could auction it off and you could autograph it to the highest bidder. We ought to triple your five dollars."

I had one photo of Mommy which I always carried with
me—it was my favorite—but as this was a worthy cause, I
gave it up. The entertainment was a huge success, mainly
because of the Creole Fashion Plate, "Known on Every
Continent." The auction on Mommy's photo was the last
big feature. The auctioneer tried to get it started on a dollar bid, but finally dropped to twenty-five cents. From there
he went to three dollars and Mommy was "knocked down"
for that amount.

It never occurred to me the bidding would stop there or
I would have bid the five dollars I first planned to give and
I would have had my precious photo back. When I looked
up Mommy was busy signing it and she said to me, "Now,
Mother, since it did not bring as much as we had hoped,
I'll still give five dollars." I gave it to them humbly enough,
for hadn't we both been taken down a peg or two by that
sale? This ignominious experience didn't spoil the joy of
her first ocean voyage, however.

All my love, dear,

Grandma

P.S.—Two of the passengers on the *Olympic* were Madame Curie and her oldest daughter. Mommy never met Mme. Curie, for I don't think Mme. Curie met anyone on that trip. Mommy used to watch her when her daughter would walk her around the deck for her constitutional, a delicate little wisp of a woman, with very thin hair drawn tightly back from her face, whose only beauty came from within. She walked as one who had not been accustomed to much exercising. A few years later when Mommy was doing her first talking picture, *The Sin of Madelon Claudet,* Mommy took out of one of those cubby-holes in her brain her recollection of how Mme. Curie looked and walked, and used it in her characterization of Madelon, when she was leaving the prison after ten years' incarceration.

While Mme. Curie had looked at brilliant lights in her laboratory, when she came into ordinary daylight she would blink as if blinded, so the prisoner who had been kept away from light and comes out into the dazzling sunlight blinks just the same, and Mommy remembered that. It caused considerable controversy at the time.

Love,

Grandma

Mary dear, When the tender took us from the ship and landed us for the first time on foreign soil, Mommy's excitement was uncontrolled. We saw an enormous white car standing close to the pier with two men in white caps and coats and goggles, one waving. It never occurred to us it was Mr. Tyler, but it was. He had just motored back from Egypt in time to meet us.

Our trunks were sent from the ship direct to the Crillon Hotel in Paris, to be held until we arrived a week or so later. We carried only what we would need on this short motor trip. The car turned out to be a fourth- or fifth-hand five-passenger open Mercedes. The chauffeur was Gabriel Marceau, an ex-soldier, who before the War had been secretary to Pierre Loti, the poet.

Gabriel handed Mommy and me a white duster each and two white veils and goggles which Mr. Tyler insisted we put on at once. Many of the passengers from the ship, while collecting their luggage, watched this procedure amusedly and Mommy was terribly embarrassed, for she pictured us creating a sensation wherever we would drive. It all seemed very conspicuous. We looked like an ad. for something. However, no one noticed us at all, for we saw many really more amazing cars, to say nothing of the gaily painted wine carts that we passed on our way to Paris. When we got in the car Mr. Tyler explained his plans for the trip. The first night we were to spend at Mont St. Michel, then proceed slowly through little villages off the

198

beaten track of tourists, then into Paris as the sun was setting behind the Arc de Triomphe.

We left the pier with girls and boys shouting, "We'll see you in Paris, Helen." This drew the remark from Mr. Tyler to Mommy, "I hope you have not planned to transfer your American acquaintances to foreign shores. I want you to know French people here." I said, "I imagine Paris will be like New York. Helen will probably never run across any of the passengers there." Mr. Tyler: "Oh, my God! Paris like New York!!"

At lunch time we stopped at a little village inn for lunch and the waiter brought with it a bottle of wine for each. Mommy said to him in English: "I don't drink wine. You can take it away." His askance look was interpreted by Mr. Tyler as one of resentment, and he said to Mommy, "You mustn't ever refuse the wine of the village. It hurts their feelings, and besides you had better get used to drinking a little light wine in Europe, for the drinking water is very bad." Well, Mommy, being thirsty and not realizing that it was going to her head, drank nearly all of the glass he had served. After lunch we got back into the car, Mommy and I in the back and Mr. Tyler with Gabriel in the front. The sun and the wine made Mommy terribly drowsy and soon she was sound asleep. She was sitting directly behind Mr. Tyler, so he didn't notice that she wasn't answering him when he pointed out some particularly beautiful farm or bit of scenery. Suddenly we came to a gorgeous view of a valley and he had Gabriel stop, so we could look down and exclaim. I was nudging Mommy to waken her before he could notice she had been asleep, but it was no use; she wasn't just asleep. The look of horror in Mr. Tyler's eyes as he said, "I bring her three thousand miles to see glorious scenic beauties and she sleeps through all of it. I expect she is tired. Did she go to bed at all on the trip over?" I was convulsed inwardly, but tried to explain it was the wine that she wasn't accustomed to and that it had made her sleepy. I just knew I would need to have my sense of humor on tap throughout the whole trip.

We arrived at Mont St. Michel an hour or so before sunset and truly that was an awe-inspiring sight. The window of our room overlooked the sea and the beautiful beach below us. Mommy said, "I am going to sneak off to watch the sun go down behind the sea. I want to see it through my eyes, and not Mr. Tyler's."

After freshening up, I met Mr. Tyler in the lobby of the hotel. He asked where Mommy was and when I told him his face became ashen and he shouted, "My God, she is walking in the treacherous quicksands," as he rushed out to find her, followed by me and the son of our hotel proprietor who sickened me as we ran with his stories of the lives lost in those same quicksands. Mommy was sauntering around the base of the rock on which the village stood, saying she had walked around it. I had to cling to the side of the rock for support. My knees were like rubber. I think if those men had not been present I would have turned

Mommy over my knee and spanked her bottom good, in spite of her twenty years.

The young Frenchman said, "Mademoiselle truly bears a charmed life, for it is at the ebb-tide that the sands are so treacherous." Mommy was thoroughly frightened and wanted to go to the church and offer a prayer of gratitude to Saint Michael, but Mr. Tyler said she had had enough wandering around alone; he was too old to climb that hundred or more steps and Gabriel had too severe a stomach wound, received in the War, to attempt it.

When I got Mommy in our room, I gave her a good talking to. I said to her, "We have just landed in a strange country and you go traipsing off alone. I'll never feel easy while you are out of my sight and I am sure Mr. Tyler will appoint a bodyguard for you from now on. I hoped this was going to be a pleasure trip." She promised me she would never do that again.

Much love,

Grandma

P.S.—We had supper that night at Mme. Poulard's, famous for her omelette, which we watched her prepare.

Grandma

MARY DARLING, I don't think I told you in any of my previous letters that Mr. Tyler before he left for Europe had asked Mr. Tarkington to write a play for Mommy. This was even before the try-out of *Golden Days* in Atlantic City. Though it had been such a hit there he did not intend Mommy to do that play in New York. Mr. Tarkington had given him a rough outline of the idea before Mr. Tyler left. During this trip to Paris Mr. Tyler talked of his hopes of the play. It was to be a young character of the ethereal type of Maude Adams. Mommy was so happy about this, for she did want to play less sprightly maidens than she had been acting in the past few plays.

As we neared Paris Mr. Tyler had Gabriel drive very slowly so we wouldn't reach the Arc de Triomphe one second before the sun began to sink. It was a breath-takingly beautiful sight. Mr. Tyler told us Miss Robson had all but swooned when she first saw it.

We drove to the Crillon and were assigned a most beautiful room, with bath, overlooking the garden, but again the enormous rate nearly spoiled its beauty for us. However, in one of our midnight chats Mommy and I decided we would go as far as our money would and then go home if necessary, but we would not complain of expense again. Through Mr. Tyler and the William Herefords we met the most charming French families who in turn took us to famous but most conservative restaurants. We roamed through Versailles and the Tuileries and every spot made historical by the French Revolution, and I had no idea Mommy had such a taste for the gory, but she knew every head that had dropped in that famous basket during that time.

After two weeks Mr. Tyler left us in Paris and we were to go immediately to London, where he had already arranged for Mommy to meet George Bernard Shaw and Sir James Barrie. He had also engaged Leslie Howard, a young English actor who had scored a tremendous success in New York the year before in a play called *Just Suppose*. He was to play opposite Mommy in the Booth Tarkington play which was to be called *The Wren*. Mr. Howard, his wife and little girl would return with us on the *Adriatic*.

Now, Mr. Tyler had taken us to all the lovely places, but they weren't exciting. Mommy wanted to see Montmartre and to go to some of the French theatres. By the way, Paris was *not* like New York. We were constantly running into passengers who had been on the *Olympic* with us. Some of them had told Mommy about the *Folies Bergères* where Mistinguette, the famous music-hall artiste, was singing in a revue.

I forgot to tell you, dear, that Mr. Tyler had left Mr. Stanhope, Mommy's old director, to see that Mommy reached London safely and on time. We were to leave Paris the following day, so as we had one free night I suggested that Freddie Stanhope take us wherever Mommy wished to go. The first place we went was the *Folies Bergères*. I was seated between Mommy and Mr. Stanhope, and while he and I didn't understand one word they said in the sketch, we could laugh at the situations, and we did, roaring with the rest of the audience, all except Mommy. She sat in stony silence, her face terribly red. Finally, she whispered to me, "I wish we could leave right away, for they are saying terrible things on that stage." At this time neither of us knew that Mr. Stanhope couldn't understand what they said, and when we came out I said to him, "Don't take us to any more places like that." And he said, "I am sorry. I thought you were enjoying it." I said, "I laughed because I didn't understand what the sketches were about." Then to Mommy's relief he said, "I didn't either, but I thought the comedians were very funny." Then he took us into many places in Montmartre before we finally fell into bed just as the sun was coming up.

The next day, just a few hours before we were to leave, Mommy told Mr. Stanhope she would like to stay a few days longer to see some of the good French actors. He arranged for us to stay. We went to two or three operas at their gorgeous opera house and one grand comedy at the Comédie Française and one tragedy at the Odéon.

In my next letter, dear, I'll tell you what a big price Mommy paid for playing hooky from London.

My love and kisses,

Grandma

Mary sweet, This is a tragic letter to write, or I should say it is about a tragedy. After a week longer in Paris than Mr. Tyler planned us to have, we arrived in London, where we were met by his London play agent, Golding Bright, and we were driven to the Garland House just back of the Haymarket Theatre, where Mr. Tyler had a suite reserved for us. All the way Mr. Bright kept saying, "Everybody" had been expecting us a week earlier. Mommy looked very smug thinking about the week she had stolen for Paris and the fun she had had.

We were greeted by a most charming English lady, our hostess, and shown to our sitting room. It had enormous vases filled with dead flowers. It looked and smelled like a deserted florist shop. There were notes from so many worthwhile people that Mr. Tyler had asked to call on Mommy, but the most awful blow was a note from Sir James Barrie's secretary, asking Mommy to have tea with Sir James one day the week previous. There was a postcard with a picture of Rodin's "Balzac" on one side and just a line on the other side saying, "Sorry couldn't wait for your visit," and signed "G. B. S." It was dated the day previous, from the Isle of Man or the Isle of something. Mommy rushed to the phone to talk to Sir James Barrie's secretary, but learned that he, too, had gone to his summer place. I think it was in Scotland. He had left for Mommy a beautiful set of his plays and stories and a copy exquisitely bound in white kid, of *Peter Pan*.

Mommy could hardly enjoy the rest of her stay in London, which naturally had to be curtailed because of that week in Paris. She tried to get up enthusiasm for everything she saw and everywhere she went but it was all tinged with a great bitterness. To have missed meeting the man whose part in *Dear Brutus* had made her and the man whose *Cleopatra* she meant some day to play was the greatest tragedy of her life. She promised herself she would go over the next year and spend the entire vacation in England.

We sailed the following week on the *Adriatic*, meeting for the first time Leslie Howard, her new leading man, with his wife and little girl.

All my love and kisses, too,

Grandma

P.S.—I have decided to tell you now of the only thing that made that trip home eventful. Mommy and I met Mr. Paul Hammond, noted yachtsman, who was returning from the International Sloop Races with his prize-winning sloop packed in enormous chests which mystified everybody for a day as to their contents. He took a great interest in Mommy, and his curiosity about her life was insatiable. It wasn't this meeting with Mr. Hammond that was so important, but it was what happened afterward, which I'll write you about when I come to that period in Mommy's career, that mattered. I told him a lot of things that really weren't true about her, but like Mommy's stories to the drama teacher, I told him what I thought he wanted to hear. I must also tell you that by this time I was awfully tired of telling the story of how she "happened" to go on the stage.

I guess that is how so many interviews that I had afterward with reporters varied. I even began to change her birthplace, by way of diversion. That is one reason I started these letters. I wanted you to know the real truth.

Love,

Grandma

Mary dear, When we returned to New York Mr. Tyler had arranged for Mommy to go for a week to Kennebunk-port to visit Mr. Tarkington to discuss *The Wren*.

She had a grand time with the Tarkingtons. He introduced her to many old sea-faring friends of his. Mommy said they were grand characters, but I gathered from what she told me of the visit there was very little discussion of the play.

When rehearsals were called Mommy became a little frightened, for Mr. Tyler explained to her she must establish the fact almost from her opening speech that she was a very practical person and that she had little wren-like qualities. You know, the wren will fight for her young against the owl. Mommy knew her characterization was not ever going to have any great charm, since she would have to use a New England twang throughout the play.

The Wren opened in New York on Mommy's twenty-first birthday, October 10, 1921. Because of this and the great number of gifts, flowers and telegrams for both occasions and the spirit of the audience, it seemed to promise a nice long run.

An enormous birthday cake with twenty-one candles was delivered to Mommy just before the performance and on the candy card in candy was written "From a Sailor Boy." Mommy was mystified about the identity of the sender, for while she knew a few Annapolis boys there wasn't one that she believed would send her that beautiful cake. The mystery was cleared up after the performance when Paul Hammond, the yachtsman of the ship, came back to the dressing room bringing a large theatre party with him. He had sent the cake. They were all most enthusiastic about the play, but the papers the next morning were dire in their comments. No one could be deceived by friends' kindly praise after reading them.

It ran about four weeks, but almost immediately after the opening Mr. Tyler put into rehearsal *Golden Days* that had been a great success when Mommy did it at Atlantic City two summers before. It had a grand cast of young people, but unfortunately this play, while timely in 1920, was dated by 1921 and it, too, had a very brief run. Its closing six weeks later left us a little worried, but we had the promise of a new play almost at once.

All my love, and kisses,

Grandma

MARY SWEET, Before the short run of *Golden Days* Mr. Tyler asked George Kaufman and Marc Connelly to write a play for Mommy. They were the rising young authors then.

When *Golden Days* closed in New York after four weeks there, and two on tour, Mr. Tyler realized that Mommy must have a play by the New Year, so she could go into rehearsals at once.

We were living on East Nineteenth Street in what had formerly been the Astor Carriage House that had been converted into a most adorable home. The sitting room that led directly in from the street was forty feet long and it seemed much longer, for we had hardly any furniture in it. Always after our trips to Europe we would have very little money left, and as *Golden Days* had been so short-lived, and that at a cut in salary, there hadn't been any augmenting of the little bank balance. Our upstairs rooms—two bedrooms, dining room, and kitchen—were very comfortably furnished, but as our former apartments had only bedroom-sitting room combinations we only had a refectory table and two Italian chairs and a very small settee that looked lost in this barn of a room. By the way, Mommy had picked up the table and chairs and settee in Europe.

One day Mr. Tyler said Messrs. Kaufman and Connelly would be down that afternoon to read the play they had written for her, called *To the Ladies*. Mommy was terribly excited at having two such successful authors (they had one of the biggest successes running in New York then, *Dulcy* with Lynn Fontanne starring) coming to her house to read a play for her. She moved our few pieces of furniture around the room until I suggested we move it all up to the end where the fireplace was and have a fire going. We pulled the curtains across the window in the front so the bareness of that end wouldn't be so glaring. Mommy had set her stage beautifully.

I have often wondered what those two men thought of that room, because they had such a distance to walk before reaching the intimate little setting. Just as Mr. Kaufman started the reading he said to Mommy, "Of course you play a piano. Your playing has an important bearing on the play." Mommy said, "Of course, I play." Mr. Connelly said, "You sing an old spiritual and accompany yourself on the piano." I was sure I wasn't going to like that play, for Mommy could do neither of these things, but the more they read of it the grander it got, and they explained it was still in the rough. I was tempted to ask them if the piano playing couldn't be done off stage, for I remembered that although Mommy had studied the piano for at least three years, an uncertain rendition of "The Scarf Dance" was her masterpiece.

After they had gone Mommy didn't wait for me to speak. She knew what I was going to say, but rushing upstairs she threw over her shoulder to me just as I had thrown the price of the pearl ring to Grandpa: "Mother, I am going out right away to rent a piano." I reminded her that renting the piano would only be a small part of her job. "How do you expect to learn to play and sing a spiritual in six weeks?" She said, "I'll do it. Watch me."

The very first place we went to look for the piano was the Wurlitzer Music Store. They sold and handled the highest grade of instruments and therefore the most expensive. The clerk recognized Mommy and said, "What can I do for you, Miss Hayes?" Mommy said, "I want to rent a baby grand for a couple of months." "Oh," said Mr. Clerk, "Why don't you buy one, Miss Hayes? You only pay as if you were renting it. Let me show you some of our beauties."

I must draw this to a close quickly, for I still feel a little sick at the memory of that awful transaction. After showing us pianos ranging from twenty-five hundred dollars down to seven hundred and fifty, no lower, Mommy said, "I am afraid I'll have to be content with the cheapest one." The clerk took us into his office and brought out a contract for Mommy to sign and said, while she was signing, "It's customary to pay a deposit of one-third the full amount and forty-seven dollars per month until the balance is paid." I said, "It is impossible for me to pay more than fifty dollars deposit just now." Mommy looked askance at me. She thought I was being penurious again. The clerk said, "That will be satisfactory. Miss Hayes is quite responsible." I took out my check-book and covered up the stub so neither Mommy nor the clerk could see I had only one hundred and fifty dollars in the bank.

We walked out of Wurlitzer's owners of a seven-hundred-and-fifty-dollar piano on which we owed seven hundred dollars, no work for nearly six weeks and one hundred dollars in the bank.

I never said a word to Mommy until she said, "Well, that baby grand is going to fill up our bare sitting room beautifully." I said, "That's one way of looking at it, but you could have furnished it completely for that amount of money and you can't sit on the piano." I never mentioned our low bank balance to her, for she wouldn't have understood.

She got a teacher who taught her just that one spiritual on the piano, and that was practically by ear. When she had gotten that thoroughly, she tried singing and playing at the same time but found her fingers and voice wouldn't work together. We had a colored cook who got very upset listening to Mommy trying to sing that spiritual. She said, "Miss Hayes, you ain't got the swing of it." Mommy said, "Ethel, you come on down here and help me." I got the meals for the next week, for Ethel had become Mommy's singing teacher. After a week Mommy discovered Ethel was only good when Mommy was not accompanying her, so Mommy sent Ethel back to the kitchen and she would stand beside the kitchen sink while Ethel would hum "Nobody Knows da Trouble I See'd" until Mommy had all the cadences of the uncultivated colored voice and she put that with the piano. It was truly lovely.

In the meantime, I got advance salary from Mr. Tyler

Helen Hayes and Alexander Woollcott

for payments on the piano and when *To the Ladies* opened and again Kaufman and Connelly had written a success and Mommy had another personal triumph, the piano took on new beauty and we bought more furniture.

All my love,

Grandma

Mary sweet, After a grand season in New York with *To the Ladies* and a not so good one on tour (the cast had been changed in very important roles and had not been benefited by this change) we closed in Chicago. Again, the stagehand union made it impossible for Mr. Tyler to continue the play without taking a big loss. It was a large show to handle and the union insisted on an enormous crew. Mommy took a cut in salary, hoping in that way to help. She was the only loser.

Mr. Tyler had planned, however, that we were to see Italy with him that summer. This time we made our own choice in a ship which was a small one and half the rate of the *Olympic.* Mommy had a real rest on that trip. It was slower and had less excitement.

After we landed at Le Havre we went direct to Paris. From there we took the express to Florence, where Mr. Tyler met us with Gabriel and another car. That was an exciting trip for Mommy through the Swiss and Italian Alps.

Florence opened Mommy's eyes to the beauties of old masters in both sculpture and painting. She never tired of walking for hours through galleries and ruins. She asked the guides the most astonishing questions, and I could only believe that she must have retained some of the memories of the art galleries to which I had taken her when she was little more than a baby.

I often accused Mommy of being stupid in so many subjects outside of the theatre, for her answers were so vague, but I found out she has cubby-holes in her brain where she keeps a lot of knowledge and brings it out when she needs it.

As it was summer there were no theatres open, so Mommy had to miss seeing any acting in Italy, but she did read all the books she could find translated about the great Duse and Salvini.

Love,

Grandma

Mary dear, After several exciting days in Rome, Mr. Tyler had planned to motor us to Chamonix at the foot of Mont Blanc and leave us there, he returning to Paris and home. We could stay as long as we liked and wherever we liked, providing we reached London in time to confer with Israel Zangwill about a play he was writing for Mommy called *We Moderns* which Mr. Tyler hoped to produce in the late fall. We had three glorious weeks at Chamonix and then on to Interlaken, Geneva, Lucerne and Basle, all in Switzerland, then Paris and London. We felt like old seasoned travelers and continentals. Mommy's favorite literature was her Baedeker and my great pastime was discovering where I would get most in exchange for my dollar. One day I boasted to Mommy in Switzerland that a bank had given me ten more centimes on my dollar than the American Express had quoted. Mommy asked me how I found the bank. I said, "Our hotel clerk gave me the address and I just took a fiacre and told the driver to take me there." Mommy said, "How much did the fiacre cost you?" I replied, "A franc and a tip." Mommy said, "Well, you are out money, for your ten centimes are only worth about three cents." I had never thought of that, but it did give us a good laugh and laid to rest any prestige I had on this trip as a financier.

When we arrived in London there were directions from Mr. Zangwill at our hotel on how to reach his summer home in Surrey. The explicitness and detail of those directions of how to buy our first-class railroad tickets which the hotel purchased for us, getting on the train and getting off at the station in Surrey, should have warned us that Mr. Zangwill loved to write.

He and Mrs. Zangwill and their two children greeted us most cordially and made us so welcome, but nothing was said of the play. Guests came in for tea, one the Honorable

Mr. Ponsonby who had been a page at Queen Victoria's Court and who was quite critical of some of the things told by Strachey who had just finished a biography of Victoria.

Mommy was having a grand time listening to one who could speak so intimately of a Queen, when Mr. Zangwill jumped up, saying, "Come, come, Miss Hayes, we must get to work," and away he whisked Mommy and me to his study. He couldn't bear that anyone else hold the spotlight.

He brought forth such a sheaf of manuscript that Mommy exclaimed, "Why, you have finished the play, haven't you, Mr. Zangwill?" He said, "No. This is only a perfect first act." He said he would read it to us, which he proceeded to do with gestures and everything. To both of us it was the most confused piece of writing we had ever heard. Whether it was because he was so terribly near-sighted and held the paper quite close to his eyes, then making strange gestures while reading, or that, because of this, we could not concentrate on the words, it seemed confused. The climax came when he jumped up on a settee and perched precariously on the back of it and began reading reams from that position. Mommy looked at me with raised eyebrows and I answered her with a shrug and a shake of the head. We didn't know until later that at that point in the scene Mommy was supposed to be seated on a settee. I am not exaggerating when I say it took two hours for Mr. Zangwill to finish that one act. He didn't even ask Mommy what she thought of it. He had already told us it was perfect.

When we left the next day it was pouring in torrents,

but Mr. Zangwill went to the station with us, for he wanted Mommy to send a cable to Mr. Tyler before we took the train saying that she "thought the play magnificent." She said, "I can't say I like it until it is finished." He tut-tutted this with, "I am a great writer, Miss Hayes, and you may be sure it will be a great play when finished." Mommy promised to send the cable from London. The train came just then, and I'll never forget Mr. Zangwill, running along beside the train as it was gaining momentum, holding an enormous umbrella which didn't prevent him from getting soaked, telling Mommy what to say in her cable to Mr. Tyler the moment she reached London. She never sent the cable. He was the greatest egotist we had ever met. But somehow he fooled Mr. Tyler, and the play was produced and failed after four weeks in New York.

All my love,

Grandma

Mary darling, Mommy was returning from an early rehearsal of We Moderns when she ran into Marc Connelly, who persuaded her to go shopping with him. It was just two or three weeks before Christmas. She called me up to say she would be late returning home as Marc was going to take her to a tea at the studio of Miss Neysa McMein, the artist.

Mommy came home in such a state of excitement and all occasioned by meeting one man: Charles MacArthur!!! I tried to find out from Mommy who the real celebrities were that she met, for Papa's name meant nothing to me when I heard it. She remembered none of the important names, and before the evening was over and she had told me again and again what Papa had said about wishing the peanuts he offered her were emeralds, and how he said it, and how he looked when he said it, and how he stood at her side all the time she was there, and she had asked him to call, and he said he would, I knew just how much the name of Charles MacArthur was going to mean to Mommy, and to me it meant Mommy had grown up.

Mommy could talk of no one else for days and days. The first thing she would ask when she would return home was, "Did anyone call?" Now, I knew it was only one person whose call she hoped for, Charles MacArthur's, but he never phoned nor called. Mommy stopped asking finally and only mentioned his name at rare intervals. I knew though, from the rising color in her cheeks when she mentioned his name, that she still thought of him with affection. I, of course, never met him, for I didn't go to any of the places he was apt to be, nor did Mommy for that matter. I did know that I wouldn't like him, for I resented his making Mommy a sort of pastime among his sophisticated friends and then forgetting her completely. I know now it was Papa's nature to be sweet to every woman and especially one as shy as Mommy who was plunged for the first time into such a brilliant gathering of people. He rescued her from being a wall-flower that day, but having done this he was not concerned any more.

I think it was while Mommy was still playing in *Quarantine* that she and I were coming out of the armory at 34th Street and Park Avenue where we had been to the Flower Show, and just as we stood on the first step a young man without a hat and whose black curly hair was flying in every direction stopped to speak to Mommy. She began stammering, couldn't pronounce his name and when I looked at her face, red as the peonies we had just seen, I knew he was Charlie MacArthur. Finally, still stammering, Mommy said, "You know, Mother, this is the Mr. MacArthur I told you about." What an admission for a young girl to make! And as I put out my hand to acknowledge the introduction, I noticed by his amused look, which I thought was also smug, that he knew and appreciated this admission. It didn't make me like him any more, I can tell you. He apologized for his appearance, said he had just left the newspaper office. To me it was just plain dirt on his hands, face and collar. He said, "I live down the street," and Mommy gurgled, "We live at Park Avenue and 35th Street." He said, "I know. May I call some time?" Just as if he hadn't asked her that the first time she met him, and then forgot it.

The moment he left us I forestalled her gushing by saying, "So that tramp is what you have been raving about all this time! What has come over you? Well, I just hope he never calls when I am home." She said, "Mother, he is one of the most brilliant men in New York." Said I, "How do you know? Just because he was clever enough to say that he wished some peanuts were emeralds doesn't make for any great brilliancy, and besides he probably heard someone else say that, and seeing how green you were just threw it to you."

I was being cruel to be kind, I thought, for to me he seemed of another world than Mommy's and I thought that was the very last she would see or hear from him. I hoped in time she would forget him entirely. But no! Mommy had invited a man friend that same night for dinner and as we were having our coffee in the sitting room the house phone rang and the doorman announced, "Mr. MacArthur on the way up." Well, Mommy fairly danced to the door, and if anyone ever wore her heart on her sleeve for the daws to peck it, Mommy certainly did that night.

He came in just as disheveled-looking, but all beautifully clean. He knew our guest, Mr. Dave Wallace, both being newspaper men, and he had coffee, and being prodded by Mr. Wallace he told one tale after another. If Mommy hadn't been so obviously enraptured, I could have liked him better, for he was a very brilliant raconteur. As it was I could almost see horns sprouting and a cloven foot. The worst of the whole evening for me was that each man was obviously determined to outsit the other. Charlie, every time he would glance at Mommy who was hanging on his every word, still seemed to me to have this smugly amused look. When they finally left together Mommy threw her arms around me and said, "Isn't he wonderful, Mother? Did you ever hear anyone talk so brilliantly?" I made the mistake of criticizing Papa to Mommy, so she stopped mentioning him to me, and I found out, later, they were seeing each other at mutual friends' homes. Now, I am glad I made that mistake, for no other man could have made Mommy so happy.

From time to time I'll tell you of their courtship and how he won me over.

All my love,

Grandma

MARY SWEET, After the failure of We Moderns which Mommy had never liked, Mr. Tyler explained to us that he had nothing in the way of a good play for her but hoped to have something in the fall. In the meantime, Mommy asked him if he would tell all the producers, as he had promised in a letter to her when she was afraid to accept a play if they had one. The cast of We Moderns was a tremendously expensive one and for this reason Mommy had taken a big cut through its entire run of about two months. Again, we had no chance to save. Mr. Tyler told Mommy that there were no plays being put on so late in the season and suggested she go away·for the summer. Mommy asked,

"On what, Mr. Tyler?" Then he said, "Haven't you any friends you can visit?" I said, "We can go home to Washington and roast all summer." Gosh, was I mad with Mr. Tyler! Mommy said, "Good-bye, Mr. Tyler, but we are not going to Washington." When we got out of his office I said to Mommy, "How do you propose to live this summer?" She said, "I am going to call up every manager I have ever met and tell him I am free." I believed Mr. Tyler when he said it was too late in the season for new productions and dissuaded Mommy from calling anyone. I said, "It'll soon get around that you are not working, and it'll be much better if they come to you."

All these years three or four of the different Equity members had been trying to persuade Mommy to resign from the Fidos and join Equity. The Fidos were just a name by this time anyway. After Mr. Tyler had told Mommy he didn't know when he would have a play for her, for he said he had no intention of putting her in any old play that would do her more harm than good, she was so depressed that I suggested that she go call on any of her contemporaries in the theatre. She said, "I am a Fido and a lone Fido at that." Rather than see Mommy unhappy over resigning from one organization to join another I took two sheets of paper and two envelopes out of the desk and wrote her resignation from the Fidelity League on one and her application for membership in the Actors' Equity on the other. I said, "Sign both of these and I'll mail them at once." She did readily enough and I sealed, stamped and dropped them in the mail chute before either of us could change our mind. When I returned to the room, Mommy looked so frightened when she said, "Mother, did you forget what Mr. Tyler once said to me: 'If ever you join a union I am through with you.'" I said, "Oh, that was long ago and besides he has gotten used to union labor by now. However, we will go this afternoon and tell him what you have done and just why. He'll understand. Besides he is too fond of you as an actress to give you up." I thought I knew him but I didn't. When we went in he was seated at his desk and almost before Mommy greeted him she blurted out, "Mr. Tyler, I have joined Equity." I'll never forget his face at this news. He stood up with his face white and said, "I am through." Mommy said, "With me?" He said, "You be-. long to the union now." We said good-bye, but he didn't answer. We managed to make a half-way dignified exit and Mommy burst into tears the moment we got in the elevator. I'd have kept her in the lobby so no one could see her, but she made me so angry by saying, "Now, what'll I do? No manager will engage me when he hears that I failed Mr. Tyler. They won't trust me." In her heart I could tell she blamed me, so I marched her into the street and said, "We'll go back to the hotel and I'll send an announcement to the newspapers saying that according to the announcement from the George C. Tyler office Miss Helen Hayes is no longer under his management." For her benefit, I said, "Then watch the demands for your services." I didn't really think there would be many offers this late in the season.

Mommy was choking back her sobs and was about to go into the Times Square Drug Store to repair the damage to her face when she espied Howard Lindsey, who was an old friend of ours.

Mommy rushed up to him, threw herself on his chest and burst into a torrent of tears, saying, "Mr. Tyler is through with me. I'll never get another job."

Really, darling, your mommy could be such a fool and most trying at times. Howard laughed and said, "With that bit of exclusive news I can make money." Apparently he didn't sell that news to the right producer, for the only call Mommy got that week was from Dudley Digges, who asked Mommy if, since she was out of work, she would join a little band of actors to go to Woodstock under the sponsorship of Hervey White, who owned a theatre and considerable property in this artists' colony. There would be no pay, just room and board and lots of fun. Mommy said, "Can I take Mother? Otherwise I can't go." Dudley said, "Of course. That is understood." Then it occurred to Mommy to ask the name of the play they would do first and how soon they would start to rehearse. Dudley said they had planned to do Lady Gregory's *The Dragon*, a sort of mythical blank verse thing. Mommy asked Dudley why they chose that type of play that would call for elaborate scenery and costumes for a summer colony. Dudley said, "This is a summer colony with a difference. They are all artists, mostly struggling. Some will paint the scenery, some the costumes and we will all pitch in to do our share too with the props." He said he had his company pretty well engaged: Edward G. Robinson, Mr. E. J. Ballantine, both fine actors who had had a run of bad breaks at an arty theatre in Greenwich Village (neither name meant a thing to us then, but a few years later Mr. Robinson was one of the finest actors with the Theatre Guild and then became one of the biggest box-office draws in motion pictures and at this writing still is), Norma Mitchell, who had been out of work for some time too, Dudley and his wife, Mary, and Mommy. They would engage native Woodstockians to play the extras. We stored most of our trunks, for Dudley said everyone being artists there, they just went round in overalls.

We left almost immediately, paying our own railroad fare. When we got to Woodstock and were driven to Hervey White's beautiful log-cabin house, where he lived alone, our bags were piled on a wheel-barrow and a young farmhand pushed them down the hill to a darling little cottage nestling in the woods. There were two bedrooms and a bath for Norma, Mommy and me. Dudley and Mary had a cottage high up on the hill near the theatre.

We were told everybody ate at a general lunch room. That was part of the White community. We went over to look at the theatre, which was only half finished and, as it was then, looked like a huge barn not meant for actors or plays. Dudley explained to the crew the stage would be necessary for rehearsals and for the men to concentrate on building that part first. There wasn't a carpenter by profession among the whole crew of workmen. That afternoon Dudley held a reading of the play at his cottage to the "music" of hammering and just loud homey visits among the men. The cast had been augmented by Miss Rose Hobart who had never been on the stage but had a real flair for it—as we found out after a few days' rehearsals.

After the reading we all went quite leisurely to our various quarters. We took our time for bathing and dressing into sports clothes and we, *The Dragon* cast, planned to meet at the lunch room for our dinner at 6:30. When we got there the waitress told us what was left in the kitchen and then she said, "You know, it's first come, first served." There were hardly two full portions of anything to go around among the seven of us. We didn't get discouraged until we wandered into breakfast at nine o'clock to be informed there wasn't even coffee left. Eddie Robinson said he was going to move his bed down to the lunch room. After that we formed a sort of breadline a good half hour before mealtimes. I eventually got over to Kingston, New York, where I laid in a stock of crackers, sardines, cookies and some fruit. Mary Digges had the necessary things for making a cup of tea for us in the afternoon, when the actors rested while the theatre builders put another brace under the stage, where during a scene the floor showed signs of not being very firm. Mommy adored those afternoons, for all the "old-timers" told their ups and downs in the theatre. Dudley's were particularly interesting, for he had been a good many years with the Abbey Players, one of the greatest organizations of actors and fine playwrights in the world. Mommy thought their art was of a much higher order than the Moscow Art Players who had just taken America by storm.

After four weeks of rehearsal of *The Dragon* they opened in a half finished barn to a packed house. There was no flooring down, so straw was spread under the seats. Just at the final curtain there was a terrific clap of thunder and one of those awful summer storms was under way. Everybody in the audience rushed for their cars, so there were no curtain calls. It rained all that night and all the next day, but by evening it cleared up.

I went out to watch it from the front that night, and when curtain time came I was the only audience that showed up and I hadn't paid for my admission. Really, I should have sued somebody, for I sat almost to my ankles in mud.

The cast refused to give a performance just for me, and I was just as happy to be spared.

We packed up and returned to New York the next day, vowing it was the best vacation we had ever had.

Love,

Grandma

MARY DEAR, I should have told you this in an earlier letter. One of the grandest things that happened to Mommy when she joined Equity, and allayed forever any regrets she might have had even though she lost Mr. Tyler, was that she was asked to play Constance Neville in Sheridan's *She Stoops to Conquer* for The Players benefit. Her part was very small, but she was with such artists as Miss Effie Shannon, Miss Pauline Lord, Miss Elsie Ferguson, Francis Wilson, President of The Players and also Equity at the time, and Henry Dixie, known as Adonis Dixie, he was so handsome.

They gave one of the classics each year and every actor considered it a great honor to be asked to appear in these plays. Walk-on parts were frequently played by stars.

The very next week after the play had been given at the Empire, The Players entertained at a big supper those who had appeared for them the week before. Each lady received a beautiful silver cigarette box inscribed with her name, character, play and date of the performance. Mommy met Miss Shannon and Miss Lord for the first time that week and loved and admired them greatly before they parted.

Mommy dressed with Miss Shannon and she kept us in gales of laughter with her subtle and kindly comments about her fellow actors.

Mommy thought she was being very astute when she said to me, "I should think this play could run for two years if some manager took it over." I explained that with this cast

Helen Hayes in *The Sin of Madelon Claudet*

it would cost thousands of dollars to run and without this cast it wouldn't run a week. She forgot they were all doing it for art and The Players.

Sweet dreams, dear,

Grandma

MARY DEAR, After our vacation at Woodstock Mommy and I came back to New York and our apartment on West Eleventh Street (we had a year's lease, that is why we had to keep it and we weren't allowed to sublet). This was in 1924. We were prepared to make the most of Washington Square Park, which was near the apartment, and live on the memory of our two wonderful visits to Europe. Mommy had lots of friends in New York either in a play or compelled to stay in town like Mommy because they weren't working.

Mommy and I were lounging around one hot day in early June when the phone rang. The operator said "Atlantic City calling Miss Helen Hayes." Mommy took the receiver and Edgar Selwyn said, "Could you and your mother come down to Atlantic City Saturday afternoon and see the last performance of my try-out, *Dancing Mothers*? I'll have rooms reserved for you at the Traymore. The part is an ingenue and you will be marvelous in it." I heard Mommy say, "Is it a flapper?" At his answer the excitement died out of her eyes and she said, "I won't promise anything, for I'm fed up with playing flappers but we will be there." I said, "Why didn't you tell Mr. Selwyn you weren't interested?" She said, "I thought this little trip down to the shore would do you good." She was lying again, for she just couldn't turn down a part sight unseen. His manager met us at the station with round-trip tickets and Pullman chairs. When we reached Atlantic City we had a lovely room overlooking the ocean, and Mr. Selwyn sent word that he and Mr. Edmund Goulding, co-author with him of *Dancing Mothers*, wanted us to have dinner with them.

We met them in the grill and they talked up the play and the part all through dinner and they both were so lovely to us it made it doubly hard, and, in fact, made it impossible for either of us to be honest with them afterward about our opinions of the play and part.

We got to the Apollo to find the house jammed with the same deceptive audience that *Golden Days* had back in that summer of 1920. Neither of us cared for the play and Mommy couldn't bear the girl Catherine that Mr. Selwyn wanted her to do in the fall in New York. Frances Howard was playing it as beautifully as that type part could be played. She was one of those awfully fresh modern flappers, but she had one very fine emotional moment that Miss Howard, for lack of experience, couldn't reach. Between each act Mommy would say, "What will I do when

Mr. Selwyn asks me what I think of it? I can't bear to hurt him. He is so proud of the play." I said, "I don't think he is that blind to its literary faults, but he thinks it will be good box office. Besides, if you do tell him you don't want to play it because you don't think it is good, I'll soften the blow by saying you don't know a good play when you see it." Mr. Selwyn was waiting in the front of the theatre with George Cohan, and when we joined them, before we could speak, Mr. Selwyn said to Mr. Cohan, "Tell Miss Hayes what you said to me just now, George." Mr. Cohan said with a very red face but a twinkle in his eye, "I said it ought to go over if Helen Hayes played the part." Mommy, trusting Mr. Cohan, felt sunk. She didn't see until I pointed it out later that he had done what we were planning to do. He had gone around Robin Hood's barn and didn't give a direct answer. Mommy and I hadn't a moment to ourselves to plan our escape, for Mr. Selwyn walked up to the hotel where he said Mr. Goulding would join us for a little supper and talk. When we were all seated and Mr. Selwyn asked Mommy if she would play Catherine for them in New York, I jumped in and said before Mommy could put her foot in it, "Helen is fed up with playing flappers, and while she thinks this is a mighty good flapper part, she wants to get away from them if she can. Let us think it over and we will come into your office Monday with our decision." Both of the men said that was fair enough, and Mr. Selwyn suggested we stay at the hotel until Monday morning. Then Mommy relaxed and had a great time dancing with both authors. The evil moment had been deferred.

All my love, dear,

Grandma

P.S.—The more we talked about how we would get Mommy out of committing herself or hurting Mr. Selwyn, the stronger her conviction came that she just couldn't play it. I suggested that she could write a nice letter to Edgar saying that she had decided to wait until a real grown-up part came along. Mommy said, "That is cowardly. I'll go to see him and be honest." Then I said, "How would it be if I asked for a prohibitive salary?" Mommy asked, "What would you call a prohibitive salary?" "Suppose I say $750.00." Mommy said, "Why, Mother, you'll never be able to whisper the figure. Five hundred dollars would be prohibitive for that part." However, she agreed that that would be the best plan. I said to Mr. Selwyn when we got there, "I'd better tell you Helen's salary regardless of the part before we take up your time." Then I said seven hundred and fifty dollars a week!! I was trying to recover from the choking sensation caused by wording this amount and looked at Mommy for approval. To her credit, her face was red with shame, but her eyes were almost popping from her head, for Edgar was inserting those figures in the contract and saying, "Helen will be worth that to me," signed his name and pushed the contract and pen to Mommy. She

232

looked as a person must look as he is drowning and knows he is doomed.

She was never happy in the part, and I always felt it was just retribution for Mommy and me for being such worms. I never felt quite comfortable with Mr. Selwyn after that for having taken advantage of one who was so sweet and guileless as he was, and I might add that Mommy never signed for her salary during that engagement with any pleasure. Mommy did work harder in that part than she ever did in any other to put as much in it as she could to justify that salary.

Love,

Grandma

Mᴀʀʏ ᴅᴇᴀʀ, This is a sort of sequel to my last letter.

When Charles Wagner was going to produce *Quarantine* and wanted Mommy to play opposite Sidney Blackmer he asked Edgar Selwyn to let him have Mommy and direct the play for him. Mr. Wagner also gave Edgar a share in the play. *Dancing Mothers* was falling off at the box office, so it was a good time to retrench on salaries. Mommy said she would do it, but only on the condition that she could leave it on two weeks' notice, if another play came along that she would prefer to do. Mr. Wagner was willing to make this concession.

We felt less guilty about her huge salary from Mr. Selwyn after that.

She left *Quarantine* to go with *Caesar and Cleopatra*, but that grand realization I will have to reserve for another letter.

Love,

Grandma

P.S.—This is just a little remembrance of Mommy's meeting with Mary Garden. Miss Garden occupied a box one night at *Quarantine* (Mr. Wagner was her concert manager) and after the play she came back to meet Mommy. Instead of shaking hands with Mommy, she put her hand on Mommy's stomach and said, "Why, she hasn't the diaphragm of a baby but her voice has extraordinary carrying powers." She didn't know at that time that Mommy was studying under the daughter of her own vocal teacher, Mme. Robinson-Duff. Mommy was very proud of that compliment.

Love,

Grandma

MARY DARLING, This is the story of my only argument about Mommy's salary with a management. One day, Mr. Munsell of the Theatre Guild called our apartment and said Miss Theresa Helburn wished to see Mommy at her office, which was then in the Garrick Theatre Building, that afternoon. Mommy was still playing in *Quarantine*. Well, we went to Miss Helburn's office at two o'clock and she said to Mommy, "Miss Hayes, we want you for Cleopatra in Bernard Shaw's *Caesar and Cleopatra*." Mommy couldn't believe her ears nor could she find her voice. To give her a chance to realize what she had heard was true, I said, "Well, about ten years ago she said she would play Shaw's Cleopatra some day." Then Mommy began to rave, "Oh, that's been the dream of my life. I know the part perfectly. In fact, I know everybody's part in the play. When do I begin rehearsals? I'll have to give my notice to Mr. Wagner." All of this in one breath and revealing the fact that as far as she was concerned salary meant nothing. Miss Helburn said she was afraid it couldn't be done for another three or four months, as the new Guild Theatre on West Fifty-second Street wouldn't be finished much before that. They wanted to open it with *Caesar and Cleopatra*.

I'd heard that the Theatre Guild paid very small salaries, yet I knew actors were glad to work for them, first of all, because they were assured a six-week run. The subscription guaranteed that much. At this time, too, everything the Guild produced was a huge success. They were the most daring of the producers. Bearing all this in mind, I said to Miss Helburn, "Before Helen signs the contract I should like to know what salary she will receive." Miss Helburn said, "The Guild wished to know first if Miss Hayes would consider playing it before they took up the matter of salary. I'll call you in a few days." Then, she added to Mommy, "I am glad you are going to have your heart's desire."

When we got out Mommy said, "Now, Mother, I am twenty-four years old and I am going to handle this in my own way." I said, "You aren't going to work for the Guild for nothing if you never play Cleopatra. Remember, the Guild isn't a struggling organization and I don't propose now that I have got your salary up, even though it was by a fluke, that you shall add to the Guild's coffers." We argued all the way down on the bus and I think Mommy had the last word, and that was, "I am going to play that part, salary or no salary."

A few days later as we were having tea at home with Miss Norma Mitchell the phone rang. I answered and a voice said, "This is Miss Helburn's secretary speaking. Miss Helburn wishes Miss Hayes to come to her office this afternoon to sign her contract." I said, "Will you please ask Miss Helburn to take the phone? This is Miss Hayes' mother speaking." Mommy was making faces and forming words with her lips without making a sound, but I understood from her face that if she lost that part through any dickering of mine, she would walk out of that door and never speak to me again. She was very like little Helen Hayes Brown then.

When Miss Helburn came on the phone I said, "What salary does the contract stipulate?" She said, "Two hun-

dred and fifty dollars and two percent over eight thousand."
I quietly hung up the receiver without a word. Mommy
fairly screamed, "What happened?" Just then the phone
rang and I took down the receiver before answering
Mommy. It was Miss Helburn, who said, "They cut us
off." I answered, "No, they didn't. I hung up. There was
no answer to such a ridiculous proposition." She said,
"Please come to the office with Miss Hayes and by the
time you get here I'll have discussed it with the other
members of the Guild." I knew my fight was lost if we
went there together, but I couldn't go on treating Mommy
quite like an incompetent, so I said we would be there
inside a couple of hours.

In the argument which followed Miss Mitchell sided
with me, thank goodness, and I promised Mommy I would
compromise with the Guild if she would promise not to
interfere. When we got there they had decided to pay
Mommy three hundred and fifty dollars per week and three
percent over eight thousand, which might amount to an
additional two or three hundred a week more. Mommy
signed the contract that day.

When we got out she said to me, "You understand how
I feel about Cleopatra, Mother. I just had to play her if
ever I got a chance." I said, "Of course, but we have still
got to eat and you have now reached a seven-hundred-and-
fifty-dollar appetite."

All my love, sweet,

Grandma

P.S.—From then on Mommy lived and breathed the six-teen-year-old Cleopatra, Shaw's flapper queen. Every word she could find out about Cleopatra at that age was grist to Mommy's mill of characterization.

When the rehearsals were called about the latter part of February, I think, Mommy probably was the first actress to be letter perfect for a director to start off with.

Grandma

Mary sweet, I want to tell you of a few things that happened to Mommy before she even started rehearsing Cleopatra to make her doubt that she had been born just to play that part.

One night shortly after Mommy had signed her contract with the Guild, and before there was any publicity given to it, Miss Ina Claire stopped by the Henry Miller Theatre, where Mommy was still playing in *Quarantine*. She remained in the dressing room until Mommy was ready to go. Miss Claire suggested she would take us home in her car. On our way home, Mommy asked Miss Claire what her plans were for next season. She said she had none but had great hopes that the Guild would let her play Cleopatra when they did it. I felt Mommy stiffen beside me, but neither of us had a chance to tell Ina anything, for she rattled on about how she would give her right arm to play it, that she would play it for nothing and had told the Guild so. Then she added, "They will probably end by giving it to a rank amateur." That was not the moment to tell Ina our secret, and in all justice to her, I don't think she dreamed Mommy was being considered. I asked, "When did you talk to the Guild?" She said, "Oh, two or three weeks ago." Now, this was before Mommy signed, so I heaved a sigh of relief that in spite of my argument with them about salary and Ina's most generous offer to play for nothing, Mommy was the one they wanted for the part.

In an article in either a newspaper or a magazine George Jean Nathan said in discussing his opinion of the cast for *Caesar and Cleopatra*, "We understand the Guild is considering Helen Hayes for the role of Cleopatra. In our opinion, while we think Miss Hayes a good actress, we do not think she is biologically suited to the part." Now this looked terrible in cold print, and Mommy just couldn't understand what he meant by this but finally decided he meant she had no sex appeal. She almost believed him, for remember, Mommy had met your Papa almost a year before and at the time he had made her think she was the only woman in the room, but he never followed that meeting up with any apparent ardor. I do believe if there had been a school for the development of "It" Mommy would have gone there.

Another time, during rehearsals, we went to a restaurant for lunch where the tables were in booths. We heard two male voices in the booth next to ours talking about the theatre and ridiculous casting of plays. They eventually came around to the Guild and its imminent opening, when one said in a voice that seemed to me could be heard on the Guild stage a block away, "For instance, Helen Hayes playing Cleopatra is the most absurd piece of casting ever done in the theatre. What does she know of life?" Then he quoted Mr. Nathan. We got out of that booth and restaurant as quickly as possible and neither of us mentioned the episode. I was curious to see the effect of these opinions on Mommy's performance, but outside of looking a bit languorous in her scene with Caesar (she mistook it for an amorous look!), she made no attempt to change her characterization. After the rehearsal she said to me, "Did I play this scene with Mr. Atwell any more sophisticated?" I told her until she had learned not to blush, she had better not try that at rehearsals but save it for the performance when she would be Cleopatra and that I was sure she would give the lie to all of them.

What worried her until the opening night was that these remarks would come to the ears of Mr. Philip Moeller, the Guild Director.

Love,

Grandma

Mary darling, Rehearsals of *Caesar and Cleopatra*, with Philip Moeller directing, were the most exciting because they were so different to Mommy from any she had ever had before. He hardly directed anyone and he is the first director we had ever met who ever gave an actor, even in the bit parts, credit for knowing his job. I don't mean he let them run wild, but he would say, "What are you going to do there?" or "Just where do you think you will stand when you say that line?"

After everyone, except Miss Helen Westley, who carried her part right up to the opening, was through studying and was working out his characterization, Mr. Moeller began weaving the cast in and out until each scene was like a beautiful tapestry. Mommy never knew whether he was a born director or a happy accident, but she did enjoy those rehearsals an awful lot.

There was such fun in knowing Miss Westley, who was adored by everyone and who had been too long in the theatre to let her work crowd out all other interests. There was no such thing as getting into the "atmosphere" with her. The moment before she stepped into a scene she would be joking and laughing about something that was entirely foreign to the theatre.

Mommy expected to be awed by every member of the Theatre Guild. They were known as members of the intelligentsia. They had been maligned. They were just human beings too, but mighty smart in guessing what the public wanted. The rehearsals were called for and held in the new theatre that was a long way from being finished, but since the enormous sets for Caesar and Cleopatra were practically being built within the theatre, Mr. Moeller thought it best to rehearse where the cast could familiarize itself with the sets.

There wasn't a place in the whole theatre where you could sit down to relax except in the front on the chairs, where I usually sat in almost perfect quiet. All noise of building, hammering and conversation was backstage.

Miss Westley was playing in another Guild play with Alfred Lunt and Lynn Fontanne while rehearsing the part of Fatateeta in Caesar and Cleopatra. She would arrive at rehearsals half dead with fatigue, and since her scenes were few and far apart she would always go out front and sit in one of the chairs in the orchestra, and relax while she waited for her cue. One day her cue came but no Miss Westley responded. The stage manager looked high and low, but she couldn't be found. Mr. Moeller said, "Skip that scene and go on to the next one." One of the cast who was in this scene with Miss Westley came out to sit in the orchestra and as he groped his way to a chair in the center he stumbled over a body. Lying on her fur coat on that uncarpeted floor was Miss Westley sound asleep. Mr. Moeller wakened her and told her since she couldn't be found when her cue came he had skipped her scene, now they would go back to it.

She stepped into it as if she was wide awake, which we

all discovered she was not, for the moment she was through with the scene she went right back to sleep again.

Love,

Grandma

MARY DARLING, It might have been ten years to the night of the opening of *Caesar and Cleopatra*, April 12, 1925, at the new Guild Theatre, since Mommy had made that promise to herself that she would play Cleopatra some day. Doesn't that sound as if the god of the actors was watching over her? Our President, Calvin Coolidge, pressed the electric button at the White House that officially opened the theatre.

The theatre was entirely completed in the front of the curtains, and what a beautiful front that was and particularly on this opening night. Ticket speculators reaped a big harvest, for people were paying any price just to get into the theatre. This, bear in mind, was in 1925 when the people were spending money as if it grew on bushes and those bushes would go on blooming gold forever.

The Diamond Horseshoe at the Metropolitan never blazed more brilliantly than the Guild Theatre shone that night. All society, every big figure in the political world, big bankers and their families, were well represented. As a matter of fact, it was a more discriminating audience than I have ever seen at an opening night in New York. I think that was the only time subscribers couldn't use their season tickets.

Mommy had the proud distinction of being the first actor to occupy the star dressing room in the new theatre. Mommy wasn't starred, of course, but she was playing one of the leading characters. It wasn't Mommy's first time to have the star dressing room but this occasion had more significance. It was as if all that had gone before in her career was the preparation for this part and this night.

After the final curtain of what was probably fifty calls—everybody was uncertain about the number—for the cast, the entire audience surged backstage, that is, they tried to, but more than half of them were in the street and waited in line to come in to congratulate everyone. The audience and actors were in a carnival spirit. It was two o'clock in the morning when we got home and we stayed awake the balance of the night waiting for the morning papers. The critics in nearly every instance proclaimed this the best performance of Mommy's career. One or two said it was the best performance of all grand performances in the play. We never knew what Mr. Nathan had to say of it. I forgot to tell you the costumes that Mrs. Aline Bernstein designed for Mommy made her look the most voluptuous little vixen you can imagine, and we both felt that would correct an awful lot of the biological defect Mr. Nathan complained of.

I hate to write this but in spite of the auspicious open-

As the aging Madelon Claudet

ing, a divided press, as far as the play and production were concerned, gave *Caesar and Cleopatra* only a fair run.

It was during this run at the Guild Theatre that Charlie MacArthur began seeing a bit more of Mommy.

All my love,

Grandma

P.S.—I think I'll add this instead of writing a whole new letter. You remember I wrote you it wasn't meeting Paul Hammond on the ship that was important, but what happened from that meeting which concerned Mommy's real fate.

Mommy had seen quite a bit of Mr. Hammond at luncheons, and teas, and we had gone down to his beautiful little house at Syosset, L.I., for visits. He had planned to enter his sloop in the races abroad again and asked if we would like to rent his house for two months that summer. The rent was pretty steep for us but certainly not for the house, so we moved down two weeks before *Caesar and Cleopatra* closed. Mommy took two guests—Halcyon Hargrove, a Washington chum, and June Walker—for the summer, bought a car and felt just like a squiress.

Now, I didn't know it at the time but Mommy was really setting a stage to capture your Papa. She invited all his friends, so that when he came he wouldn't be bored by seeing too much of her alone. Besides these, Halcyon and June had their friends down. I protested against such expenses as this amount of entertaining entailed but Mommy said, "I'll have a play when the summer is over" and went right on spending all the money she had saved.

This plan really worked beautifully, for Papa fell truly in love with Mommy that summer and so began their beautiful courtship.

Grandma

M ARY SWEET, This is going to be a letter about the last time Mommy ever allowed herself to be broke, or even sad, unless she had a contract, "I don't have to worry. I have a play for next season." As a matter of fact, not even when she had a contract and until that play opened and was a sure success did she permit herself to spend a dollar extravagantly.

As I told you, our summer at Syosset was one orgy of spending and this mostly in entertaining. So when Mr. Hammond returned and we came back to town in September it meant intensive play-hunting, and at once. However, Edward Childs Carpenter and James Forbes, who had organized a producing company called Dramatists Theatre, Inc., sent for Mommy for a play called *Young Blood*. It wouldn't be ready until late October. Mommy didn't care particularly for either the part or play, but was afraid to refuse it. In the meantime, Mommy drew all the dividends which we had allowed to accrue on her insurance, so this tided us over until *Young Blood* opened in late November. It ran two months, in spite of very bad notices, and then went on tour, but the tour was a short one, too.

When we returned to New York in early spring it looked like a long lean summer. I keep bringing up the subject of money and its scarcity with us to point out that great weakness with actors: never thinking of the precariousness of the profession and that rainy day that is bound to come.

One day we were discussing our financial situation with James Whittaker who had married Halcyon, another romance that began in Syosset, and he suggested we go abroad, as he and Halcyon had planned to do, on a freighter. He had spent many years in Paris, and, as he said, we could live all summer long for what it would cost us to live one month in New York.

He and Mommy started out one morning to shop for the best passage for the least money and I stayed at home to go over our wardrobe. The phone rang; it was the William A. Brady office calling Miss Hayes. I explained she was out to buy steamer tickets. This information was evidently relayed to Mr. Brady, for he came on the phone and asked me if I couldn't reach her before she made her reservations. He explained he wanted her at once for a revival of *What Every Woman Knows*, that his lease on the Bijou Theatre had six or eight more weeks to run and this revival would just fill in that time. I told him I didn't know what steamship line Mommy was going to but would have her call him the moment she returned. He said, "I don't want to talk to her over the phone. Have her come to my office, no matter how late, as I want to go into rehearsals at once." He was that sure Mommy would do it.

When she finally came in she was so tired and wan-looking I hadn't the heart even to mention the call. I felt she needed the rest more than anything in the world just then. She told me that she and Jimmy had gone from freighter office to freighter office. Some were all booked up or some had such poor accommodations that they wouldn't consider them at all. They planned they would start out early the next day and try all the other lines. She was lying across the bed so exhausted when the phone rang that she said, "I won't talk to anyone. Say I'm out." It was Mr. Brady, asking if I had located Mommy, and I told him she hadn't returned yet. When I hung up, Mommy asked me who it was. Then I told her about the call. She said, "I wouldn't mind working for three or four weeks. I imagine that is as long as it will run. I wouldn't have the temerity to attempt a part that Maude Adams had made famous, if it weren't that I am superstitious about turning down a Barrie part." Just the same, there was a smugness about her, for she was flattered that Mr. Brady had considered her. I said, "Not only has he considered you, but he is quite sure you will play it. He just said he would wait in his office until midnight if you didn't come there before then."

She jumped up, began taking her dress off. I asked, "Are you going to bed?" She answered, "No, I'm going to freshen myself up, and you and I are going to call on Mr. Brady."

The interview was most one-sided. Mr. Brady did all the talking and never heard one of Mommy's reasons for not daring to play the part. She did say, almost as she was signing the contract, "I can't speak with a Scotch burr, Mr. Brady." He said Miss Adams hadn't used an accent when she played it.

When we got outside she found that she had a run-of-the-play contract at five hundred dollars a week. She said, "This will give me two thousand dollars more for our vacation."

Love,

Grandma

MARY DEAR, Rehearsals were called immediately for *What Every Woman Knows* and Mommy was horrified when she received her script that most of her lines were written in Scotch dialect. She spoke to Lumsden Hare, who was directing it and had played the same part he was to play with Mommy in Miss Adams' company, about this dialect, and he, too, assured her Miss Adams had only used good English. Two of the Wylie brothers were real Scotsmen and one was English, and from the first reading they spoke their lines with a Scotch accent. Mommy said to Kenneth

McKenna who was to play John Shand, "We can't let those men show us up. We must speak with an accent." I told you in my last letter Mr. Brady was only putting this play on to fill in the balance of his lease in the theatre and therefore doing it as cheaply as possible. Rehearsals were held in a large room next to his office, thereby saving the cost of lights in a theatre. Mr. Brady never attended a rehearsal, but one day as he was passing to go to his office he stopped in the doorway to listen to Mommy and Kenneth struggling with an accent and at the same time trying to play the scene with the spirit of Scots people. His only comment as he turned to go into his office was, "You sound like a couple of Harps." Then everyone realized it was a brogue and not a burr those two had. Mommy said, "Kenneth, we have got to find a cultured Scotsman or woman to talk to before we open." They couldn't imitate the brothers, for they were supposed to be illiterate.

Kenneth was told of a Scotswoman who had once been an actress but in lieu of any work in her profession she had turned to fortune telling (you know the Scots and Irish believe they are more or less fay).

She was wonderful for their accent, for she was cultured, but she did so want to read their palms or tea leaves. She volunteered a prediction one day just before their Scotch lesson that they were going to have a long run, but this marked her as an absolute fake to Mommy, unless she considered four weeks at the most a long run. Mommy said, "Now, if she had told me I would be crossing the water shortly I would have had more faith in her." She did serve her purpose grandly though, for by the time the play opened in Stamford, Conn., Mommy's Scotch accent was just enough to be noticed without being affected. On Thursday night, April 9, 1926, *What Every Woman Knows* opened in Stamford and was so enthusiastically received that the entire cast, except Mommy who had seen too many big out-of-town openings flop in New York, planned either to take cottages or go to hotels near enough to New York to commute all summer.

By Saturday almost the entire audience was made up of New Yorkers who had heard of its success. Still, Mr. Brady hadn't come to see it, but Miss Grace George (Mrs. Brady) who had suggested Mommy to Mr. Brady for Maggie Wylie carried the glad tidings to him.

At the scenic and dress rehearsal Sunday at the Bijou, where it was to open, Mr. Brady was there before anyone else and was as proud as a peacock over *his* foresightedness. Every time Mommy made an exit he would rush over to her saying, "If you stay with me, I'll make you the greatest actress in the country. I'll get all the Barrie plays for you." Mommy who was horribly nervous about the New York opening asked me to talk to Mr. Brady. When she made her next exit I got between him and Mommy and said, "Wait until you see her tomorrow night before you make any rash promises, Mr. Brady." He said, "I trust my wife's judgment against anyone in the theatre and she says Helen will be a sensation." Having watched all the performances in Stamford, I agreed with Miss George, but I still thought it would not run over six weeks.

Monday night, April 13, 1926, at the Bijou Theatre, was, I guess, the real turning point in Mommy's career, for up to that time producers only saw her as a flapper or an ingenue. Thanks to Miss George's keen perception and Mommy's intense desire to do something besides these light types, there isn't a part now that she is afraid to undertake.

That night I was in my old place in the wings and after each act until the final curtain Mommy suffered from her old opening-night deafness. She thought she and the play were failures. My heart was so full of happiness that I couldn't reassure her without bursting into tears, which she mistook for shame and disappointment. The applause and the cheers at the final curtain very nearly deafened Mommy for life. The audience just wouldn't let her go, and when they finally went into the street they were all still cheering. I won't attempt in this letter to tell you of the encomiums heaped on her, without exception, by every critic in New York. You have Mommy's press book.

What Every Woman Knows played sixty-two weeks in New York and on tour and closed in June, 1927. In every city business was enormous and as Mr. Brady gave Mommy a percentage of the gross, she made a grand income that year and saved a nice nest egg. When the play closed in New Haven Mr. Brady arranged to have it do so on Friday night, as Mommy, Jean Dixon and I were sailing the next day on the *Duillio* for Italy. We were going on our own, this time. I think you will enjoy hearing about that trip.

Much love,

Grandma

MARY DARLING, I guess I have told you often enough how difficult it always was for Mommy ever to say "no" and what I am going to tell you about was one of the times that this weakness might have been very disastrous.

One day she got a letter from Mr. Brady while she was still playing Maggie Wylie in New York, telling her of his plans for her future. He said he was going to secure all of Sir James Barrie's plays that Miss Adams had made famous. The first was to be *Quality Street* which he would produce in the fall following the closing of *What Every Woman Knows* on tour in June. He intended to live up to his promise to make her the most beloved actress in the country. It was such a sweet and generous letter that Mommy sat down and wrote a reply saying, in effect, that she wouldn't ever leave him and signed her name, I believe in full. Now, I had never seen his letter nor her reply to it. I just heard of this correspondence afterward. It wouldn't have made any difference, however, for I wouldn't have known that Mommy's letter was as binding as a contract.

After writing the letter Mommy completely forgot about it and her promise to remain with Mr. Brady.

Some time after this Jed Harris sent Mommy a play called *Coquette* by Ann Bridges and George Abbott. Two seasons before Mr. Abbott had sent the same play, but the title then was *Norma's Affair*, a comedy. At that time Norma was a flapper and Mommy had vowed she wouldn't do another one, so I returned it with a note, saying, "Miss Hayes wasn't interested."

When the new version was sent to Mommy she refused to read it, but I did and was astonished at the drastic changes that had been made in it. While not a classic by any means, it was one of the most poignant tragedies of modern youth I had ever read and I was sure would be good box office. I told Mommy of this, but she said, "How can they make a good tragedy out of a bad comedy, for you said it was bad when you read it?" I denied saying it was bad, but that it wasn't what she wanted to play. She read it that night and felt that with a few more changes it could be a good vehicle for her next season. There were numerous conferences with Miss Bridges, Mr. Abbott and Mr. Harris about these changes and they were promised to Mommy before it would be put in rehearsal.

One night after her performance in *What Every Woman Knows* we—Mommy, your papa, and I—went to Crosby Gaige's office (he was co-producer with Jed Harris in this play) and Mommy signed the contract to play Norma Besant in *Coquette* the following season.

Immediately, tremendous publicity was started from the Gaige-Harris offices and immediately Mr. Brady produced the forgotten letter and preferred charges against Gaige and Harris with Equity.

Mommy was called over to the Actors' Equity before an arbitration board and, much to everybody's surprise and confusion, Mr. Brady insisted that his fight was with Gaige and Harris, that Mommy was innocent. Sam Harris, who was one of the arbitrators, tried to explain to Mr. Brady that neither Gaige nor Harris knew of any former contract and that Miss Hayes was the guilty party. Mr. Brady would not hear a word against Mommy and out-shouted everyone, even Mommy, when she tried to tell him she had forgotten her written promise to him. Finally, Mr. Gilmore, the President, said, "Well, there is only one thing we can do and that is suspend Miss Hayes for six months from appearing on the stage." That was Mr. Brady's cue for a speech, and he made the most amazing but also kindest one for Mommy you ever heard. This is what he said, "Helen Hayes is the finest, the squarest little lady that has ever stepped on a stage and anyone who ever touches a hair of her head will answer to me." This was directed to Gaige and Harris. Turning to Mr. Gilmore he said, "If you persist in carrying out your sentence against her I'll never rest until I break Equity." With this he grabbed Mommy's arm and to the amusement of the entire board walked Mommy out.

Mommy became like a daughter to Mr. Brady. He would be waiting at the stage door when we arrived at night, then climb three flights of stairs to her dressing room (she chose that one because it was larger and cooler than the downstairs one). He would frequently bring up the "underhand" methods of Gaige and Harris and he would never allow Mommy to shoulder the guilt. Do you wonder Mommy has always adored him?

Much love, sweet,

Grandma

MARY DEAR, Did I ever tell you how Jean Dixon came to be a sort of sister to Mommy and a real daughter to me? I don't think I ever did. I'll have to go back to Golden Days. Just before Mr. Tyler sent it on tour he put Jean in a part that had been played by a young girl who did not want to leave New York. Jean's father had been an old friend of Mr. Tyler. This was Jean's first part outside of school theatricals, but I saw a spark there I was sure could be fanned into a flame.

After Golden Days closed she very wisely went into stock and in those days that was the best schooling for the theatre. I think it was in 1927 Jean replaced Norma Mitchell in To the Ladies and whether I took her under my wing or she adopted Mommy and me, we were almost inseparable after that. In fact, we three always had a suite of rooms together on tour. Mommy and Jean occupied one room and I learned an awful lot about each of their frailties in their arguments and frank sisterly quarrels they would have after we had gone to bed.

In 1925 or '26 Jean came to live with us, and what an outlet she became for not only Mommy's problems, but mine, too. You see, I still didn't think your papa was good enough for Mommy and was constantly criticizing him. So Mommy stopped talking to me about him, and Jean became her adviser. After one of those confidences, Jean would come to me and say, "By your tactics, Brownie, you are just making her that much keener about him, and besides if she is truly in love with him, why try to break it up? You want her to be happy and you know Helen also has a bunch of faults."

Now, to go back to the first trip abroad of the Three Musketeers, as we called ourselves, I have never quite understood how we three ever returned together, for we were constantly getting separated. Mommy with her vagueness about directions, I with my belligerency (I always presupposed foreigners wanted to take advantage of us) and Jean, who was so level-headed and whose French was like a native's, seemed to take on Mommy's and my irresponsibilities and wasn't much help either.

We landed in Naples and after two weeks there of intensive sightseeing for Mommy and Jean, and my daily hunt for the bank that would give me the most lire for my dollar, and having myself a heated argument with everyone who couldn't understand me, we traveled on to Pisa, Pompeii, and ruins, ruins, ruins. I finally suggested we find a place where there were no galleries or ruins to see, a resort, in other words, where I could get away from dates and periods, and rest. Mommy's faithful Baedeker, when consulted, told us of Strazza, a summer resort which was on our way to Rome.

The girls were in ecstasy over the beauty of this little spot (by the way, I don't think it is even on a map), but undoubtedly the Italians knew of it and vacationed there when they wanted quiet with great scenic beauty. There were no amusements, but a little boat took passengers on the lake in front of the hotel to a little island on which were ruins of an old palace.

That afternoon we were asking the clerk, or rather Jean was in her beautiful French, just where we could take a short walk before dinner, when two enormous cars drove up and from the way the clerk and the entire menage brushed us aside we suspected no less a personage than Mussolini had come to the hotel. First of all we could just glimpse through the cordon that surrounded him a magnificent-looking sheik in an exquisite heavy cream silk burnoose followed by, we learned afterward, his wife, her attendants, and a nurse carrying a tiny baby. All wore beautiful Arabian costumes.

They had no sooner gone up in the elevator than Mommy and Jean rushed to the desk to find out who they were. The clerk said the sheik was a great Arabian prince. Mommy amused Jean and me by saying he looked like your papa. She changed her mind that night when he came down in

European dinner clothes, and looked very common and ordinary. He spent the entire meal ogling the girls, for he hadn't failed to notice their excitement when he first came into the lobby. He didn't know that by the change of clothes he had lost all glamor as a sheik for them.

All my love,

Grandma

MARY DARLING, Rehearsals for *Coquette* started almost immediately after our return from abroad in September. Mr. Harris planned to open it in Atlantic City about the middle of October. He had gotten a great cast for it, with George Cukor directing. From the very first days of rehearsals it was most hilarious and later became most confused and unpleasant. In the beginning, Mommy and George Cukor were responsible for the lack of seriousness in the rehearsals. You see, Mommy and George had been close friends ever since they had been together in *Dancing Mothers* (George was stage manager for that) and they would stand in the wings and tell jokes and stories. George was a great wit.

I think I told you Mommy was never impressed by the script of *Coquette* and when she and George got together, with their sense of humor going full blast, it struck them as a little ridiculous with its terribly broad Southern accent, its "Miss Nomah being a belle of the Southland, suh" and its Southern "cunnels, suh" bouncing in and out and being very proud and most "honahble, suh." Mommy, George and I would go out to lunch together and both of them would vow and declare they would be serious and sincere about everything, but they would no sooner get back to rehearsals than one of those lines such as "Miss Nomah, would you do me the honah to become mah wife" then off they would go again into derision about the whole thing.

The cast was becoming demoralized, not so much from the behavior of Mommy and George as by the necessity of re-writing and serious handling. George Abbott was angry with Jed for taking the direction of the play from him and refused to come for a rehearsal. Miss Bridges, whose first play it was, knew nothing about re-writing, but she agreed with Mommy that something should be done and that re-writing was the most important thing. She had returned from one of the rehearsals to our apartment one day when things had been going particularly bad. After they came to this decision Mommy called Jed on the phone and told him that she and George Cukor were aggravating each other's unsympathetic attitude toward the play and that they needed someone there who believed in it and who could make them believe in it and she said, "George Abbott's the only one."

Jed agreed to get Abbott, and Cukor was most amenable and bowed out for Abbott. Rehearsals took on new life,

Helen Hayes in *Victoria Regina*, with Brian Aherne

though Mommy still felt much that wasn't sincere in the play could be corrected. The cast had been rehearsing under Abbott for about ten days when Jed came in for his first rehearsal. It was only about four days before the opening in Atlantic City and the cast was in fine shape, had reduced the Southern accent to a natural one, when Jed began to tear practically everyone apart, Mommy included. Ordinarily, Mommy's entrance would be about five minutes after the curtain was supposed to rise, but this day it was nearer two hours before Jed reached Mommy's entrance cue. She had been watching from the side the process of pulling down, so when she spoke her first line which was a simple "Hello" to her brother Jimmy, Jed stopped her and said, "What are you going to do with that 'Hello'?" her anger began to rise and she said in that quiet voice of hers that generally preceded an explosion, "Just nothing."

Mommy thought this would head Jed off, but no, he wasn't going to let her get away with that and proceeded to give a long dissertation on the meaning of the line. I could see Mommy's lips tightening and would have warned Jed, but she went into her next speech when he again stopped her with a long explanation of reading. Well, dear, the fireworks were on with a vengeance. Mommy turned on Jed, threw down her part and fairly screamed, "I didn't know this was Euripides. I thought it was a simple play about plain people. I won't go on until you get out of here!" It was a very ugly scene, but when Mommy came down to the footlights and apologized to me for making

261

it, she said, "It isn't for myself alone but I know the cast will never survive a whole day of such direction."

As I have written you before, I think Mommy could always be told her faults and would admit them, but in this she was quite sure she was right.

At this point Jed rushed out of the theatre, and the cast, first thanking Mommy for her stand, went on with the rehearsal, which went along smoothly only up to the curtain of the second act, which Mommy had discussed with both authors, Miss Bridges and Mr. Abbott, as being false in its conception.

Jed stayed away until the dress rehearsal in Atlantic City and when he came in and took charge he began to function superbly. Mommy observed an extraordinary thing about Jed and that was he was most nerve-racking as a director during the building days of a performance, but he was great at picking flaws and finding the exact treatment for a scene, after the groundwork had been done.

They worked on it diligently, but they had reached the opening in Atlantic City without making it ring true to Mommy. That opening night, October 17, 1927, was what Mommy felt it would be. The audience was just lukewarm about her and the play, and unimpressed. In the meantime, Jed and I had been holding secret conferences (he stayed away from Mommy entirely) and he agreed with Mommy that it was the second-act curtain that was wrong. While Mommy knew what she would do under the circumstances she couldn't tell the authors what to write. Jed knew and begged me to have Mommy insist on George re-writing that scene that night with him. I went into Mommy's dressing room after the play and was greeted with, "Now, I guess you'll believe Charlie. It is a bad play and if I am roasted in Philadelphia I positively will not appear in it in New York, contract or no contract." I told her what Jed had said and she said, "I don't care who re-writes it, so long as I don't have to play in it."

Mr. Abbott called the cast on the stage that night and asked Mommy what she thought of its reception. She said, "That second-act curtain is the chief offender. This is the way I feel about it: If my own father killed the man I loved, at that moment I would want to see him hanged. What I would feel later on, I don't know." George said, "But you will lose the sympathy of the audience if you denounce your father." She said, "I lost the sympathy tonight and the bottom dropped out of your play from then on." She added, "I want to tell you right now, George, if I get bad criticisms in Philadelphia I'll not open in New York in this play." Jed and I were sitting together in the back of the theatre and he whispered, "Tell her to stick to that and George will be willing to fix it. I know just what she means." I said, "She will stick to that and nothing will change her." The two authors and Jed worked all night in the hotel, but the change was not put in until the opening night in Philadelphia. They rehearsed for it in Atlantic City and Jed had worked a miracle on that second act curtain.

Coquette opened October 24th in Philadelphia, and it seemed to me that all New York was there, every theatre owner, all the ticket agents, newspaper representatives, playwrights and authors. This, despite the bad word that was taken to New York from Atlantic City. Mommy insisted that I sit out front. Your papa and Sidney Howard who were collaborating on a play for Pauline Lord called *Salvation* were out front, too. The response of the audience to the first act was the same in Philadelphia as it had been in Atlantic City—very good. But it was that second act that was the hazard for all of them.

When the curtain came down on that act with Mommy beating her fists on the couch and screaming, "I hope he hangs. I hope he hangs," I don't think I have ever heard any audience go quite so wild before. Everybody was standing up yelling, "Hayes, Hayes," and when I finally got to the lobby I rushed to your papa and Mr. Howard and I triumphantly asked, "Now what do you think of it?" Your papa said, "I still think it stinks." Mr. Howard said, "It'll run two years in New York."

After the play that night there wasn't one dissenting voice about it, and Mommy was called by her friends who came back the greatest young emotional actress on the stage.

After we got to the hotel Mommy seemed very happy and we were quite sure that the critics would acclaim the play.

To our amazement and my horror the critics the next

day were unanimous in condemning the play, but praised Mommy to the skies. They said it was far from the usual pattern, but deplored its tragic ending. They all held out little hope for a run in New York, then, too, proceeded to compare it with *Behold This Dreamer* which had opened the night before *Coquette* with Glenn Hunter starred, and they certainly gave *Coquette* the worst of the comparison.

We found out that Philadelphians believe implicitly in their drama critics, for *Coquette* was a decided flop in Philadelphia. No business at all, and *Behold This Dreamer* played to packed houses for the two weeks it was there. Again, we were fooled by a first-night audience.

Good night, dear. Sweet dreams,

Grandma

Mary darling, After the two awful weeks in Philadelphia *Coquette* went over what you might call a week of dress rehearsals in Newark, New Jersey, for it was to be left entirely as it was to be played in New York. Jed and George Abbott decided not to make another change, and besides their faith in it was undiminished and they felt it couldn't be improved upon.

In Newark the press and public were just as cold to the play as Philadelphia, and undoubtedly influenced your godfather, Alec Woollcott's opinion. He was to give a lecture on the Monday night *Coquette* was to open in New York, so he came to a matinee in Newark to write his review for the New York *Evening World*. It would appear the following Tuesday, as if he had seen the New York opening.

He came back after the matinee and told Mommy she had given a great performance but he feared the play was hopeless. He wrote his review along those lines, and four days later *Coquette* opened in New York. That is so thrilling that I think I'll have to make that a letter all by itself.

All my love,

Grandma

Mary sweet, On November 8, 1927, *Coquette*, with Mommy starred, opened at the Maxine Elliott Theatre in New York City. Mommy said to me, "Since your faith is still unshaken in the success of *Coquette* I am going to let you sit out front tonight. I don't believe you feel so sure, Mother, but you are trying to cheer me up. I am not quite an idiot and I can see through you." Mommy couldn't believe I meant what I said. She had allowed the out-of-town critics to get her down, and then, Uncle Alec's opinion given to her in Newark completed her demoralization. She said, "I am glad Charlie won't be here to see my humiliation."

I rushed out and bought a new evening gown, for it would be my first night out front with New York's "first-nighters" and I wanted to do Mommy "proud" and then, too, I wanted to look my best when our friends came up to congratulate me after the play.

At the last minute she got frightened and asked me if I minded not seeing the play from front but standing in the wings as always. I can't tell you how happy that made me. It is an awful feeling when a mother begins to realize her opinions are no longer important to her child, no matter how old that child is. I don't know how much of this feeling Mommy guessed or whether she thought the ordeal of watching the play flop from an orchestra seat would be too much for me, but she did make me feel necessary to her. I took my old place in the first entrance all dressed up in my new evening gown.

After the play was over the applause and cheers were so thunderous that they penetrated even Mommy's first-night deafness, though she said, "I must be crazy. I can't be hearing that commotion out front." She was pushed again and again onto the stage to take curtain calls. She walked on as one in a dream vaguely seeing people on their feet across the footlights yelling and stamping, she told me afterward. Crowds began surging back to the dressing room, each one trying to be first to reach Mommy and me. It had gone around that I had literally picked *Coquette* out of an ash can and forced Mommy to play it. These people were crying, kissing both Mommy and me and being pretty hysterical, but Mommy seemed to be walking in her sleep and nothing said seemed to penetrate her mind.

After the dressing room was cleared out and Mommy, still unbelieving, got her make-up off, she, Jean and I went home together. We sat up nearly all night eating apples and Mommy wondering just what had hit her. The next morning the reviews were the most ecstatic Mommy had ever gotten, all except Uncle Alec's. Percy Hammond in his review said he had never witnessed an entire audience go so completely haywire that even the ermine-cloaked behaved like the gallery gods.

When we arrived at the theatre the next night there was a line reaching from the box office to, and around on, Sixth Avenue. Ticket speculators had rented veritable slits in buildings on Thirty-ninth Street and were selling tickets for *Coquette* at fabulous prices. There was an agency buy of sixteen weeks in advance—an unheard-of thing. Everybody concerned with *Coquette* waxed rich, for that business lasted for a year before the standees began to be one less than the fire laws allowed.

On August 17, 1928, Mommy and Papa were married. Mommy still continued in the play until September, when Jed Harris gave Mommy a two weeks' vacation for her honeymoon. *Coquette* reopened in October and business was enormous. They played until the following July, 1929, and without a break started on tour. In the meantime, Mary Pickford bought the picture rights and had had it re-written so as to pass the censors. It was ruined by the changes, I always thought. However, it was not released until Mommy opened in San Francisco and because of these changes only affected business for the balance of the tour. Up to that time, Mommy had played forty-five weeks on tour to tremendous business.

Because of your coming into Mommy's life I insisted that she close her engagement with *Coquette* in Los Angeles.

Mommy and your papa returned to New York, I think some time in September, and I followed shortly after that. I wanted to be with Mommy when you came into the world.

I have passed over Mommy's and Papa's marriage, for that is for them to tell you about some day, but this I will say, it was the culmination of all the hopes I had had for Mommy's happiness.

Grandma

M ARY SWEET, While you and Mommy were still in the hospital, where you were born, Jed Harris brought her a play called *Mr. Gilhooley,* dramatized by Frank Elser from a novel by Liam O'Flaherty. Mommy read it and liked it enormously and the idea of doing a character (it was an Irish harlot) so different from anything she had ever done before appealed to her tremendously. She agreed to play it the following season.

Though the whole subject of Mr. Gilhooley was a sordid one, there wasn't one of us who read it that didn't feel it would be a great play. Papa and I were strongly convinced that it would be a success.

Rehearsals began in August under Jed's direction and they rehearsed violently and endlessly and didn't stop until an hour before the curtain rose in New Haven. That night Mommy had a sandwich in her dressing room while she was putting her make-up on, which, because of lack of time, had to be a hurried one. *Mr. Gilhooley* was launched under those conditions.

So strong was Mommy's faith in this play that when it was coldly received by the Yale undergraduates who began slamming seats and stomping up the uncarpeted aisles of the gallery before the last act was over, she was completely floored.

Thornton Wilder who had attended the first performance took Mommy and me to a beer parlor afterward, and talked to her for two or three hours about the merits of the play and her performance, over numerous cups of coffee. His encouragement restored Mommy's confidence and carried her over to the opening in Atlantic City. There she received another blow. It was a failure there, too. Again the audience left the theatre before the play was over. Uncle Alec Woollcott came down there to see it and came backstage afterward, proclaiming it a great play and Mommy a great actress. This plus the general feeling among those concerned that Atlantic City wouldn't know anything anyway about a play like this buoyed Mommy up again, and she was sure when they opened in New York before a sophisticated audience its reception would be equal to that of Coquette.

On September 30, 1930, at the Broadhurst Theatre, Mr. Gilhooley opened in New York, and while there was no applause between the acts as there had been in Coquette Mommy was quite sure it was because the audience was too moved by the play and performances to applaud, but expected and was prepared for cheers, no less, after the final curtain. Mommy got the greatest shock of her life in the theatre. For when the company stepped onto the stage for the first curtain call they received only polite, perfunctory applause and most of the audience had their backs turned to the actors on their way out.

Mommy refused to read a review the next day, but I did, and they were dire, all except for Arthur Sinclair, an Abbey Theatre player, who was acclaimed as great in the part of Mr. Gilhooley.

However, though Mr. Gilhooley ran only four weeks it didn't do Mommy any harm, for it was seeing her as Nellie Fitzpatrick in that play that led Maxwell Anderson to write Mary of Scotland for Mommy. He realized she could play other types besides sweet young ingenues.

Before Mommy closed in Mr. Gilhooley she signed with Gilbert Miller to play Peggy Chalfont and with the signing of that contract began the finest, happiest and most satisfactory managerial association of Mommy's whole life in

271

the theatre. That association has continued unbroken, except for the year Mr. Miller loaned Mommy to the Guild for *Mary of Scotland.*

The first four years of their association were pretty confusing, for Mommy was dashing back and forth to Hollywood, fulfilling movie contracts, but Gilbert was very understanding and very helpful. Mommy will have been with Gilbert Miller nine years in December, 1939.

All my love,

Grandma

MARY DARLING, Mommy opened in *Petticoat Influence* at the Empire Theatre, December, 1930, occupying for the first time the star dressing room that her two idols had used —John Drew and William Gillette—when she was with them.

I don't think Mommy had felt so secure or so happy in years. You came to her in February of that year. Gilbert Miller had become her manager and she was going to appear at the Empire, which still held memories of the great in the theatre. Associated, too, with Mommy were Henry Stephenson and Reginald Owen. It was during the run of this play that these two signed contracts for motion pictures and have practically been lost to the theatre ever since.

Petticoat Influence wasn't an outstanding success, but it

had a very good run in New York and finished the season on tour. The entire cast was English except Mommy, but as she was constantly watching her diction there was no noticeable difference in her speech from theirs.

I really think diction is the most important thing in the theatre, for nothing annoys an audience so much as not being able to understand every word spoken. After the closing of *Petticoat Influence* in the spring of 1931, Mommy went to Hollywood to fulfill her motion-picture contract.

Much love, dear,

Grandma

Mary sweet, These letters about Mommy's entire career in pictures are going to be about the hardest I have ever written you, because I always felt Mommy was temperamentally unsuited to that medium of histrionic expression and therefore I was prejudiced against them.

I have told you how much Mommy depended on her audience's reaction to a performance and how quickly she sensed a friendly one. She explained to me after her first day at the studio her conviction that she would never be a success in pictures. She said, "Mother, what would you do if, on the first shot, half a dozen camera men got in a huddle and discussed the best way of lighting your face, which from their pantomiming I gather must be the ugliest face they had ever had to work on. Why, I began to think I had a hare-lip and warts like horns sprouting on my nose. I know I am no beauty, but on the stage with a simple make-up I have been complimented on my looks. It makes me self-conscious and you know I have never been that on the stage. Consequently, I just can't be happy here."

Another thing that happened on that first picture to disturb Mommy was this: Edgar Selwyn had made the adaptation of *Lullaby* from the stage play that Florence Reed had done for David Belasco. After several days of "shooting" scenes from his adaptation, the powers that be decided it wouldn't do and called your papa in to write an entirely new version.

Now, you aren't too young to have noticed one of your papa's idiosyncrasies is that he writes inspirationally and cannot be pinned down to a typewriter and told to turn out a story and a great one in a week. In the theatre, Mommy had always had the finished play manuscript sometimes months before the play was produced, but here in the pictures, though Papa was writing day and night, frequently an entire day's output would be discarded the next morning. Mommy would arrive at the studio by seven-thirty only to find the sequences that Papa had written the night before weren't playable. Then all work would be suspended while they sat around waiting for Papa to send a scene over to the studio. When it would finally arrive, Mommy was not given time enough to find out what it was all about. She would find herself standing before the camera, and it was do or die. She worked many times on that picture until nine o'clock at night. She would fall into bed with a tray before her, and Papa would read to her, while she ate, what he had written that day. Whether it was good or not, Mommy wouldn't know, for her brain would feel so tired nothing seeped into it.

Mommy and Papa were in a very trying situation, for this was the first thing he had ever written for Mommy, and she, knowing how anxious he was that it should be the best thing he had ever done, took on his nervousness and anxiety and would burst into a heated argument with him about what and how it would be done on the stage. Then Papa, whose brain was as tired as hers, would tell her in no uncertain terms that she didn't know what she was talking about.

That their marriage survived this experience proved how real their love was, for after ten of the most nerve-racking weeks, the new *Lullaby* now called *The Sin of Madelon Claudet* was previewed at Huntington, California. All the executives of Metro-Goldwyn-Mayer, except Irving Thalberg who had gone to Europe before the picture was started, went over to see it.

Mommy told Papa to sit by himself, and she and I would sit by ourselves. Both their nerves were at the breaking point, and she knew this would be too much of an ordeal for them to watch together. It was, without a doubt, the worst thing you have ever seen from every point of view— production and performance. When it was over Mommy literally crawled out of the theatre and we rushed over and got into the car, where she sat in stony silence until Papa sneaked over to the car just as heartsick as she was. Two or three of the executives came over to us to give Mommy a word of cheer, one saying that "good acting methods on the stage went for naught in the films."

The picture was promptly shelved and it was entered in the records as a "colossal" mistake all around. Mommy and Papa, feeling they had failed each other, were drawn closer together and just tried to forget all about pictures, the thing they thought had nearly been their undoing.

It did rankle in Mommy's mind that a medium of entertainment that reached millions of people had defeated her on her first attempt.

Much love, and kisses,

Grandma

Mary darling, I don't know whether you would call it Hayes luck but Mr. Samuel Goldwyn had seen a couple of the scenes from Lullaby run off in his projection room and had liked Mommy enough to offer her the part of the wife opposite Ronald Colman in Arrowsmith. He said the script was complete and he would send it to her at once. Mommy jumped at the chance to have at least one picture to her credit before she came back to New York and the theatre.

M.G.M. made no objection to her going over to Mr. Goldwyn. As a matter of fact, I think they had no intention of ever using Mommy in another picture.

With a script that she could take home every night to study, then be on the set next day letter perfect and knowing exactly what she was going to do, the picture went along swimmingly.

About the middle of August, Irving Thalberg returned from abroad and immediately ordered *Madelon Claudet* dusted off. When it was run off for him, he said, "There is more than two-thirds of a picture there." He got Papa back to re-write many of the scenes with really brilliant suggestions.

Mommy was still working on *Arrowsmith*, but she went every Sunday to the M.G.M. studios to remake *Madelon Claudet*. This had been going on for three or four weeks, when Mr. Goldwyn found it out and threatened to take Mommy out of *Arrowsmith* if she didn't take her Sundays for rest. So again *Madelon* was put away until the last shot of *Arrowsmith* was taken. Then work was resumed on *Madelon*.

Each day Irving would look at the "rushes" and reported that it was going to be one of his best pictures, but Mommy refused to go near the projection room, for she was quite sure that nothing could be done to help that picture.

Some days Mommy was on the set for twelve or fourteen hours. So is it any wonder that when it was finally finished Mommy took to her bed and was quite sick?

The second preview of *The Sin of Madelon Claudet* was held in Glendale, California. Mommy was too sick and too frightened to go over, so I went alone. Ruth Chatterton asked me to go with her, but I couldn't bear the thought of anyone commiserating with me. Ruth was taking Lois Wilson, and, knowing they both loved Mommy personally, I was not going to put them in the position of saying things they couldn't possibly mean. You see, darling, I was sure it was still a bad picture, though I had only Mommy's word for it.

I saw a miracle happen in that Glendale Theatre that night. *Madelon Claudet* was almost a masterpiece of scenario writing and Mommy gave one of her finest performances. Men and women all over that theatre were sobbing and crying unashamed.

I rushed out immediately after the picture was finished, with the wildest applause ringing in my ears, something unbelievably strange in a motion-picture theatre.

When I reached Mommy I started screaming the news to her the moment I opened the door. When I got to her bedside she looked at me and said, "Mother, what has happened to you? Have you gone mad?" I tried to tell her how great she came over in that picture, but she just stared at me with a frightened look. Just as she decided to call for help, so sure was she that I might become violent, Ruth Chatterton and Lois burst in, with Ruth saying to Mommy,

"You are the biggest damn fool and the best actress I have ever seen. The preview was a sensation. When Lois and I left the theatre the audience was still applauding into the news reel."

While we three were trying to get it through Mommy's head that she and her picture were a triumph the phone began ringing. It was the executives of the studio taking it in turn, adding to what Ruth had said and telling Mommy how great she was. She remained decidedly unimpressed. Irving wanted Mommy to see the picture before she returned to New York, but she said there would be too many scenes she would want to do over again. She preferred to remain unenlightened.

A week later she returned to New York and rehearsals of *The Good Fairy*, still doubting she and *Madelon Claudet* were what everyone was saying: "Magnificent." Can't write any more now, dear, but I am sending you much love.

Grandma

P.S.—I think I had better tell you this now before I forget it: Do you know you appeared for a brief scene in the first version of *Madelon Claudet* when you were just a year and a half old?

This is how it happened. You would be asleep in the morning when Mommy would leave the house for work. You would be asleep when she returned home at night.

She was afraid you wouldn't recognize her by the time

the picture was finished, so she had Nana bring you to the studio during the afternoon a couple of days a week.

There was a scene in which Madelon's little son ran across the lawn to greet her, and Edgar tried any number of children, but they all ran out of the camera or just didn't do anything he told them to. When you arrived at the studio you invariably would run to Mommy and throw your arms around her neck, the very thing Edgar wanted the child to do in the picture. He asked Mommy if she would let you do it, so their troubles would be over. At first Mommy objected but Papa said he thought it would be cute to have you in Mommy's first talking picture, and so you were. I was sorry that scene was cut out in the new version, for you were adorable.

Now, wasn't that a strange coincidence? Mommy's first part on the stage was as a boy and your first part in a picture was also as a little boy.

Love,

Grandma

P.P.S.—I forgot to tell you Mommy hadn't seen *Madelon Claudet* when it first opened at the Capitol in New York, but when it was at the end of its two weeks' run there she and Papa got up enough courage to go and see it. She told me that night when the memory of all the pain and heartaches that had accompanied its making swept back over both of them and they began, quite unconsciously, to groan and mutter, a man sitting behind them leaned forward with a tear-streaked face and said, "If you don't like the picture, other people do, so please keep quiet or I'll have to call the usher." They were both so unnerved by this that they stole out and she never saw the picture through.

Love,

Grandma

Mary sweet, I think in this set of letters I will just clear up the years Mommy had in pictures, that is, six months each year, spread over four years.

When both *Madelon Claudet* and *Arrowsmith* were being proclaimed, before they were ever released, Paramount offered Mommy the beautiful part of Katherine opposite Gary Cooper in *Farewell to Arms*. M.G.M., not anticipating the great success of *Madelon Claudet*, were not prepared with another story for Mommy, so they were glad to lend her to Paramount. Mommy promised to do this picture when she would close in *The Good Fairy*, but she had no heart in it.

That play opened at the Henry Miller Theatre, November, 1931, simultaneously with the showing of *Madelon Claudet* at the Capitol Theatre. Mommy was treated to the penalty of movie fame, for after the opening night of *The Good Fairy*, in which Walter Connolly co-starred, and we came out of the stage door, the sidewalk was solidly blocked with young men and women all presenting autograph books and fountain pens to her for her signature. Shortly after this *Arrowsmith* was released and then it became impossible for Mommy to leave by the stage door, because of the crowds. Sometimes they would catch a glimpse of her running from the front entrance into a taxi. They would jump on the running board and hold on until she signed their books. Mommy wasn't free to walk in the streets any more —something she dearly loved to do, window shopping and staring at people.

Mommy hated to be on show outside of the theatre, for she never dressed up to it. She disliked being stared at very much, since it had been her habit from early childhood to do the staring. These admirers had no qualms about following her for blocks and finally walking up to her and saying, "You are Helen Hayes, aren't you? I saw you in such and such a picture," then mentioning her in a picture she had never even heard of. It was pretty awful for Mommy.

The Good Fairy ran for fifteen weeks in New York and then toured for fifteen weeks. At its conclusion Mommy flew to·California to do *Farewell to Arms*.

Loads of love, dear,

Grandma

MARY DEAR, After Mommy finished *Farewell to Arms*, though she had enjoyed doing that picture with Gary Cooper and under Frank Borzage's most sensitive direction, she began dreading her next picture. As I told you before, every woman is sort of tabulated in pictures, one for her glamor, one for her beautiful figure, one as wholesome family appeal, etc., etc. Mommy was to be typed The Great Actress. She was made uncomfortably aware of this in her first interview with Mr. Louis B. Mayer. She had never met Mr. Mayer. All her dealings had been with Irving Thalberg and Mr. Harry Rapf who had produced *Madelon Claudet*. Mr. Mayer sent for Mommy to come to his office. He stared at her as she sat opposite him across the largest desk she said she had ever seen.

Finally, he shook his head most solemnly and said, "What are we going to do with you? All that wonderful acting. If only you had a Norma Shearer face." Mommy agreed with him that her face would never be Metro's fortune. Then he said, "Have you any sex appeal? We don't even know that, yet. You have always been so bundled up in old-fashioned costumes, rags and nurse uniforms. How about having a test made in one of those slinky white satin gowns, so we can see? Mommy assured him that even as Lady Godiva she couldn't compete with the Harlows, the Crawfords and Shearers, and she advised him to dismiss that angle of her right away. "Well," he said at last, "we will just have to keep you acting every minute." As a result of this decision Mommy was put into a series of ranting roles and tragic stories. One fan wrote, "For Heaven's sake, can't Helen Hayes do anything but die in pictures? I am so sick of seeing her get the worst of it." These new stories got Mommy so bewildered that she didn't know just what was expected of her, but she went through her paces like a circus pony, suffering all the while from its unreality. She felt herself becoming thoroughly dishonest in her work and she got frightened.

She persuaded Irving Thalberg to buy *What Every Woman Knows* for her. There was no ranting or tragic sequences in that and, furthermore, it was a real honest character. Because Mommy had made such a success with Maggie Wylie she knew that, given the chance and with a good scenario, she could do the same in pictures and thereby open another avenue for herself. She reckoned without the scenario department.

After Mommy left *Mary of Scotland* she went back to Metro to find that the script of *What Every Woman Knows* was twisted and changed because someone had the great idea of modernizing the story. They had Maggie Wylie, the sly little Scotch lass who in the stage version never left her knitting and her chair by the fireside, barging into 10 Downing Street, bearding the Prime Minister in his den, alone and single-handed, practically putting England off the gold standard and saving the British Empire. Darling, it was terrible!

Mommy was furious and tried to have it re-written with

284

some semblance of its former charm, but she got the same answer she always heard when she tried to argue in Hollywood: "My dear, you just don't know anything about pictures or the picture public." They had Mommy there!

Much, much love,

Grandma

M<small>ARY</small> <small>DEAR</small>, To show you how well grounded Mommy's fears were for her dear Barrie, when the picture was finished à la Metro-Goldwyn-Mayer, it was previewed at Huntington Park, where the audience is made up mostly of oil-field workers who want even their entertainment a "red-hot" gusher.

Mr. and Mrs. Thalberg took Mommy over to see it. Her picture had been slipped into a bill that featured Jean Harlow in *The Red-Headed Woman*, and that was what those tough young lads in the audience preferred. After this Harlow picture finished to loud and ribald applause, along came the Wylie family with their sly Barrie humor that hadn't been entirely removed in the rewriting. Mommy told me the audience first sat dumbly, then they began to get restive, then positively rebellious. They clapped, howled and just jeered the whole thing. Mommy said the only thing that kept her from going stark mad that night was a baby in its mother's lap who sat directly behind her and the Thalbergs. The child, instigated, Mommy was sure, by its mother, took to climbing over their heads during the picture, and Mommy was kept so busy disentangling herself and pushing it back onto its mother's lap that it served as a counter-irritant to what was going on in the rest of the theatre.

The Thalbergs dropped Mommy off at her home, and she was so numb with despair that when Thornton Wilder called her on the phone to ask how the preview had gone her voice must have told him the state of mind she was in. He told her not to go to bed, that he would be right over. Papa was in New York, so I was waiting up for her, for I knew Mommy would have to unburden herself to someone, no matter how the picture was received. The first thing Thornton said when he arrived a few minutes later was, "Let's have a drink." Mommy was considerably jolted by this, for she knew Thornton, like herself, was a teetotaler. She said she was in no mood to refuse anything that would make her forget what she considered her shame. They had a drink and immediately it took effect, and their tongues were loosened. Thornton talked about anything and everything but the picture. Then they had another drink and still another and I expect that that is the first time in their lives that two well-known teetotalers got good and tipsy. Poor Thornton was certainly a hero that night, for I am sure he made himself sick just for Mommy.

The next day Mommy was called to the studio for retakes, and when they handed her the first rewritten scene she discovered it was full of cheap Scotch jokes lifted right out of vaudeville. Mommy was good and mad and said to the director, "You can't put lines like this into this picture. It isn't Barrie." He said, "Yes, we can. Barrie laid an egg in Huntington Park last night and you had better just forget him." Mommy was horrified, but at that moment something clicked in her brain and she knew she could never make a success of pictures and was through with them. As soon as she realized this she dropped all arguing, didn't make any objections to any of the stupid things they did, went through all the retakes without a murmur.

I sat on the set and saw much of what was going on. Because I loved *What Every Woman Knows* and knew Mommy had been great as Maggie Wylie, I begged her to put her foot down and insist on the picture being kept as close to the original as possible. She said, "Not I. When I am through with this picture I shall shake the dust of Hollywood from my heels forever."

She was returning to New York to go on tour with *Mary of Scotland*, but just before leaving she went up to the office of Eddie Mannix, who was managing director of Metro, and told him of her decision never to return to pictures. She was sure after this last fiasco they would be glad to be rid of her. But he said, "Oh, yes you will. You are coming back in six months to make *Vanessa*, or we are going to sue you for ninety-six thousand dollars that we have spent so far on the preparation of the script. And we will also close *Mary of Scotland* by injunction. Mommy rushed to her only friend at court, Irving Thalberg, for help, and he did everything in his power to get her out of her contract, but to no avail. You know, darling, Metro wanted to cash in on Mommy's tremendous success in *Mary of Scotland* and so were determined to bring her back. Irving advised Mommy to come back the next summer and make *Vanessa* with the understanding they would not hold her to the balance of her contract. All the executives agreed to this compromise. Mommy returned to New York and her tour with *Mary of Scotland*.

Love and kisses, dear,

Grandma

P.S.—On her return when Mommy received the script of *Vanessa*, it was a new low in script writing, because the Walpole novel had been rejected by Mr. Breen, head of the Censor Bureau. A few days after Mommy arrived she was called to the studio for some purpose so mysterious they wouldn't even tell her over the phone. At the studio they told her she was to see Mr. Breen and put in a plea for *Vanessa*. She was told, "He is the father of a family and you are well known as a good wife and mother, so lay heavily on that angle. Tell him you think it would be a splendid moral lesson for the young." Mommy told me by this time every move she made in pictures was so crazy that she was in a mood to do anything, just to get it over with. So she agreed. She and Mr. Breen met in an office at Metro. She put on as good a show as she could, pleading for Vanessa. She said to me she had an almost irresistible impulse to blurt out: "Look, Mr. Breen, I can't agree with you on rejecting this script on moral grounds, but if you will only reject it on the grounds of art, I am right with you." She had to curb this impulse, for she felt the eye of David Selznick on her and she couldn't indulge in her sense of right. Mr. Breen finally agreed, after several changes which incidentally demolished the story, that they could go ahead with it.

Vanessa took eleven seemingly endless weeks. The moment it was over Mommy left Hollywood and pictures for good.

Grandma

MARY SWEET, While Mommy was in Hollywood, I think it was in 1932, Maxwell Anderson who was also out there writing for pictures, called her up and told her he had a rough draft of the first act of Mary of Scotland, which he was writing with her in mind for the star role. If he sent it over, would she read it, and if she was interested in playing it, he would finish it. Mommy told him she would be glad to read it. Well, the script came just as she and Ruth Gordon were going to the studio. She gave it to me and said, "Will you read this, Mother, and see if your old play-picking prowess is still working?"

I could not put it down, though it was a very long first act, for I was enchanted with it. When Mommy came home I told her what I thought, and she read it that night. She, too, loved it and told Max the next day that she would be delighted and honored to play Mary Stuart. She, however, told him she was committed to do three or four more pictures before she would be free for her six months in the theatre. He said it would take all of that time to complete it. Mommy returned to New York after her six months in Hollywood and began rehearsing in Mary of Scotland for the Theatre Guild.

Mommy had been reading a great deal about Mary Stuart. Several of the biographers spoke of her as being around six feet tall. Mommy, as you know, is only five feet. She had heard before she left Hollywood that Mae West, who wasn't any taller really than Mommy was, wore built-up shoes and appeared to be very tall on the screen. She was also told that was why Miss West walked so strangely —four-inch heels and two-inch soles were like stilts. Mommy knew that, as a queen, she must have a queenly carriage, so she had these shoes made at once and wore them from almost the beginning of the rehearsals, so she would accustom herself to the difference in height. Miss Theresa Helburn directed the play and really did a mighty fine job of it.

Because there was considerable cutting to be done, the Guild decided to open the play out of town and stay out four or five weeks until it was perfect for New York. They opened in Washington, D. C., and though critics and audience raved about it, Max and the Guild knew it could be better, so rehearsals were called for every day while on tour.

By the time it reached New York five weeks later, Mommy had forgotten the confusion and unhappiness of her year in pictures. She was back on familiar ground, back to reality, and Hollywood seemed a vague dream.

Much love.

Grandma

P.S.—I want to tell you a funny thing that happened to Mommy and me during our week in Washington, and also our first meeting with our President's wife, Mrs. Franklin Delano Roosevelt.

Lurena Hickock was a mutual friend of Mrs. Roosevelt and mine, so through her, Mommy and I were invited informally to tea at the White House. Mommy was rehearsing all day each day, but because of this honor Miss Helburn excused her. I attended the rehearsals every day to see that none of Mommy's ingenue mannerisms crept into her characterization of Mary Stuart.

The tea was at four, but as Mrs. Roosevelt knew we would have to come direct from rehearsals she sent word to come as we were. It would be almost a family party.

When Mommy and I came out the stage door we had to walk half a block to find a taxi. When we got in the cab the driver asked, "Where to, Lady?" I said, "The White House." He said, "Is there a public reception there today?" I said, "No. I don't think so." Then he said (and by this time we were at the East Entrance where public receptions are held), "Lady, you can't get in here. It's closed." I was having a grand time, and Mommy by her silence and evident enjoyment was encouraging me. I said to the driver, "We want to go to the main entrance." In the most despairing way he said, "Lady, if you haven't got a card you won't be allowed inside the door." I said, "I tell you what, when we get out don't drive away at once because you may have to pick us up afterward. We may be ejected." As Mommy and I stepped out of his cab Mr. Roosevelt's secretary, followed by a couple of footmen, helped us up the steps and onto the red carpet leading to the door. My last glimpse of the driver was of him still sitting there with his mouth wide open. This bit of foolishness kept me from having a bad case of stage fright, for this was the first time I had ever been in the White House and my first meeting with the most gracious First Lady who has ever occupied that position, I am sure.

Love,

Grandma

Mary DARLING, Mommy opened at the Albin Theatre in *Mary of Scotland* with Helen Menken as Queen Elizabeth and Philip Merivale as Bothwell, November, 1933. That

As Queen Victoria in *Victoria Regina*

was another great triumph for Mommy and play. The critics were unanimous in praise of both and spoke of it as the most perfectly cast play of the season.

Mommy had been terribly worried about her small stature, especially since she was playing against Miss Menken and Mr. Merivale, both quite tall. One critic said she was every inch the statuesque Queen of Scotland. Four inches in her shoes had helped, but it wasn't that altogether that deceived the eye. Dr. William Lyon Phelps of Yale came backstage one night shortly after the opening. I was in Mommy's dressing room at the time and he said, "Miss Hayes, how do you get the effect of being so tall?" Mommy explained about the added inches in her shoes. He said, "It can't be that, for you grow before our very eyes and appear every inch of Mary Stuart's six feet." Mommy then said, "Well, if you must know, I *think* myself tall." She expected him to laugh but he didn't, for he believed that was exactly what she did.

I asked Mommy afterward if that was another "drama school" answer and she said it was absolutely true. It was a theory she worked out for herself to make her mentally more content when she walked on the stage, but she didn't expect it to get across the footlights.

Another thing that worried Mommy was the questions that would be raised by the author's white-washing of Mary Stuart, who according to all biographers was no better than she seemed. Max took poetic and theatrical license with that lady, but it was such a beautifully written play that

Mommy made herself believe Mary Stuart the tragic maligned woman Max had written her.

She must have put that over too, for no one ever questioned the authenticity of her characterization. *Mary of Scotland* was still playing to capacity at the end of April when Mommy received word from M.G.M. Studios they would expect her to return to do *What Every Woman Knows*, according to her contract with them, by June 1st. Her Equity contract with the Guild automatically ended on that date. When Mommy notified the Guild management that she would have to leave there were, of course, loud outcries from them at this desertion. Mommy, of course, had no choice in the matter, but she realized then that this attempt to do pictures and stage was unfair, particularly to theatrical producers. It is impossible for a star to leave a play and have it run on. This was proven when Mommy left *Mary of Scotland* and the Guild tried to keep it running with another actress in Mommy's role. Business dropped terribly and the play closed in one week. You see, Mommy had become so identified with Mary Stuart in the minds of the public that they refused to accept another star, no matter how good she was. This frightened Mommy, for she feared that theatrical producers would be wary of engaging her if her time with them would be limited to six months. This was the situation when she went to Hollywood and found her beloved Barrie ruined in the scenario department.

All my love and kisses,

Grandma

M<small>ARY</small> <small>SWEET</small>, I don't know whether it was wise to separate Mommy's stage from her picture experiences in my letters to you, for now that I have done that, I find them a bit confused. You will remember I wrote you Irving Thalberg promised Mommy if she returned to do *Vanessa* the next summer he would release her from her contract with them. She left Hollywood joyously to have a most triumphant tour of six months in *Mary of Scotland*. This was Mommy's first real trouping since *Pollyanna* and as the company broke box-office records everywhere she found that she enjoyed it just as much at thirty-four as she had at sixteen, especially the one-night stands. They played huge auditoriums along the route where eight and nine thousand dollars at the box office for one performance was a frequent occurrence. Then, too, the company was such a happy one that it was just the tonic Mommy needed to put her back deep into the theatre again.

June 1, 1934 crept up on her and with it her dreaded Hollywood commitment. They closed *Mary of Scotland* in Chicago to packed houses. It could have run on indefinitely to big business there, but Mommy had to fly on to California to start her picture on time. She told me her heart was so heavy at leaving she was surprised the plane was able to take off.

Much love,

Grandma

Mary dear, This is just a short letter about Mommy's two stock starring experiences. Since she has gone under Gilbert Miller's management she has been busy each year with a play or picture commitments in the summer. If she had any idle time she and Papa fled abroad, where they would get away from all discussion of their work and would become like other tourists dashing about adventuring.

She had a few weeks after returning from Hollywood, and having no plans for that winter (this was July, 1935), she was going to stay with you and Papa in Nyack, read all plays sent to her and rest. Robert Cutler, who is a friend of Mommy's and who conducts a stock company at his lovely County Theatre in Suffern, New York, every summer, asked Mommy if she would star for a week or two for him in any play she chose. Now, she who had said she didn't want to see the inside of a theatre for months jumped at this chance, to satisfy a secret worry she had been carrying around for just ten years. She would do Shaw's *Caesar and Cleopatra* and settle once and for all in her own mind whether George Jean Nathan was right that she couldn't play Cleopatra. Now, this was a pretty ambitious production for a small summer theatre, but Mommy never thought of that and there would be no Aline Bernstein costumes to help her with "It." She was going to have one more try at a part that she had always loved. She gave ten performances, and the opening night every drama critic came from New York to see it and reviewed her performance the next day as if she had just added another triumph to a long list and as if she had never played it before. Ten years had ripened Mommy's understanding of Cleopatra. She realized that she had been too obvious when she first played it.

They played to capacity those ten nights and Mommy was so happy about it that she gave a big party for all of the company at your home. It was a grand finish. Last summer she played Barrie's *What Every Woman Knows* for two weeks at the same theatre at Suffern and there was another ghost laid. It was so bad in the picture Mommy almost doubted whether it was a good play after all!

Good night, dear, and kisses,

Grandma

MARY DARLING, When Mommy returned to New York she had no play for the next season, even though Gilbert Miller had promised to have one for her, and it was now late in August. She wasn't worried, and thoroughly enjoyed her new freedom at Nyack with you and Papa. Max Gordon had sent her *Pride and Prejudice*, which she liked best of all the plays she had been reading.

The theatrical season was drawing on apace, but Mommy, for some unexplained reason, couldn't bring herself to give a definite answer to Max Gordon. During these negotiations with him a book arrived for her, entitled *Victoria Regina* by Laurence Housman.

Gilbert Miller, who was in London, had his New York office send it on to her. With it came the explanation that there were thirty-two short plays or scenes in the book, but Mr. Miller had said that about ten could be used for a stage production. Mommy told me she was in such a lazy mood and the book was so thick she couldn't bring herself to read it at once. She tossed it on a shelf and forgot all about it. A couple or more weeks passed and Max Gordon was getting impatient, so he came out to Nyack to pin Mommy to her final word. She still couldn't make up her mind; that undefined something stood in the way of her decision. As Max was leaving the house Mommy said to him, "I'll call you in the morning and I think my answer will be 'yes'. But let me sleep on it one more night." It was a hot, lazy afternoon. She had nothing particular to read, so she took *Victoria Regina* down by the pool. She became completely enthralled by it after the first few pages. Half way through it she heard some people in the garden on their way to take a swim in the pool, and as she just couldn't bear an interruption at this point she fled to the shower room, locked the door, stood against the wall and finished reading the play. Tears were streaming down her face as she read the last scene. Three weeks had passed since she had received it and the dreadful thought came to her that maybe Gilbert had given it to another star or that some other producer had bought it or maybe Gilbert, not hearing from her, had abandoned the idea of producing it altogether. She became so frantic at this thought that she could hardly unlock the door. When she did she rushed out and went streaking by those people sitting at the pool (she said she never did find out who they were). They certainly must have thought her completely mad.

She sent a cable to Gilbert reading "I must do *Victoria Regina*. Cable me immediately if o.k." The next few hours of waiting were agony, but when his answer finally came it read, "Everything all right. The play is yours."

This turned out to be the greatest adventure in Mommy's career.

Much love,

Grandma

P.S.—When Mommy first read *Victoria Regina* she hadn't noticed the scenes marked that had been done by the Gate Players in London. You know, because it was an authentic history of Victoria's reign and members of her family were still living, it was not allowed to be done commercially in England. The Gate Players put it on every Sunday night without admission charges for their own pleasure and their friends'. Mommy was a little dismayed when she found that the last two scenes depicted Victoria at the age of sixty and then twenty years later at her Diamond Jubilee. She decided she would persuade Mr. Miller to finish the play on the death of Prince Albert if, and when they did it in America. She cabled Gilbert to that effect. He replied that Mr. Housman, a man in his seventies, was adamant about the same ten episodes being done in America that were done at the Gate Theatre. He suggested that she hop on a boat, come to London and discuss this change with him herself. Also, he believed she could get all the data on Victoria's character almost at first hand.

I was in California at the time, but Mommy sent the play for me to read with the request for my immediate opinion. When I finished reading it I called Mommy on the phone and said, "It is a beautiful lace handkerchief, but certainly no play there that would interest an American audience." I added, "I have heard that Victoria was a very smug woman, no imagination and certainly no romantic background." Mommy answered, "I don't know your authority but everything I have read about her made her to me a great woman and certainly her love for Albert was as romantic as it was beautiful. Anyhow, I want to play her for my own satisfaction. I have promised Gilbert and I am sailing in a week or two to discuss the play with Mr. Housman."

The die was cast but I, with my reputation of being a good picker of plays, couldn't resist giving Mommy this final bit of advice, "By all means do what you want to do, for you can afford to dally with a series of lovely pictures. I do hope, however, you have a play to go into that has some backbone in it when *Victoria Regina* closes after a few weeks."

Everyone knows how mistaken I was, for *Victoria Regina* ran nearly three years in New York.

Love,

Grandma

M<small>ARY</small> <small>SWEET</small>, Whenever Mommy anticipated an argument about an important point she always wanted someone very close to her to be along to lend moral support or it might be just a sympathetic ear. Papa was away, I think, and I was in California, so when Mommy was going on this trip to London to confer with Mr. Housman you were the only one at home, and so she decided she would take you along. While you were too young to help in any argument, you were someone very dear to turn to if the argument went against her. Even at the ripe age of five years you were beginning to have your share in Mommy's career. Then, so she would have someone to tell her "she was absolutely right in her requests and to stick to them," she took Ruth Gordon along, too.

I suppose you remember that trip on the *Normandie*. Mommy told me how wonderful the French Line was to her in giving her one of the *Normandie's* de luxe suites named "Le Havre." It was the second or third trip of this enormous liner and the vibrations were so terrible, she told me, you all but had to be strapped in your beds to keep from rolling around the floor with the many statuettes, vases and huge furniture that refused to remain put. The climax came when you all had been out two or three days. She and Ruth were lying in their beds, Mommy was rehearsing what she would say to Mr. Housman "if he were this type of man or if he were that type" when a huge vase, filled with roses that she had brought from Nyack and also filled with water, toppled over onto her bed and formed a big pool there. She was soaking wet, but she was thankful that she hadn't been killed.

Do you remember the tender coming out to the ship at Southampton loaded with people who had learned that Mr. and Mrs. Fredric March were landing? They had come out on the tender to get autographs. Do you know that Mr. March first started signing his autograph with a flourish "Sincerely yours, Fredric March" then he reached the stage where he just signed "Fredric March," finally just "F.M."? Mommy said it looked as if every person carried autograph albums for entire families. She was a bit surprised to find what she thought a very restrained people, the British, just as keen about the cinema stars as Americans were. Another thing that surprised Mommy was that they recognized her, for, after all, her career in pictures was a very limited one. She had made only seven, and four out of that seven were pretty bad.

This is where the British people differ from us Americans. They have a sincere loyalty to their artists. Once having liked them, they still keep actors in their hearts despite subsequent failures. In America if an actor has two or three bad plays or pictures the public begins to pick flaws in him or her. Decidedly, "The play's the thing" over here.

Forgive this digression, but I just had to pay this little tribute to the English theatre public.

All my love, dear,

Grandma

Mary darling, Ruth Gordon told me much of what happened to Mommy while you all were in London.

After you and your governess, Margaret, would start off for visits to Kensington Gardens and Hyde Park, Mommy and Ruth would sally forth in Mr. Miller's car, which he had put at Mommy's disposal. They would make a round of the museums and galleries for her data on Queen Victoria, especially in her later years. I don't know whether you noticed them or not when you would go out, but Ruth told me from the first day you all arrived a crowd collected around the Hotel Claridge, where you were stopping, to wait for Mommy to go out. You remember, you were on the third floor of the hotel and Ruth said when the French windows were open they frequently heard voices calling very softly, "Helen, Helen Hayes." The porter was constantly bringing stacks of autograph books up to Mommy's

room for her to sign. Now, catch an American porter doing that! Over here they go on the principle that the guests
must be protected from all annoyance. It is funny it didn't
annoy Mommy. On the contrary, she was extremely flattered. This is a good place to tell you one of Mommy's
reasons for not caring for pictures. All her life in the theatre
she has depended on and understood an audience's reaction to her performance, not necessarily applause, but a
feeling that goes across the footlights. That's why Mommy
wasn't annoyed by the cinema fans' admiration, for that
was the only recognition she could get from her work in
pictures.

Most of these waiting fans rode bicycles, and as Mommy
and Ruth would enter the car, these cyclists would ride
close to them, and as traffic would be halted for a minute
would thrust fountain pen and autograph book through the
window of the car shouting, "Sign my book, Miss Hayes"
or "Miss Hayes write something nice in mine." When the
traffic would start up again the cyclists would be hanging
with one foot over the cycle and the other foot over the
running board of Mommy's car. She would throw pens
and books helter-skelter out of the car window, screaming
meanwhile, "Oh, you are going to be killed!"

Mommy had eight full days of this, but Ruth said she
never seemed to tire of it. All the English actors that
Mommy had met in America rallied to give her the most
glorious time while she was there. It is too bad you were

too young to be at some of the parties, for you would have met many of the celebrities who had never been to Nyack. For instance, Mommy told me that Charles Laughton and his wife, Elsa Lanchester, were giving a party in her honor and asked her if there was anyone in particular that she would like them to ask for her. Mommy said, "I want all your great actors and actresses who are in town *and H. G. Wells.*" When Mommy and Ruth arrived at the party they found many old friends they had known in America and she also met several of the best in the English theatre that night, along with three or four well-known writers. She also had her heart's desire—H. G. Wells.

Much love,

Grandma

P.S.—Charles Laughton took Mommy to the museums and art galleries, where she could see relics of the Victorian period and portraits of Her Majesty at all ages. He took Mommy one day to Kensington Palace and as they were standing beside the bed the young princess had shared with her mother, the Duchess of Kent, before her accession to the throne, Mommy remembered that Mr. Laughton was a past master at the art of character make-up. She told him the difficulty she anticipated in making her tiny little face faintly resemble a full moon with sagging cheeks, as she must, to portray Victoria at the age of sixty. He told her that to get that effect over the footlights he usually put a good-sized slice of apple inside each cheek. Mommy thought this would be a grand idea and not at all unpleasant, for you know she loves apples.

Grandma

MARY DEAR, An appointment was made for Mommy and Rex Whistler, who was to design the scenery, sets and costumes for *Victoria Regina*, to discuss the play with Mr. Housman. Mommy told me about this meeting after she returned, and I only wish I could describe it half as comically as she did.

She told me Mr. Housman plunged into a discussion of the merits and beauty of the scenes as played at the Gate Theatre and then proceeded to act these scenes à la Israel Zangwill. Every once in awhile when he would stop for breath she would try to give her reason for not wanting to play the Queen at sixty years. He never allowed her to get beyond just opening her mouth. He was quite sure America would flock to the theatre if only to hear his play read. "Anyone," said he, "could act it." Mommy and Rex found themselves outside Mr. Housman's door, still followed by a barrage of beautiful adjectives about his play, and neither of them had been able to get in a word about his or her desires.

Another thing that had worried Mommy and which she had hoped to discuss with Mr. Housman was what she was going to do with her decided American accent in the role of an English Queen. She was told by someone that Victoria spoke with a sort of guttural sound and Mommy hoped that this might cover up that strange Americanese of hers. At the museums and galleries she concentrated more on Queen Victoria from the age of forty to the age of eighty. At the galleries most portraits of the Queen between those ages made her look very plump and her face was quite red. Rex Whistler said he would have a heavily padded bodice made to wear under her black silk dresses in her last two scenes and said they would add enormously to her bodily size.

Everything seemed to be rounding out beautifully, and Mommy made it quite clear that nothing now could stop her from playing *Victoria Regina* at all ages. Mr. Miller then arranged for Mommy to meet the Marchioness of Milford-Haven for help on some of her grandmother's mannerisms.

Mommy was invited for tea at Kensington Palace with the Marchioness. She was a charming little old lady and was excited about an American actress playing her grandmother. Mommy said, "That had frightened me terribly at first, for I was afraid I would be criticized for my decided American accent, but I have learned that Her Majesty spoke with a real German accent. The Marchioness said, 'Vy, my grandmutter spoke chust as gut Anglish as I do.' " This delighted Mommy and from then on she practiced speaking with the same amount of accent. She was in

London only eight days but she absorbed every little thing she could about Victoria and her time.

Again, everything was working in Mommy's favor to do the play she wanted most of all.

Good night, dear,

Grandma

MARY DARLING, The visit to London planted more firmly than ever the seed of a queenly complex that Mommy had felt growing in her after she played *Mary of Scotland*. She had been seeing so much and talking so much of all the things and habits that closely concerned Victoria that gifts, relics some of them, of Victoria's time were given to her. Charles Laughton gave Mommy a piece of lace that had been worn by the Queen. Vincent Price, who had played the Prince Consort at the Gate Theatre and was returning for the same role with Mommy in America, took her to an antique jeweler's near the British Museum, where she purchased many of the jewels that she wore afterward in the play. They were exact copies of some Victoria had worn or pieces worn by the royal family of that time. At the British Museum she saw all the robes of kings and queens of England dating way back to the old days. There, too, she saw and visualized Victoria in her coronation robe. Come to think of it, I believe Mommy told me you were

Charles Mac Arthur, Mary Mac Arthur and
Helen Hayes Mac Arthur

with her when she went there. Oh, well, when you read this some time it will freshen your memory of it.

Do you remember seeing on your way out a little white celluloid make-up tray not a bit better than the one Mommy used when she toured in *Pollyanna*? It was in a little glass case all by itself like a jewel. The card beside it read, "Make-up tray belonging to Anna Pavlova as it was found on her dressing table after her last appearance." She was the greatest ballerina of all time.

Mommy's completed absorption of Victoria's personality came with the last fitting at the Claridge of the authentic copies, even to the materials, of the gowns which Victoria wore and which Mommy would wear in the play. She told me that mentally she felt as if she had a crown on her head and fully expected Rex and the fitters to back out of her presence (she was only joking, of course).

                        Much, much love,

                                    Grandma

P.S.—Mommy told me if it hadn't been for the radio contract she would have remained in England until *Victoria Regina* opened in the middle of December. She was having such a glorious time and so much fun. Noel Coward, entertaining her as a house guest at his place in Kent, read three of his plays from *Tonight at 8:30* which she adored. By the way, his play opened in New York practically at the same time *Victoria Regina* did and was an enormous hit, too.

I have just remembered a funny story Mommy told me about her first and only time to "dip snuff," as the darkies say in the South.

Did you know the driver of Mr. Miller's car had been the chauffeur for the Prince of Wales before he became king? Well, whether it was this intimacy with royalty that made him take more liberties with commoners he volunteered information or corrected Mommy and Ruth if they were inaccurate about a place of interest. Mommy said they were riding along when she noticed a sign over a shop reading "Tobacco and Snuff." Mommy said to Ruth, "Do you suppose anyone uses snuff these days?" The chauffeur said, "Oh, yes, Ma'am. It is much used among the nobility." Mommy, still addressing Ruth, said, "Mercy, I wonder what it is like?" The chauffeur said, "Pardon me, Ma'am, would you care to try some now?" and gallantly passed an ornate silver snuff-box to her. Mommy, always willing to oblige, took a good pinch and put it all in one nostril. From then on, she said, he didn't need to use his siren once. Her sneezes were so loud and they kept up until they returned to the hotel.

As soon as Mommy returned home she began studying her role of Victoria, so that when rehearsals were called Mommy was prepared to go right on.

On the 12th of December, 1935, Mommy opened in *Victoria Regina* in Baltimore, playing there one week, then to Washington, and there was something about the triumph of Mommy and play in both cities that presaged its reception in New York.

Love,

Grandma

P.P.S.—This is a lovely experience Mommy had that week in Washington. She wrote to Uncle Ned Sheldon about it and he gave me her letter. I quote it verbatim:

"Last night I dined at the White House. There were only the Secretary of State and Mrs. Hull, three Governors, the President and Mrs. Roosevelt, their daughter and I. Wasn't that thrilling? That was before my broadcast. I went over to the studio in the President's car and then returned to the White House for the diplomatic reception, which was a magnificent show. Then I finished off the evening up in the President's study having a glass of beer with him and his military aide, while Mrs. Roosevelt stayed downstairs and took care of the 'little' ambassadors, etc. It was so wonderful to remember how I used to go trailing through that same White House on the 'Open to Public' days with the rest of my class at school."

Grandma

MARY DEAR, Again, Mommy gave me a memorable night when she opened in *Victoria Regina*, December 26, 1935, at the Broadhurst Theatre.

Every scene was received with a burst of applause, and when the curtain went up on the tenth scene at Balmoral, with Victoria at the age of sixty seated at a table with her widow's bonnet on over her heavy red face there wasn't a sound for a few seconds but the whispers of the audience, one saying, "That can't be Helen Hayes," another saying, "My God, it isn't possible for an actress to change like that." Then Mommy spoke and the applause broke out like a clap of thunder. It was a great triumph of make-up.

As the last act finished with Victoria being wheeled on in her chair after her drive in the procession of her Diamond Jubilee, I really thought the roof would fall in or the theatre collapse when Mommy, Prince Albert and Disraeli received their first curtain call. Those curtain calls, by the way, lasted long after I reached Mommy's dressing room.

When Mommy got to her room finally, she grabbed her bonnet and wig off, and without removing her make-up insisted on having everyone who wanted to come back and tell her more and more lovely things about the play and her performance. Gilbert and Mrs. Miller were the first to arrive, and they just couldn't speak. They were so moved and happy by the reception of Mommy and the play. The crowds kept coming and going in an unending line, and Mommy drank in more praise that night than most heads are able to hold without bursting. The climax came when a Russian countess who had never seen Mommy before said to her, "It is so extraordinary, Miss Hayes, how you make yourself look so girlish in the first scenes." Mommy shrieked with laughter, but was considerably flattered to think the bugbear of looking sixty and more was more convincing than her own youth. Not so, Gilbert. After the lady had been told by him that she was ridiculous he turned to Mommy and said, "No more visitors in the dressing room until you have your make-up off entirely." Mommy was still chuckling over this when we reached a wonderful party that Gilbert gave at Club 21 and Mommy spoke to the countess who looked at her without recognizing her as Helen Hayes. This really rounded out Mommy's great night.

The business of *Victoria Regina* never lessened and when Mr. Miller closed the play on June 20, 1936, to give Mommy a rest for two months, the crowds were so great for that last week one would have thought it wasn't going to open again, and at the same theatre, too. It was advertised to open August 31, 1936, and before that date the theatre was completely sold out weeks in advance. It ran to capacity until May 29, 1937. That was the full New York run.

Loads of love, dear,

Grandma

P.S.—This was one play that I never tired of seeing,

especially the last two scenes, for Mommy was always adding little touches to her character that were surprisingly like Graddy Hayes at that age.

Love,

Grandma

Mᴀʀʏ ᴅᴇᴀʀ, This letter tells of Mommy's radio experience. You weren't a year old when a weekly magazine asked Mommy if she would broadcast a fifteen-minute talk for them or do a short scene from one of her plays.

Mommy, I have told you time and time again, never knows when to say "no." She dreaded the idea of speaking lines into that microphone with no chance of retracting if she made a mistake. Still she said she would do it.

Papa wrote her a short talk and as the time neared for her to go on the air she became so frightened I believe that if she hadn't given her word, she would have backed down. However, after the first few words (I sat with my ear glued to my radio) you would have thought she had talked into that little black box for years.

I was curious to know her reaction to this new medium of expression and when she returned home I asked her all about it. She said then that she didn't think that she could ever do it again. At that time audiences were not allowed in the studios, so it seemed to her that she was orating on a desert island. You know Mommy has a funny little way of hesitating in her speech, but since time, tide and the radio wait for no man, she was limited in making any pauses.

She said then she thought she would be as great a failure on the air as she expected to be in pictures. However, she got numerous offers from sponsors for other broadcasts but she refused them all.

In 1934 she appeared in a sketch on the air for Hinds' Honey and Almond Cream. Then she guest-starred twice on the Rudy Vallee Hour.

Mommy also substituted at an hour's notice for Margaret Sullavan in a radio presentation of *Peg O' My Heart*.

Mommy had a dress rehearsal in Philadelphia for *Mary of Scotland* that Sunday night. They were opening there, beginning their road tour the next night. Mommy was just lounging around, resting preparatory to leaving in the afternoon for Philadelphia when the phone rang at about eleven o'clock in the morning. It was the Lux Theatre asking Mommy if she would substitute for Miss Sullavan at two o'clock. Mommy explained that she had never read nor seen *Peg O' My Heart* and furthermore she couldn't speak with a brogue. They assured her that she could read it from the script, but that they would explain and apologize before she went on the air. Mommy just couldn't let them down, so she promised that she would come as soon as possible. She arrived at the broadcasting station at one o'clock, read half way through the script and was told she would go on the air that minute.

Now, let me tell you how I sat listening to this broadcast, for one solid mystified hour. I was in California and my clock was five minutes slow, so by the time I turned on and tuned into the station the announcer had finished telling of the substitution and why, and he was telling the story of Peg. When Peg said her first speech I said aloud, though I was alone, "Why, she is imitating Helen." The longer I listened the surer I was that I was going crazy or that my great wish to hear Mommy's voice had made the resemblance of tone so sure in my mind. When it was over and the announcer said, "Lux Radio Theatre wishes to extend our most sincere thanks, Miss Hayes, for your magnificent performance and hope that we will have the honor and privilege of having you with us again." Not one word about Miss Sullavan. I just waited long enough for Mommy to reach home when I called her to ask for an explanation and to tell her it is a wise mother who knows her own child's voice three thousand miles away. She told me that Miss Sullavan had developed a bad case of laryngitis and that she had gone on the air without any rehearsal. She then said, "Was I terrible?" I told her that I had never heard a more delightful, lilting brogue nor a better-acted sketch, and bear in mind, I thought all the time that it was Margaret Sullavan giving a great imitation of her.

In 1935 she had signed a contract with Sanka Coffee as sponsors for twenty-six weeks in a serial called *The New Penny*, beginning October 1st. She had signed this contract before she had read *Victoria Regina*. It was a half-hour program from eight-thirty to nine, and since it would be impossible for her to do *Victoria Regina* and her broadcast the same night, Gilbert closed the Tuesday night performance of *Victoria Regina*, and Mommy gave an extra matinee in its stead. Because of the difference in time she gave another half hour at midnight for the West. She renewed her contract with the same sponsors, Sanka Coffee, for twenty-six more weeks the following September, 1936, in a new serial called *Bambi*. This time the half hour was from eight o'clock to eight-thirty every Monday night.

Mommy made her first entrance in *Victoria Regina* at exactly eight-forty. She would go to the theatre by seven, make up and dress. She wore a long cloak with a zipper up the front and a hood that covered her wig of long hair. She would go up to her studio in a private elevator and when the half hour was up she would hurry down to her car, where Herman would have the motor running and be at the wheel all ready to go; a policeman stood on the running board and while Herman kept the siren going full blast a path was opened for Mommy from the Radio Theatre, Forty-ninth Street and Sixth Avenue, to the Broadhurst Theatre, Forty-fourth Street near Eighth Avenue. Priscilla and Ada, her maids, would hand Mommy her powder puff and mirror, give the zipper a pull; Mommy would give her nose a dab, step out of her cloak and onto the stage.

After that, up to the present time, Mommy has only done guest-starring on the radio.

Grandma

Mary darling, There were many nice things always happening to Mommy during the run of *Victoria Regina* and I want to tell you some of them.

Mommy had never been satisfied with her little widow's bonnet that she wore as Victoria in the last act. The design was absolutely authentic, but the material on Mommy's was a thick net and rather stiff. She was so happy in all her other costumes, even to the jubilee bonnet which was designed after Graddy Hayes' best bonnet, which Mommy described to the London costumer. Graddy's wasn't as elegant as Victoria's but it was of that period.

One day Mommy received a letter from a lady who said she had been to the play several times and loved it. She described herself as quite old and wrote that she became a widow some years before. The milliner who had made Victoria's bonnets in London made her ten of these same widows' bonnets. She had seven of them packed away in a box and she wrote it would give her great pleasure if Mommy would accept and wear them in the play. When they were received at the theatre Mommy was overjoyed to find they were made of the finest net and were exactly like those worn in every portrait Mommy had seen of Victoria at that age. It was amazing what a difference that bonnet made in Mommy's performance. She was really sixty-year-old Victoria. She begged this lady who had sent them to come to see her or let Mommy call and thank her, but she received the reply that no thanks were necessary, that the wearing of one in the play was sufficient. Mommy was constantly receiving anonymously some treasured souvenir of Victoria. All these things will be a wonderful heritage for you some day.

They had played *Victoria Regina* one hundred performances and the cast and crew decided they would give Mommy a surprise party on that occasion. I had been called down to the theatre by Harry Essex, Mommy's manager, but he cautioned me not to dress up so I wouldn't arouse Mommy's suspicions. I thought Mommy would never get her make-up off and get dressed, I was that curious. At last we were ready to go, and then Harry said to Mommy, "The boys have made something and they want you to see it. Do you mind running downstairs a minute before you go?" I made Mommy precede me, and when she reached the bottom of the stairs the orchestra began playing first our own national anthem, "The Star Spangled Banner," with the entire company and stage crew assembled, the orchestra and every attaché from the front of the theatre standing under American and British flags. Little Shirley Porriere, who played Princess Ena in the play, made a curtsy and presented Mommy with a beautiful old-fashioned bouquet. Then the orchestra struck up, "God Save the Queen." By the end of this Mommy was crying. She was so touched.

The crew had had their wives prepare a buffet supper the like of which I have never tasted or seen before, and this was surrounding a very gorgeous though truly Victorian birthday cake. On one side of the cellar was an easel with a red cloth draping it, and as everyone stood with a glass in his hand of his favorite beverage from water to champagne, Mr. Zucco who played Disraeli, said, "Let us drink a toast to Queen Helen Hayes, whose reign over us has been such a happy one and to whom it gives us great pleasure to present this portrait of the beloved Queen Victoria that she has so magnificently portrayed these one hundred times." Then he removed the covering to disclose a beautiful original etching, signed by the queen herself. Everyone from the front of the theatre to the back of it had contributed to the purchase of this lovely gift to Mommy and it was truly one of love.

Mommy danced then, first with Freddie, her head carpenter who has been with Mommy so many years in that capacity and without whom she doesn't believe her curtain could go up.

It was the most wonderful night for me to see Mommy so loved for herself.

This birthday occurred on the night of March 21, 1936. One hundred performances later Mommy gave a big party for all of her big theatrical family at Sardi's. Then another big party was given by Mr. Miller on its five-hundredth-performance birthday. But none of them was so perfect as that first one. The spirit remained the same, however.

Loads of love, dear,

Grandma

320

P.S.—One night a card was sent back to Mommy bearing the name of Count Cavadonga, the great-grandson of Queen Victoria, with the request that he be permitted to meet Miss Hayes. Mommy was very excited and not at all worried that he would question her performance, for she knew he had never known his great-grandmother. When he did come to the dressing room after the play, and though he complimented Mommy on her performance, he did say she made Victoria a much sweeter woman than his mother had told him she was. He said he understood her to be a very irascible old lady. You see, from one's own family the truth comes out.

Love,

Grandma

Mary sweet, This is a short note about history repeating itself unto the third and fourth generation. Do you remember the present which Mommy promised you for your seventh birthday? You remember she promised to let you go on in Victoria Regina as the Princess Ena in the last scene of the play.

You talked of nothing else for weeks and I think what delighted you most about this promise was that you would be permitted to stay up until midnight. Your disappointment was terrible to see when Mommy said she had planned to have you go on in a matinee, so it wouldn't interfere with your routine. I took Mommy aside and told her that going on at a night performance was the best part of the gift to you. Then I reminded her that she had played six nights a week when she was your age and it hadn't done her any harm. She said, "Of course, she can go on Saturday night and can sleep late the next morning."

You insisted on dressing in Shirley Porriere's room down in the basement, though Mommy had planned to have you dress with her. You wanted no extra privileges. How you carried me back to the days when Mommy accepted every hardship and inconvenience because it was part of being a good trouper. Do you remember the great number of telegrams of good wishes for the success of your debut in the theatre and that very funny one from Papa, who was in Hollywood, asking you if you would consider playing Scarlett O'Hara in *Gone with the Wind?* You took his wire very seriously and said to me, "Could I play that part, Grandma?" That was like Mommy, too, only she would have said, "I *can* play that part." There were so many lovely flowers, gifts and that beautiful cookie jar from Mr. Miller with a card reading, "I want to place you under a long contract." Really, I don't think Mommy ever had more excitement crowded into one night than you had on February 15, 1937.

You, of course, were made up and dressed before the first act.

When the curtain went up on the last scene and you

were standing on the stage holding the hand of your stage mother, you were truly a most beautiful little Princess Ena. From then on, like Graddy Hayes when she watched Mommy at your age, the tears in my eyes blotted out every bit of that final scene. I found myself instead of looking at the stage turning first to the right and then to the left to find out if I could hear anything people were saying about you and wanting to tell them you were my granddaughter. So truly was I Graddy Hayes at that moment that I began looking to see if I had both my gloves.

Thank you, darling.

Love and a heartful of pride,

Grandma

MARY DARLING, This is about honors paid to Mommy by two queens. Word of the success of *Victoria Regina* was being carried back to England by visiting English people who on arrival in this country came to see Mommy in the play, and a whisper came to Mommy that Queen Mary had expressed a wish that she could see her in it, so Mommy had a most royally bound book made up of photographs from every scene in the play. On the fly-leaf was inscribed "Victoria Regina. To Her Most Gracious Majesty, Queen Mary. From Helen Hayes." On the next page was the cast of characters and the autograph of every member of the cast.

The book was sent at once and a few months later Mommy received that beautiful photograph of the Queen that occupies the place of honor in Mommy's drawing room.

On the photograph is written in the Queen's own hand: "Mary R, 1937."

The next honor bestowed on Mommy by royalty was when the former Queen of Spain came to a matinee of *Victoria Regina*. Between the first and second acts, Mommy received a note written by the Queen's secretary, asking Mommy if she would see the Queen after her performance. Mommy was terribly frightened and excited, frightened for fear something in the play might give offense to Her Majesty and then, too, Mommy knew that the Queen was not too young when her grandmother died to remember things about her.

Mommy asked Harry Essex to escort the Queen and her attendants backstage through one of the boxes. So Mommy wouldn't keep the Queen waiting she stood at the door leading from the box with her make-up on. She waited and waited, and finally Harry came to Mommy and said "I don't know what happened, but the Queen rushed out a side door before I could reach her and was in a taxi and gone before anyone realized it." Mommy was heartsick, for she was quite sure the Queen had been offended. For two days Mommy really suffered from this thought. Then she got a phone call from the secretary, saying, "Queen Victoria of Spain desired Miss Hayes to come to her apartment at the hotel for tea the next afternoon."

Mommy looked very lovely when she arrived at the suite and was met most graciously by the Queen, who explained why she hadn't gone back to see Mommy after the matinee. She said that the crowds waiting at the stage door had frightened her. She then plunged into the most amazing number of questions which concerned how Mommy had ever learned so many things about her grandmother. "Why," she said, "you laugh like her, talk like her, and who told you of her having a little impatient shrug if anyone tried to sympathize with or help her when she was old?" Mommy said, "I guess all old people do the same things, for they were all the mannerisms of my Graddy Hayes."

The Queen then complimented Mommy on her performance and said, "What a pity you can't do this in England! It is such a lovely treatment of my grandmother's reign."

Good night, dear, and sweet dreams,

Grandma

MARY DARLING, After almost three years in New York Gilbert Miller sent *Victoria Regina* and Mommy on tour, starting September 15, 1937. They were to go from coast to coast, practically the same route she had taken with *Mary of Scotland*. It was the same story everywhere, only now *Victoria Regina* broke even *Mary of Scotland's* records. I ran on to many of the towns she was to appear in and really I was proud all over again, for her receptions were as great as if she were a real queen, and, at that, I expect she is a real queen of the theatre.

There were two important changes made in the cast before *Victoria* started on tour—Werner Bateman for Vincent Price in the role of Prince Albert and Abraham Sofaer for George Zucco's role of Disraeli. Zucco had left the cast a few months before *Victoria* closed on June 25, 1938, in New York. Mr. Sofaer and Mommy were talking one day about the coming tour and the danger of monotony descending on the entire company from being in the same play so long. Mommy said, "I would like to do one of Shakespeare's plays at a few matinees during our tour, for we have a large cast and each one can be in the play. The frequent rehearsals would give us something to do to occupy our time and then the tour couldn't possibly become monotonous." They began reading the different plays, but all the star parts for women were so long, and Mommy said she didn't want to have too much to study. Mr. Sofaer suggested *The Merchant of Venice*. He had played Shylock in England and he said Portia was about the shortest female star role in any of the Shakespearian plays. Mommy got very enthusiastic and started the ball rolling at once. Guy Moneypenny, who as you know was in the cast of *Victoria*

326

and had been in *Mary of Scotland*, was told to submit some designs for costumes. He has a great flair for designing and he had shown Mommy some of his work. Then came the casting, which was all settled before they left New York. Sofaer was to direct.

Victoria Regina's great tour started October 3, 1938, in Philadelphia and they settled down almost immediately to rehearsals of *The Merchant*. Costumes and sets were all ready and beautiful, and Mommy planned three daily rehearsals until they would reach Chicago where they would give just two matinees during the run of *Victoria* there.

Mommy wrote me so enthusiastically about her characterization of Portia. She was going to play her as one with a great sense of humor.

I was to go to Chicago for the first matinee, but Mommy called me up to come on for three or four rehearsals before she opened.

The first rehearsal I saw was a little confused, but I was overjoyed at finding Mommy playing Portia so gaily and with a great economy of gestures. I was worried about "the quality of mercy" speech, for in my day I had seen the greatest Portias, but every last one of them, when they reached that speech, was invariably ponderous and lyrical. You felt them, moments before that speech, getting all set for it.

Mommy was speaking those beautiful lines almost before I realized it, for she was just as colloquial with them as she had been with the other lines. It was as if she were figuring

327

out in her mind an argument that would reach Shylock's mind.

Do you know, dear, for the first time I understood what Portia was trying to say? I told her all this after the rehearsal and begged her not to change one inflection. *The Merchant* opened on a Thursday matinee and the theatre was jammed with the most friendly audience, and something I have never seen happen to any of the great Portias I had known, they laughed heartily *with* Mommy's Portia.

The critics were most enthusiastic in their praise of production and performance, and Mommy came in for the greatest encomiums for her Portia mainly because she was the first one who hadn't intoned the famous speech. A few days later Mommy was deluged with letters from professors, teachers and students, begging her to give a Sunday-night performance so they could attend. She did, to another packed theatre the next Sunday night. Because it had gone so well at these two performances, and, bear in mind, half of the cast was miscast, Mommy decided she would give no more on tour, but would do it the following season in New York. This was her very first Shakespearian role and she liked it.

I needn't tell you of any more of the wonders of that tour of *Victoria Regina*, for you joined the cast in Seattle, Washington, playing Princess Ena at two matinees a week. From then until it closed in Los Angeles you, too, enjoyed the triumphs and earned five dollars a performance. Mommy gave one performance of *The Merchant* in Los Angeles by request, and Frank Hogan, the great lawyer who was in town and saw it that Sunday night, told me it was the first time he had seen a Portia who he thought could pass a bar examination.

Victoria closed in Los Angeles, California, June 25, 1938, for what Mommy thought was the end. It wasn't, but that is another letter.

Much, much love,

Grandma

MARY SWEET, Gilbert suggested to Mommy a few months after she closed in *Victoria Regina* that she could establish an unheard-of prestige in the theatre by reopening *Victoria* in New York for a few weeks the beginning of the next season. Mommy said, "It will establish me as an actress with an enormous ego! We have milked this town dry of *Victoria* audiences." He finally talked her into doing it, but she first exacted a promise from him that she would be allowed one year's rest from plays and discussion of plays.

Victoria Regina opened at the Martin Beck Theatre October 3, 1938, and repeated the same business it had done on its premiere back in 1935. After ten weeks of playing to standees, Mommy insisted on closing, so she could begin her sabbatical year. Just before this decision out-of-town theatres where *Victoria* had been the year before wrote Gilbert beseeching him to give them a return engagement of *Victoria*. Gilbert showed these appeals to Mommy and, as you no doubt have discovered by this time, Mommy has no will power. She agreed to play six more weeks on tour.

She closed in *Victoria Regina* January 28, 1939, but this time she didn't say it was for the last time. She said, "I am like Adelina Patti, who, I have been told, was always giving her farewell concert but would bob up again the very next year."

I, for one, would hate to think that your Mommy would never play *Victoria Regina* again.

Au revoir, my sweet,

Grandma

Mary dear, This letter might be called "Mommy's Awards" for I am going to confine it to just the honors she received throughout her theatrical career. I think I wrote you how she was frequently being given the prize for her studies in school, but it was not until she received the gold statuette, first award of the Academy of Motion Picture Producers for her performance in *The Sin of Madelon Claudet* that the award cycle started again. This first award was in 1932. In 1936 she received a bronze plaque for being the favorite actress of the Radio Guide. The same year, 1936, she was notified that Elmira College for Women was to confer the Degree of Doctor of Letters on her for her work in the theatre. Papa was very sweet to me on this occasion, for he insisted on my going up to Elmira and being present when Mommy, in the loveliest costume I think she ever wore—the cap and gown—received this degree from the dean. Katharine Cornell was honored with the same degree but because she was in a play at the time and couldn't get up to Elmira, her father acted as her proxy and received it for her.

This is a secret I never told Mommy, but I was glad Miss Cornell couldn't come so Mommy wouldn't have to share any thunder.

In 1937 Mommy received the Radio Stars' award for distinguished service. I think it was in the same year the Drama League award honored her for the best diction in radio. In 1938 Mommy received the Degree of Doctor of Humane Letters from Hamilton College, Uncle Alec's Alma Mater. I wasn't present on this occasion, for Mommy was on her second tour of Victoria Regina and left Boston, where she was playing, for Hamilton on the midnight train. It was bitter cold when Mommy arrived at Hamilton at seven o'clock in the morning, but Uncle Alec met her and they had breakfast in the little station together. After breakfast Professor Rudd met them. Then all three went for a long walk and a discussion of the exercises. Uncle Alec thought it would be an excellent idea if Mommy recited the "Quality of Mercy" speech instead of the usual acceptance speech. She did this, much to Uncle Alec's delight. I told you how colloquial she made that speech when she did *The Merchant of Venice* and I was told everyone present at the exercises was pleased by this interpretation.

Mommy had to dash for her train right after the exercises in order to make Philadelphia in time for the play that night. She had no time to learn how well her speech had been received.

I think this is going to be a rather nice ending for the letters, after all. There will be other honors for Mommy, I am sure, in the years to come, and I hope you will always be present, darling, when she does receive them, for it will make you very, very proud.

Much love,

Grandma

P.S.—Mommy also received a plaque for diction once, which reminds me of an unconquerable weakness in her make-up. This is a strange use of words. I will have to explain this by giving instances.

One day she and I were discussing a woman who had married a man for his money, and she said, "Don't you think she is horrid to be so mercantile?" Another time she and Jean Dixon returned home in a taxi, and Mommy was terribly excited, for their taxi had jammed into another taxi, and she said, "While no damage was done to either, the drivers hurled the most horrible epitaphs at each other." This last one I remember I really think the best of them all. We were moving from a large apartment to one that had a very small living room and we had no place for the grand piano. Mommy was at luncheon with George Kaufman, Edna Ferber and Uncle Alec Woollcott, and she was telling them about her wish to dispose of the piano. She said, "Anyone who wants my piano is willing to it." Kaufman replied, after a pause, "That is very seldom of you, Helen." If it hadn't been for this funny answer, Mommy would never have realized that she had spoken strangely. You see, her brain is quite clear about what she intends to say but words get in the way of her thoughts. Because of this peculiarity Mommy has always been shy about talking to people she doesn't know well.

Grandma

M<small>ARY</small> <small>DARLING</small>, Back in the summer of 1938, I think it was (by this time you surely have discovered how hazy I am about dates), Mr. and Mrs. Ladislaus Bus-Fekete came out to visit Papa and Mommy at Nyack. I was there too. Mommy to most eyes was enjoying her idleness. No talk of plays or theatres. I, who had gone through two or three other "happy" vacations with Mommy could discern the old restlessness popping out every once in a while. Honestly, I couldn't bear the idea of Mommy being out of harness a whole year, so when I heard Bus, Papa and Ben Hecht discussing a play, I just cocked my good ear to listen.

I had also had a little bug in my head for the last five or six years that kept buzzing to have your Papa write a play for Mommy.

Driving home with the Bus-Feketes that night I asked if it was a play for Mommy. Bus said, "Oh, no! It is not a star part." I said, "Couldn't it be made a star part?" "No," said he. "It would throw the play out of gear to build the part of the woman any stronger." Well, that was another hope shattered.

Mommy came home from that tour to be with you all Christmas Day, and Gilbert and Mrs. Miller and I were there for dinner. Gilbert, who had always been such a delightful raconteur, was strangely silent all the afternoon. Suddenly, out of a clear sky, Mommy said, "Gilbert, are you looking for a play for me?" Darling, I don't think Mommy ever said a line on the stage that had such a startling effect as that one little question had on all three of us. Gilbert perked up at once and was his old hale and hearty self again, and I, who had been planning to go away just as soon as Mommy closed in *Victoria* so I wouldn't have to watch her restlessness all summer, breathed easier again.

It turned out to be a most glorious Christmas Day for all of us. A load was off all of our minds. Gilbert said he would get busy right away and find a play for Mommy next season. So much for Mommy's sabbatical year.

All my love, dear,

Grandma

Mary sweet, One day after Mommy had closed in *Victoria Regina* she said to me, "Charlie is rewriting Bus's play and I think it is grand. I'd like to play the girl in it. Will you read it?" I did, and although it was only a rough outline I was crazy about it.

You know when Mommy first met your papa she would blush terribly at every little frank expression, and your papa accused me of having a thousand inhibitions and transferring them to Mommy. Well, I am inclined to think he was right, but like all inhibited people I enjoy frankness in others. For this reason I just love the characters that your papa writes about. They are such real, open and above-board folk. The size of Mommy's part in the play didn't worry me, for I had never been one to judge a part by quantity but by quality. I knew this wasn't a part that could play itself. It required natural and human acting, and I knew Mommy would bring that to it.

I am not going to tell you much about the worries and anxieties for both Papa and Mommy that went into the finishing of *Ladies and Gentlemen* except to tell you that out of this combination came another conviction for me, that your papa was truly Mommy's man.

The play had a four-week try-out in California, with Herbert Marshall co-starring with Mommy. It closed in Los Angeles in August and Papa and Ben Hecht began practically to rewrite the last act. Herbert Marshall left the cast in Los Angeles and Philip Merivale was Mommy's choice to co-star with her in New York.

Ladies and Gentlemen opened in Philadelphia, September 18, 1939, after four very hectic weeks of rehearsal. Your papa and Ben Hecht were still rewriting. I went down for the opening and I was proud all over again for Mommy and Papa. Papa had a brilliant idea for the final curtain which he planned to write in immediately, and when I saw it in Washington I was satisfied that he had turned the trick. The audience loved it. *Ladies and Gentlemen* opened October 17, 1939, at the Martin Beck Theatre, seven days after Mommy celebrated her thirty-ninth birthday.

I was out front, but the first scene wasn't over before I wished Mommy had asked me to stand in the wings as of old. That first-night audience wasn't anything like as enthusiastic as I had expected, and I know Mommy would need to be told she was all right. However, I knew your papa would be with her to encourage her, so I remained seated until the play was over.

I guess I was over-anxious, for the critics acclaimed Mommy all over again, and *Ladies and Gentlemen* promptly became one of the biggest hits of the season.

Mommy is still having her sabbatical, for it is like a vacation being in this play, still under Gilbert Miller's management and best of all starring in a play written by your papa.

All my love, dear,

Grandma

Mary darling, From this letter on I am delegating to you the carrying on of Mommy's career in a book, and since it is the first time she has ever appeared in a play of Papa's you can make it a joint biography for their grandchild.

When Mommy opens in her next play, which will be a long time from now, I know, I hope to be sitting out front. While you are too young to criticize her performance, I hope she will want you standing in the wings so that when she makes an exit yours will be the hand she will hold and you will tell her how well the play is going, whether it is or not. On an opening night a little white lie, when necessary, is forgivable. You are the only one, I am sure, Mommy would want to give this glorious privilege to.

As you watch Mommy at work in the theatre or when she discusses that work with you, jot every little thing down, for as long as she lives that work will always be interesting to you and yours.

So it is hail but not farewell and many happy years watching and growing up with Mommy.

All my love,

Grandma

Index

342